3302524081

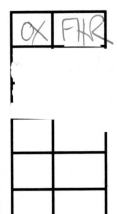

OX FHR

1L

D 98/734

3

The Northern Counties

Cumberland, Westmorland, Durham, Northumberland, Lancashire and Yorkshire

Edited by

PETER SUMMERS, F.S.A.

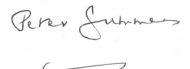

PHILLIMORE

1980

Published by
PHILLIMORE & CO. LTD.
London and Chichester

Head Office: Shopwyke Hall,
Chichester, Sussex, England

ISBN 0 85033 329 6

*The General Editor and the Publishers wish
to acknowledge with gratitude the generous
Grants from The British Academy and the
Manifold Trust, without which publication of
this volume would not have been possible.*

CENTRE
for OXFORDSHIRE
STUDIES

Printed in Great Britain by
UNWIN BROTHERS LTD.
at the Gresham Press, Old Woking, Surrey

and bound by
THE NEWDIGATE PRESS
at Book House, Dorking, Surrey

CONTENTS

ILLUSTRATIONS

GENERAL INTRODUCTION

Hatchments are a familiar sight to all those who visit our parish churches. They are not only decorative, but of great interest to the herald, genealogist and local historian. It is therefore surprising that — apart from local surveys in a few counties mostly in recent years — no attempt has yet been made to record them on a national scale. This series will, it is hoped, remedy the deficiency; it is proposed to publish separate volumes covering all English counties as well as Wales, Scotland and Ireland.

It is probable that no volume will be complete. Previously unrecorded hatchments will turn up from time to time; many have already been found in obscure places such as locked cupboards and ringing chambers. There are likely to be some inaccuracies, for hatchments are often hung high up in dark corners, and the colours may have faded or be darkened with age and grime. Identification is a problem if the arms do not appear anywhere in print: and even if the arms are identified, pedigrees of the family may not always be available. But enough has been done to make publication worth while; the margin to the pages will perhaps allow for pencilled amendments and notes.

Since I began the survey in 1952 many hatchments, probably evicted at the time of Victorian restorations, have been replaced in the churches whence they came. On the other hand, during the same period just as many hatchments have been destroyed. An excuse often made by incumbents is that they are too far gone to repair, or that the cost of restoration is too great. Neither reason is valid. If any incumbent, or anyone who has the responsibility for the care of hatchments which need attention, will write to me, I shall be happy to tell him how the hatchments may be simply and satisfactorily restored at a minimal cost. It is hoped that the publication of this survey will help to draw attention to the importance of these heraldic records.

The diamond-shaped hatchment, which originated in the Low Countries, is a debased form of the medieval achievement — the shield, helm, and other accoutrements carried at the funeral of a noble or knight. In this country it was customary for the hatchment to be hung outside the house during the period of mourning, and thereafter be placed in the church. This practice, begun in the early 17th century, is by no means entirely obsolete, for about 80 examples have so far been recorded for the present century.

Closely allied to the diamond hatchment, and contemporary with the earlier examples, are rectangular wooden panels bearing coats of arms. As some of these bear no inscriptions and a black/white or white/black background, and as some otherwise typical hatchments bear anything from initials and a date to a long inscription beginning 'Near here lies buried . . .', it will be appreciated that it is not always easy to draw a firm line between the true hatchment and the memorial panel. Any transitional types will therefore also be listed, but armorial boards which are clearly intended as simple memorials will receive only a brief note.

With hatchments the background is of unique significance, making it possible to tell at a glance whether it is for a bachelor or spinster, husband or wife, widower or widow. These different forms all appear on the plate immediately following this introduction.

Royal Arms can easily be mistaken for hatchments, especially in the West Country where they are frequently of diamond shape and with a black background. But such examples often bear a date, which proves that they were not intended as hatchments. Royal hatchments, however, do eixist, and any examples known will be included.

All hatchments are in the parish church unless otherwise stated, but by no means are they all in churches; many are in secular buildings and these, if they have no links with the parish in which they are now found, are listed at the end of the text. All hatchments recorded since the survey began are listed, including those which are now missing.

With only a few exceptions all the Yorkshire hatchments have been recorded and checked by Mr. D. M. Hallowes, and with meticulous accuracy; dealing with the hatchments of such a vast area has been a tremendous task, and it is over 25 years since Mr. Hallowes and I first corresponded on the subject. Mr. Hallowes has also checked and amended all the South Lancashire hatchment records, and made new discoveries. Mr. Robert Boumphrey has dealt most efficiently with the Cumbrian hatchments, checking and amending the original recordings, and also those in North Lancashire. Most of the hatchments of Durham and Northumberland were originally recorded by Dr. C. H. Hunter Blair, who was sending me his blazons in the early 1950s. All these have been carefully checked, in Durham by Mr. T. H. Brown, and in Northumberland by Mr. and Mrs. Alan Gardner; many of the blazons needed amendments and additions, and hitherto unknown hatchments have been added. I am also glad to acknowledge the valuable help given by Mr. James Blundell in the identification of a number of hatchment details in both Lancashire and Yorkshire which had previously defied solution. Finally, I must not forget to thank all those who sent the original hatchment blazons at the start of the Survey, far too many to mention, but without whose help and enthusiasm this volume might well not be published now; it would certainly have been less complete.

The illustrations on the following two pages are the work of the late Mr. G. A. Harrison and will provide a valuable 'key' for those unfamiliar with the complexity of hatchment backgrounds.

PETER SUMMERS
Day's Cottage, North Stoke, Oxford

1. MARRIED MAN
2. MARRIED WOMAN
3. BACHELOR
4. WIDOW
5. WIDOWER
6. SPINSTER

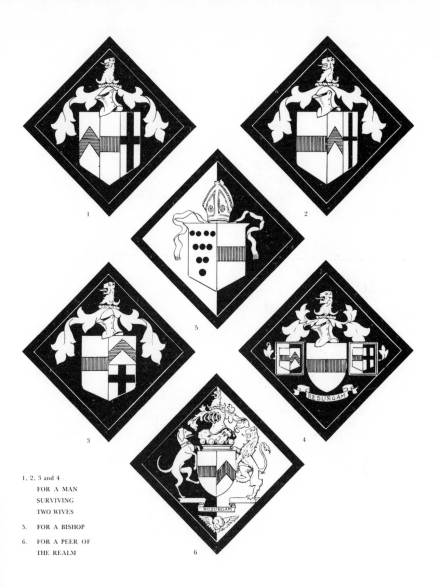

1, 2, 3 and 4
 FOR A MAN
 SURVIVING
 TWO WIVES

5. FOR A BISHOP

6. FOR A PEER OF
 THE REALM

ABBREVIATIONS

B.P.	= Burke's *Peerage, Baronetage and Knightage*
B.L.G.	= Burke's *Landed Gentry*
B.E.P.	= Burke's *Extinct and Dormant Peerages*
B.E.B.	= Burke's *Extinct and Dormant Baronetcies*
Hunter Blair	= Dr. C. H. Hunter Blair
Foster	= Foster's *Lancashire Pedigrees* or Foster's *Yorkshire Pedigrees*
Whitaker	= T. D. Whitaker, *History of the Parish of Whalley*, 1872/6
Baines	= Edward Baines, *History of the County Palatine of Lancaster*, 1888/93
Bloom	= J. H. Bloom, *Heraldry in the Churches of the West Riding of Yorkshire*, 1892

NOTE

Blazons throughout are exactly as noted at the time of recording, not as they ought to be.

CUMBERLAND

by

Robert S. Boumphrey

Witherslack 1: For the Very Rev. John Barwick, 1664
(*Photograph by J. Hughes*)

INTRODUCTION*

All who love Westmorland or have the good fortune to live in this delectable county will approve of the Editor's decision to record its hatchments separately from those of its sister Cumberland. Nevertheless, the existence of the new county of Cumbria cannot be ignored, and it seems an eminently sensible compromise to group the two counties together for the purpose of an introduction for it must be admitted that the number of hatchments in both is very small in proportion to the size of the area covered, only 17 in Cumberland and 20 in Westmorland.

But though small in number, they are in no way lacking in interest. The earliest seems to be that at Millom of Joseph Hudleston, of Millom Castle, who died 10 September 1700. It was at first thought that the hatchment at Greystoke showing Hudleston impaling Fleming might be that of Andrew Hudleston, of Hutton John, who married Dorothy, daughter of Daniel Fleming, of Skirwith, and died in May 1672, which would have made it even earlier, but the palaeographical evidence forced us reluctantly to attribute it to his descendant, Andrew Hudleston, of Hutton John, who married Elizabeth, 2nd daughter of Sir William Fleming, 3rd Bt., of Rydal, and died 2 February 1822. It is not without interest in its own right, however, owing to its unusual shape, that of a fusil rather than a tilted square or lozenge, and the same applies to the fusil-shaped hatchment of Robert Milbourne, of Armathwaite Castle, at Armathwaite.

The latest hatchment is of considerable interest owing to its modern date, that at Lorton Hall for Margaret Dixon, née Wright, who died 12 November 1951.

The hatchments at Grasmere are perhaps unusual in being painted on wooden panels instead of canvas, and on one of them there are signs of the paint blistering somewhat. In general, however, most of the hatchments in the area are in good condition and well cared for, with one notable excep-

*This Introduction covers both Cumberland (pp. 6-10) and Westmorland (pp. 12-17).

tion, that of Aglionby at Ainstable; exposed to the elements in an open porch, it has deteriorated to such an extent that the Aglionby arms can be deciphered only with difficulty, and the impaled coat has disappeared completely. One of the hatchments at Lowther would benefit by some slight repair.

The hatchment of Thomas Strickland, of Sizergh, who died 12 September 1835, is of interest in impaling a foreign coat, that of his wife, Gasparine Ursule Ida, youngest daughter of Baron de Fingerlen de Bischinsen. Another hatchment recalling a foreign marriage is that in Orton church of Joseph Burn, formerly Teasdale, of Orton (1770-1818), illegitimate son of John Burn, of Orton Hall (1743-1802), who changed his name to Burn on inheriting his father's estate. A merchant in Barcelona, he married Eulalia (d. 1813, aged 31), daughter of Joseph Vila, of Barcelona, and on obtaining a grant of arms for himself in 1810, obtained one for his wife also.

Most interesting of all, and very unusual, if not unique in design, are the two Barwick hatchments in Witherslack church. The hatchments themselves are conventional in shape and size, some 4½ft. x 4½ft., but each lozenge is painted on a much larger framed rectangular wood panel, approximately 8ft. wide and 5ft. high with cherubs' heads in each corner, both of them in excellent repair.

The hatchment of Jarrard Strickland is more like an early 17th-century memorial panel than a late 18th-century hatchment, for not only is it rectangular, but it also bears an inscription. However, in view of the black/white background and the fact that the inscription is a simple one relating to the date of death only, it has been included. On the other hand, a diamond shaped 'hatchment' for the Rev. Richard Hutton, at Bootle, who died in 1704, has been omitted; it bears a long inscription under the shield and was probably intended as a simple form of permanent memorial. I understand that a separate volume is to be published on all transitional hatchments and memorial boards as soon as the hatchment series is completed.

I am most grateful to the Rev. J. A. Woodhead-Keith-Dixon, of Lorton Hall, for checking many of the hatchments in Cumberland, and to my good friend, Mr. C. Roy Hudleston, for help not only in recording but also in identifying many of the hatchments in both counties. Most of all am I grateful to my dear wife whose keen eyesight so often noticed details which I might otherwise have missed, and who never complains of my frequent absences on heraldic jaunts.

R. S. Boumphrey,
22, Mitchelgate, Kirkby Lonsdale

AINSTABLE

1. Dexter background black
Argent two bars and in chief three martlets sable (Aglionby), impaling, Argent .... indecipherable (   )
Crest: A demi-eagle displayed or   Mantling: Gules and argent
Motto: Quand Dieu playea
Unidentified

ARMATHWAITE

1. All black background
Sable a chevron between three escallops argent (Milbourne)
Crest: A griffin's head erased proper beaked or   Mantling: Gules and argent
For Robert Milbourne, of Armathwaite Castle, d. 1782. (Hudleston and Boumphrey, Cumberland Families and Heraldry)

2. Dexter background black
Qly, 1st and 4th, Azure three escallops in pale or between two flaunches ermine (Clarke), 2nd, Barry of six argent and azure three chaplets or (Greystoke), 3rd, Sable a dove argent between three crosses formy or (Williams)   In pretence: Qly, 1st and 4th, Lozengy or and gules (for Pearman), 2nd, Argent on a bend cotised azure a lion passant guardant or (? Tothill), 3rd, Per pale gules and vert a fleur-de-lys argent (Elstob)
Crest: On a gem ring or set with a stone azure a pheon argent
Mantling: Azure and or   Motto: Trust in God
For Anthony William Clarke of Armathwaite Hall, and Queen Street, Cheapside, who m. Mary Pearman, and died at Pau, 1875. (Clarke family papers)

ARTHURET

1. Dexter background black
Qly, 1st and 4th, Or on a chief sable three escallops or (Graham), 2nd and 3rd, Argent a fess chequy argent and azure a chevron gules (Stewart)
Crest: Two wings addorsed or   Mantling: Gules and argent
Motto: Reason contents me
For the Rev. Robert Graham, D.D., Rector of Arthuret, who m. 1752, Frances, dau. of Sir Reginald Graham, 4th Bt. of Norton Conyers, and d. 2 Feb. 1782.   (B.P. 1949 ed.)

2. Dexter background black
Graham, impaling, Lozengy argent and gules a chevron azure (Gorges)
Crest (on a knight's helm): Two wings addorsed argent
Mantling: Gules and argent   Motto: In coelo quies
For Charles Graham, son of the Rev. Robert Graham, who m. 1781,
Elizabeth, dau. of Richard Gorges, of Eye, co. Hereford, and d. 15 Feb.
1782.   (B.P. 1949 ed.)

3. Dexter background black
Qly, 1st and 4th, Graham, 2nd and 3rd, Argent a fess chequy argent and
azure a chevron gules (Stewart), over all the Badge of Ulster, impaling,
Or a fess chequy argent and azure a bend engrailed within a double
tressure flory counter-flory gules (Stewart)
Crest, mantling and motto: as 2.
For Sir James Graham, 1st Bt., of Netherby, who m. 1782, Catherine
(d. 20 Sept. 1836), dau. of John, 7th Earl of Galloway, and d. 13 Apr.
1824.   (B.P. 1949 ed.)

GREYSTOKE

1. Dexter background black
Qly of six, 1st, Gules on a bend between six cross crosslets fitchy argent
the Augmentation of Flodden (Howard), 2nd, England with a label of
three points argent (Brotherton), 3rd, Chequy or and azure (Warren),
4th, Gules a lion rampant argent, armed and langued azure (Mowbray),
5th, Gules three escallops argent (Dacre), 6th, Barry of six argent and
azure three chaplets gules (Greystoke), impaling, Qly, 1st, Sable a lion
passant argent armed and langued gules, on a chief argent three cross
crosslets fitchy at the foot sable (Long), 2nd, Per fess or and gules a pale
counterchanged three choughs proper (Tate), 3rd, Gules ten bezants a
canton ermine (Zouche), 4th, Argent two chevronels gules a label of
five points azure (St Maur)
Crest: On a chapeau gules and ermine a lion statant guardant tail
extended or ducally gorged argent   Mantling: Gules and argent
Motto: Sola virtus invicta
For Henry Howard, of Greystoke Castle, who m. 1849, Charlotte
Caroline Georgiana, dau. of Henry Lawes Long, of Hampton Lodge,
Surrey, and d. 7 Jan. 1875.   (B.P. 1949 ed.)
(There is an identical hatchment in the parish church at Thornbury,
Glos.)

2. Dexter background black
Gules fretty argent (Hudleston), impaling, Gules a fret argent (Fleming)
Crest: Two arms embowed the hands proper holding a chapeau gules
feathered sable   Mantling: Gules and argent   Motto: Soli Deo
honor et gloria

For Andrew Hudleston, of Hutton John, who m. 1794, Elizabeth, dau.
of Sir William Fleming, 3rd Bt., of Rydal, and d. 2 Feb. 1822.   (B.L.G.
1937 ed.)

3. All black background
Hudleston arms only
Crest: Two arms embowed vested azure, cuffed argent, the hands holding
a man's scalp proper   Mantling: Gules and argent   Motto: Resurgam
For Andrew Fleming Hudleston, who d. unm. 2 Sept. 1861.   (B.L.G.
1937 ed.)

HUTTON-IN-THE-FOREST

1. Dexter background black
Argent a cross engrailed sable between four roundels sable each charged
with a pheon argent, the Badge of Ulster (Fletcher), impaling, Argent a
stag lodged gules, in the mouth a sprig of oak leaved and fructed proper
(Bowerbank)
Crest: A horse's head erased argent   Mantling: Gules and argent
Motto: Martis non cupidinis
For Sir Frederick Fletcher Vane, 2nd Bt., who m. 1797, Hannah (d. 17
Dec. 1861, aged 93), dau. of John Bowerbank, of Johnby, Cumberland,
and d. Mar. 1832.   (B.P. 1875 ed.)
(The hatchment is at the house, not in the church)

LORTON HALL

1. Sinister background black
Gules a fleur-de-lys argent, on a chief ermine a crescent or for difference
(Dixon), impaling, Sable on a chevron argent three spearheads gules, in
chief two unicorns' heads argent erased gules, armed and maned or, in
base on a pile or issuing from the chevron a unicorn's head erased sable
(Wright)
For Margaret, dau. of James Wright, of Glossop, Derbyshire, who m.
1911, James Dixon, of Millom, Cumberland, and d. 12 Nov. 1951.
(Rev. J. A. Woodhead-Keith-Dixon)

MELMERBY

1. All black background
Argent on a fess sable three fleurs-de-lys or, in chief a label of three
points gules (Pattenson), impaling, Azure three ears of guinea wheat
slipped and bladed or (Grainger)
Crest: From a ducal coronet or a camel's head proper

Mantling: Gules and argent   Motto: Pie repone te
For Thomas Pattenson, of Melmerby Hall, who m. 1768, Barbara (bur.
9 Dec. 1781), dau. of John Grainger, of Bromfield, and was buried 23
Nov. 1811.   (MS ped. by C. R. Hudleston)

2. Dexter background black

Pattenson, impaling, Sable an antelope salient argent armed crined and
hoofed or (Harris)
Crest, mantling and motto: as 1.
For John Pattenson, of Melmerby Hall, who m. Mary Anna Frances
Antoinetta, eldest dau. of Stephen Harris, and d. Mar. 1817. (Source,
as 1.)

3. All black background

On a lozenge surmounted by a cherub's head
Arms: As 2.
Motto: As 1.
For Mary Anna Frances Antoinetta, widow of John Pattenson, d. 1837.
(Source, as 1.)

MILLOM

1. Dexter background black

Gules fretty argent (Hudleston), impaling, Hudleston with crescent for
difference
Crest: Two arms counterembowed vested argent holding in the hands a
scalp proper   Mantling: Gules and argent   Motto: Soli Deo honor
et gloria
For Joseph Hudleston, of Millom Castle, who m. Bridget, dau. of
Andrew Hudleston of Hutton John, and d. 10 Sept. 1700. (B.L.G.
1937 ed.)

2. All black background

Hudleston arms only
Crest, mantling and motto: As 1.
Unidentified

BRUNSTOCK House, nr. Carlisle

1. All black background

Azure a lion rampant or (   )
Crest: A lion rampant or   Mantling: Gules and argent
Motto: Intro ut exeam   A very small hatchment on wood panel, only
14ins. x 14ins.
Unidentified

(This beautiful little hatchment, in the home of the late Mr J. W. Milbourne, a well known Cumbrian collector of antiques, is the smallest in the county. As it has not been identified, we do not know whether it is associated with any Cumbrian family.)

WESTMORLAND
by
Robert S. Boumphrey

APPLEBY Castle

1. All black background
Sable an eagle displayed ermine a bordure argent (Tufton)
Earl's coronet   Crest: A sea lion sejant proper   Motto: Ales volat
propriis   Supporters: Two eagles wings expanded ermine
c. 4ft. x 4ft., but mounted on a wooden frame, c. 5ft. x 5ft., to which
traces of black cloth are still attached
Probably for Charles, 10th Earl of Thanet, who d. unm. 20 Apr. 1832,
or for his brother Henry, 11th and last Earl of Thanet, who d. unm.
12 June 1849.   (B.E.P.)

BROUGHAM

1. Sinister background black
Gules on a chevron between three lucies hauriant argent a molet gules
for difference (Brougham), impaling, Gules two bars gemel and a chief
or (Richmond)
Crest: A cubit arm in armour the hand proper grasping a lucy argent
Mantling: Gules and argent
For Elizabeth, dau. of Christopher Richmond, of Highhead Castle, who
m. Peter Brougham, and d. 1729. He d. 1732. (Trans. C. & W.A. & A.
Soc. vol. lxi)

2. All black background
On a lozenge   Qly, 1st, Gules a chevron between three lucies hauriant
argent (Brougham), 2nd, Or a fess chequy gules and or between three
garbs gules, a label of three points azure (Vaux), 3rd, Argent a bend
chequy gules and or (Vaux), 4th, Gules a cross flory or (De la More)
In pretence: Gules a chevron argent between in chief two spur rowels
and in base a battleaxe or (Syme)
For Eleanora, only child of the Rev. James Syme, who m. 1777, Henry
Brougham, and d. 31 Dec. 1839, aged 89. He d. 13 Feb. 1810, aged 68.
(B.P. 1949 ed.)

3. All black background
Qly, 1st, Gules a chevron between three lucies hauriant argent
(Brougham), 2nd, Or a fess chequy or and gules between three garbs gules,
a label of three points argent (Vaux), 3rd, Argent a bend chequy or and
gules (Vaux), 4th, Gules a cross flory or (De la More), impaling, Gules
on a chevron argent between three garbs or three escallops sable (Eden)
Baron's coronet
Motto: Pro rege lege grege

Supporters: Dexter, A lion rampant vert collared chequy or and gules
Sinister, A stag argent attired or
For Henry, 1st Baron Brougham and Vaux, who m. 1819, Mary Anne,
eldest dau. of Thomas Eden, and widow of John Spalding, and d. 7 May
1868. She d. 12 Jan. 1865.   (B.P. 1949 ed.)

GRASMERE

1. Dexter background black
Gules a fret argent, the Badge of Ulster (le Fleming)   In pretence: Qly,
1st and 4th, qly, i. Gules on a bend between six cross crosslets fitchy
argent the Augmentation of Flodden (Howard), ii. Gules three lions
passant guardant in pale or a label of three points argent (Brotherton),
iii. Chequy or and azure (Warren), iv. Gules a lion rampant argent
(Mowbray), 2nd and 3rd, qly i. & iv. Or on a chief sable three escallops
or (Graham), ii. & iii. Or a fess chequy argent and azure in chief a
chevron gules (Stewart)
Crest: A serpent nowed holding in his mouth a garland of olive and
vine proper   Mantling: Gules and argent   Motto: Resurgam
For Sir Michael le Fleming, 4th Bt., who m. 1782, Diana, only dau. and
heiress of Thomas, 14th Earl of Suffolk and 7th Earl of Berkshire, and
d. 19 May 1806.   (B.P. 1949 ed.)

2. All black background
On a lozenge surmounted by a cherub's head
Gules a fret argent, the Badge of Ulster (le Fleming)   In pretence: As
1st quarter of 1.
For Diana, widow of Sir Michael le Fleming, 4th Bt. She d. 20 June
1816.   (B.P. 1949 ed.)

3. All black background
On an asymmetric lozenge surmounted by a cherub's head
Gules a fret argent, the Badge of Ulster (le Fleming)   In pretence: Qly,
1st, Gules a fret argent (le Fleming), 2nd, Howard, 3rd, Brotherton,
4th, Warren
For Anne Frederica Elizabeth, dau. of Sir Michael le Fleming, 4th Bt.,
who m. 1807, her cousin, Sir Daniel Fleming, 5th Bt., and d. 5 Apr.
1861.   (B.P. 1949 ed.)

4. All black background
Qly, 1st and 4th, Gules a fret argent (le Fleming), 2nd and 3rd, Qly or
and argent a lion rampant azure between three fountains (Hughes)
Crests: Dexter, as 1.   Sinister, A lion couchant or, the dexter paw
resting on a fountain   Motto: Resurgam
For Major-General George Cumberland Hughes le Fleming, d. 7 June
1877. (B.L.G. 1937 ed.)

(All four hatchments are on wood panels; there is also a rectangular panel with the arms of a Fleming baronet.)

LOWTHER

1. All black background
Or six annulets sable (Lowther)
Viscount's coronet   Crest: A dragon statant argent
Mantling: Gules and argent   Motto: Magistratus indicat virum
Supporters: Two horses argent each gorged with a wreath of laurel proper
Probably for Henry, 3rd Viscount Lonsdale, who d. unm. 12 Mar. 1750/1.   (B.P. 1949 ed.)

2. Dexter background black
Or six annulets sable, the Badge of Ulster (Lowther)
In pretence: Argent on waves of the sea a three-masted ship sails set flags and pennants flying proper (Hereditary Admiral of the Coasts of Cumberland and Westmorland) Also impaling, Per pale azure and gules three lions rampant argent a crescent for difference (Herbert)
Earl's coronet   Crest, mantling, motto and supporters: As 1.
For St George Henry, 4th Earl of Lonsdale, who m. 1878, Constance Gladys, dau. of Sidney, Baron Herbert of Lea, and d. 8 Feb. 1882. (B.P. 1949 ed.)

3. All black background
On a lozenge suspended from a true lover's knot
Qly, 1st and 4th, Azure a cross moline argent (Bentinck), 2nd and 3rd, Sable three stags' heads cabossed argent attired or, a crescent for difference (Cavendish), in fess point a martlet or, impaling, Or six annulets sable (Lowther)
Supporters: Two lions double-queued, the dexter or the sinister sable
For Mary, 2nd dau. of William, 1st Earl of Lonsdale, who m. 1820, Major-General Lord William Frederick Cavendish-Bentinck, C.B., youngest son of William, 3rd Duke of Portland, K.G., and d. 21 Oct. 1863.   (B.P. 1949 ed.)

MORLAND

1. Dexter background black
Argent a chevron between three eagles displayed azure (Nevinson), impaling, Azure a fess dancetty gules between three cross crosslets fitchy or a bordure or (Stanwix)
Crest: A leopard passant argent collared and lined or
Mantling: Gules and argent

For William Nevinson, of Newby, who m. Mary, sister of General Stanwix, and d. 1742. (Nicholson and Burn, Hist. and Ant. of Westmorland and Cumberland, 1777)

ORTON

1. Sinister background black
Vert a chevron or ermined sable between three lions rampant or, on a chief or ermined sable three fountains, all within a bordure wavy argent (Burn), impaling, Argent a cross couped gules between three crescents azure (Vila)
Motto: Resurgam   Two cherubs' heads above
For Eulalia, dau. of Joseph Vila, of Barcelona, who m. 1806, Joseph Burn, of Orton Hall, and d. 6 May 1813, aged 31. He d. 12 July 1818. (B.L.G. 5th ed.)

SIZERGH Castle

1.   Dexter background black
Sable three escallops argent (Strickland), impaling, Argent a fess and in chief three molets sable (Towneley)
Crest: A holly tree proper, in front on a scroll the motto 'Sans mal'
Mantling: Gules and argent   Motto: In coelo quies
Supporters: Dexter, A stag proper collared and chained or   Sinister, A bull proper charged with a molet sable
For Charles Strickland, who m. 1762, Cecilia, only dau. of William Towneley of Towneley, and d. 6 Oct. 1770. (Burke's Commoners, Vol. 1, p. 59; Strickland family papers.)

2.   Sinister background black
Qly, 1st, qly i. & iv. Sable three standing dishes argent (Standish), ii. & iii. Sable three escallops argent (Strickland), 2nd and 3rd, Strickland, 4th, Standish, impaling, Argent a chevron between three martlets sable (Lawson)
Crest: A holly tree proper
For Anastasia Maria, elder dau. and co-heir of Sir John Lawson, 5th Bt., of Brough Hall, Yorks, who m. as his 1st wife, Thomas Strickland, who assumed the name and arms of Standish. She d. 2 June 1807. (Sources as 1.)
(There is another hatchment for Anastasia Standish at Standish, Lancs.)

3.   Dexter background black
Qly, 1st and 4th, Argent billetty and a fess dancetty sable (Deincourt), 2nd and 3rd, Sable three escallops argent (Strickland), impaling, Qly, 1st and 4th, Or rising from a cloud in base proper a cubit arm sleeved

gules the forefinger pointing upwards proper, 2nd, Azure a demi-man in
armour holding a curved sword in his dexter hand proper, 3rd, Azure
four molets of six points one, two and one argent; in pretence, over
sinister quarterings, Per fess argent and gules in chief a demi-horse rampant proper, in base a bezant (Fingerlen de Bischinsen)
Crest: A holly tree proper fructed gules   Mantling: Gules and argent
Motto (below shield): Sans mal
For Thomas Strickland, who m. 1824, Gasparine Ursule Ida, dau. of
Baron de Fingerlen de Bischinsen, and d. 12 Sept. 1835. (Sources, as 1.)

4. All white background
Qly, 1st, Sable three escallops argent (Strickland), 2nd, Argent billetty
and a fess dancetty sable (Deincourt), 3rd, Argent a saltire gules (Neville),
4th, Per pale argent and gules a cross botonny counterchanged (Ward)
Crest and both mottoes: As 1.   Skull and crossbones to dexter,
winged hourglass to sinister, cherub's head in base
Unidentified

5. Dexter background black
Sable three escallops argent a crescent or for difference (Strickland),
impaling, Argent a fess and in chief three molets sable (Towneley)
Helm, but no crest   Mantling: Gules and argent
Motto: Requiescat in pace   Also on same scroll: Obiit 23 Mar
1795 Ann: Aetat 54
On a rectangular wood panel, c. 24ins. x 21ins.
For Jarrard Strickland, who m. 1779, Cecilia, widow of Charles Strick-
land, and only dau. of William Towneley of Towneley, and d. 23 Mar.
1795.   (Sources, as 1; inscr. on panel.)

WITHERSLACK

1. All black background
Gules two swords in saltire points upwards, blades per pale and per
chevron argent and sable counterchanged, hilts and pommels or, in
centre chief a capital D or (Deanery of St. Paul's), impaling, Argent a
rose gules barbed and seeded or between three bears' heads erased
sable muzzled gules (Barwick)
Crest: A bear's head erased proper muzzled gules   Mantling: Gules
and argent
For the Very Rev. John Barwick, M.A., D.D., Dean of St Paul's 1661-
1664, who d. 22 Oct. 1664.   (Trans. C. & W.A. & A. Soc., LXV,
241-4)

2. All black background
Barwick arms only
Crest and mantling: As 1.

Attributed to Dr Peter Barwick, physician to Charles II, younger
brother of Dean Barwick, d. 4 Sept. 1705, aged 85.   (Sources, as 1.,
224-5; Guide to Witherslack church, 1971.)

(These hatchments are most unusual in that, although of normal size,
each forms part of a much larger panel, on which outsize cherubs' heads
are painted. Despite the attribution of No. 2 to Dr Peter Barwick, who
died 41 years after his brother, both hatchments are identical in style
and would appear to have been painted at the same time. Machell, in
1692 (Antiquary on Horseback, p. 76) recorded that the Dean's arms
were painted 'in diamond frames on the backside of the Creed and
Commandments'; if these are the same as those now recorded, then
clearly Machell was right in his attributions)

ADDENDUM

BOWNESS-ON-WINDERMERE

1. All black background
On a lozenge with a gold border Qly, 1st and 4th, Gules a fess or between
three cocks' heads erased argent combed and wattled or (Allicocke), 2nd
and 3rd, Sable two bars ermine and in chief three crosses formy or
(Bathurst), impaling, Argent three calves passant sable (Metcalfe)
Crest: A cock argent combed and wattled gules membered or
Mantling: Gules and argent   Motto: Mors iter ad vitam
Despite the arms being on a lozenge, assumed to be for Benjamin
Allicocke, of Loddington, Northants, who married a Metcalfe and d.
1683.
(In the possession of Lt. Col. R. A. Allicocke Young, Bowfell, Bowness-
on-Windermere)

DURHAM

by

Thomas H. Brown

Durham Castle: For the Rt. Rev. William Van Mildert, 1836
(*Photograph by Dr. C. W. Gibby*)

INTRODUCTION

The recording of hatchments is both daunting and time-consuming. Daunting, as at one church I could not screw up enough courage to climb more than half-way up a long and unstable ladder with an armful of dusters, lamps and camera to view a very high and very dirty hatchment—I had to call in a member of a Mountain Rescue team, also interested in heraldry, to complete the job for me. On another occasion, I had to don boiler suit and rubber gloves to tackle the hatchments in the triforium of Durham Cathedral. These have now been cleaned and I hope they will at some time be put back on display. Time-consuming, because of the number of churches which are now kept locked, often with no indication as to where the key may be found (three miles away in one case). Then begins a Sherlock Holmes investigation to find the location of the key and also the location of the key's guardian. They rarely seem to be together when I call! Oh, for the days when all churches were open or the key was in an easily found hiding place in or around the porch door. As compensation the task is extremely interesting. This work, organised and edited by Peter Summers, will not be regarded just as an immense record but as a display of family history and so of local history.

Co. Durham is often supposed, like Northumberland, to be a desert when it comes to the smaller items of historical interest, but here we have churches with four, five and even six hatchments while Durham Cathedral has ten. There are 50 examples in the county (three others have disappeared since the Survey began), including those of a general, two bishops, two knights, four baronets and of each rank in the peerage, ending with the four dukes of Cleveland (2nd creation), showing their descent from King Charles II and Barbara Villiers, Countess of Castlemaine, Duchess of Cleveland. Two charges are unusual: semy of golpes—golpe

is a Spanish word for knock or injury, very appropriate for
a purple roundel; and cross crosslets which are rotated
through 45° into the saltire position (Crosier family).
Quarterings of note include Bowes and Lyon, Byron and
Milbanke, while Conyers is associated with perhaps the
earliest 'Worm' story in the Kingdom. The Rev. Sir George
Wheler (Durham Cathedral) was born at Breda in Holland
during the royal exile and was later knighted by Charles II,
the monarch who had previously placed John Cosin, a fellow
fugitive, into the chair of Prince-Bishop of Durham. The
earliest person commemorated died in 1637, while the most
complicated hatchment is that of the Marquess of Londonderry with two cartouches, the first surrounded by the collars
of the Garter and Bath, with eight 'medals' pendent, the
second overlapping the first and quarterly of twenty. There
are examples of the Eden family (Lord Avon was, before
his elevation, Sir Anthony Eden), one of whom was both a
4th and 6th baronet.

There are four oblong panels in contrast to the usual
diamond shape and the most curious of these is at Bishop
Middleham. The arms appear to be quarterly of six, two,
two and two. They are really three generations of the Hutton
family and their marriages.

When Peter Summers started this mammoth task I think
he must have taken as his motto a few words from Ovid—
'Teloque animus praestantior omni' which, very freely
translated, reads 'and with courage greater than any sword'.
The amateurs of heraldry and history are pleased to see that
his courage is being rewarded by the actual publication of
his collection.

Thos. H. Brown,
65, Low Lane, Middlesbrough

AUCKLAND ST ANDREW

1. All black background
Argent a cross engrailed gules between four water bougets sable
(Bowser)
Crest: A Moor's head and shoulders facing the dexter proper wreathed
about the temples or   Mantling: Vert and argent
Motto: Resurgam
Skull and crossbones below
Possibly for Ralph, son of Richard Bowser of Bishop Auckland, d. 18
Jan. 1690.   (M.I.)

AUCKLAND ST HELEN

1. All black background
Gules on a chevron argent between three garbs or three escallops azure,
the Badge of Ulster (Eden)
Crest: An arm in armour couped at the shoulders proper, garnished or,
grasping a garb or   Mantling: Gules and argent
Motto: Si sit prudentia
Skull and crossbones below
Lettered on frame: S.I.E. Aged 72, 1812.
For Sir John Eden, 4th Bt. of West Auckland, who d. 23 Aug. 1812.
(B.P. 1949 ed.)

2. All black background
Qly, 1st and 4th, Eden, 2nd and 3rd, Per bend gules and azure between
two bendlets or a rose argent between two fleurs-de-lys or (Smith), over
all the Badge of Ulster
Crests: Dexter, An arm in armour couped at the shoulder proper grasping
a garb or   Sinister, A lion rampant per pale azure and gules
Mantling: Gules and argent   Motto: In coelo quies   Skull and
crossbones below
Wide frame covered in brown felt
For Sir William Eden, 4th Bt. of Maryland and 6th Bt. of West Auckland,
who d. 21 Oct. 1873. (Hunter Blair; B.P. 1949 ed.)

BRANCEPETH

1. Dexter background black
Argent on a chevron between three cross crosslets fitchy sable an escallop
or (Russell), impaling, Gules a bend ermine, on a canton or a lion's head
erased gules (Milbanke)

Crest: A goat passant argent armed and unguled or
Mantling: Gules and argent   Motto: In coelo quies   Skull below
For William Russell, of Brancepeth Castle, who m. 2nd, Anne, dau. of
Edward Milbanke, and d. 8 June 1817.   (B.L.G. 2nd ed.)

2. Dexter background black
Russell, impaling, Gules three leopards' faces jessant-de-lys or, over all
a bend engrailed azure (Tennyson)
Crest: A goat passant argent   Mantling: Gules and argent
Motto: Resurgam
For Matthew Russell, of Brancepeth Castle, who m. Elizabeth, dau. of
George Tennyson of Bayous Manor, Lincs, and d. 8 May 1822.   (B.L.G.
2nd ed.; Hunter Blair.)

3. All black background
Russell arms only
Crest, mantling and motto: As 1.   Skull and crossbones below
Probably for William Russell, son and heir of Matthew Russell, buried
8 Feb. 1850.   (Hunter Blair.)

4. All black background
On a lozenge surmounted by a cherub's head
Qly, 1st and 4th, Argent a chevron azure between three fleurs-de-lys
gules (Bellasis), 2nd and 3rd, Argent a pale engrailed between two pallets
sable (Bellasis)
Motto: In coelo quies   Skull and crossbones below
Unidentified

5. Sinister background black
Qly, 1st and 4th, Argent a cinquefoil between two chevronels, all
between three cross crosslets fitchy sable (Russell), 2nd and 3rd, qly i.
& iv. Gules three cinquefoils pierced ermine (Hamilton), ii. & iii. Argent
a galley sable (Arran)   In pretence: Russell, as above
Viscountess's coronet   Supporters: Two mermaids proper each
holding a mirror or
For Emma Maria, dau. of Matthew Russell, of Brancepeth Castle, who
m. 1828, Gustavus Frederick, 7th Viscount Boyne, and d. 29 Apr. 1870.
(B.P. 1949 ed.)
(This hatchment was recorded since 1954, but is now missing)

6. All black background
Qly, 1st and 4th, Argent a chevron gules between three fleurs-de-lys
azure (Bellasis), 2nd and 3rd, Argent a pale engrailed between two
pallets sable (Bellasis)   In pretence: Argent on a cross voided
between four lions rampant five estoiles sable (Billingsley)
Crest: A stag's head erased holding a sprig of oak leaves in his mouth
proper   Mantling: indecipherable

For William Bellasis, of Brancepeth Castle, who m. Bridget, dau. and
heir of Rupert Billingsley, and d. 1769.   (Hunter Blair)
(This hatchment was in a dilapidated state when recorded by Hunter
Blair in Archaeologia Aeliana, 1954, but is now missing)

7. All black background
Argent a chevron gules between three fleurs-de-lys azure (Bellasis),
impaling, Argent a pale engrailed between two pallets sable (Bellasis)
Motto: In coelo quies   Two cherubs' heads above and skull below
Unidentified
(This hatchment was recorded by Hunter Blair in Archaeologia Aeliana,
1954, but is now missing. It was perhaps No. 4, incorrectly blazoned)

DURHAM Cathedral

1. All black background
Argent on a bend sable three pheons or (Bland)
Crest: From a ducal coronet or a leopard's head proper
Mantling: Gules and argent   Skull and crossbones in base
Badly damaged and frameless
For the Rev. Henry Bland, Canon of Windsor, Dean of Durham, and
Headmaster of Eton, d. 29 May 1746.   (Alumni Cantabrigienses)

2. All black background
Chequy azure and argent on a bend argent three lions passant gules, a
crescent argent for difference (Chandler)
Crest: A pelican in her piety or   Mantling: Gules and argent
Skull and crossbones in base   At top of frame W.C., at sides 17 & .7,
at bottom a cherub's head
For the Rev. Wadham Chandler, Prebendary of Durham, d. 2 June
1737.   (Alumni Cantabrigienses)

3. All black background
On a lozenge surrounded with gilt scrollwork
Or a fess wavy between six cinquefoils gules (Davison)
Mantling: Gules and ermine, with gold cords   Skull and crossbones
in base
On top of frame A.D., at sides 17 & 90; frame also decorated with metal
angels
For Anne Davison, youngest dau. of William Davison of Beamish, b.
1717, d. unm. 12 Apr. 1790.   (M.I.)

4. All black background
Qly, 1st and 4th, Sable a helm between three pheons argent (Dolben),
2nd and 3rd, Ermine on a bend sable three goats' heads erased or (Mulso),
over all the Badge of Ulster, impaling, Azure a fleur-de-lys argent (Digby)

Crest: A wyvern sejant proper   Mantling: Gules and argent
Skull and crossbones in base   On frame, the letters I.D. and the date
1756, also two metal cherubs and two metal angels
For the Rev. Sir John Dolben, 2nd Bt., who m. 1720, Elizabeth, dau. of
William, 5th Lord Digby, and d. 21 Nov. 1756.   She d. 1730.   (B.E.P.;
Surtees Soc. Vol. 34.)

5. Sinister background black
Gules on a chevron between three garbs or three escallops sable, in
chief an annulet argent (Eden), impaling, Argent on a bend cotised sable
three annulets argent (Dawnay)
Crest: An arm embowed in armour the hand proper holding a garb or
Mantling: Gules and argent   Skull and crossbones in base
Frame decorated with cherubs and crossbones, and at bottom, 1734
For Dorothy, dau. of Henry Dawnay, 2nd Viscount Downe, and widow
of Robert Shafto of Whitworth, who m. Thomas Eden, Prebendary of
Durham, and was buried 30 Nov. 1734.   He d. 3 Mar. 1754. (Bur. Reg.)

6. Sinister background black
Sable a cross engrailed between four spearheads argent (Prosser)   In
pretence: Qly, 1st and 4th, Argent a fess engrailed between three
annulets sable (Wegg), 2nd, Sable on a chevron between three goats'
heads erased argent three roundels sable (Cowper), 3rd, Sable a chevron
engrailed ermine between three beehives or (Lehook)
Motto: Be ye ready also   Cherub's head above
At the top of the frame are the letters S.P., and at the sides 18 & 24
For Sarah, youngest dau. of Samuel Wegg, who m. 1796, Richard
Prosser, Archdeacon of Durham, 1808-1831, and d. 4 Mar. 1824, aged
70.   (M.I.)

7. Dexter background black
Azure a pheon argent on a bordure or nine roundels gules (Sharp),
impaling, Or a saltire sable (Dering)
Crest: An eagle's head erased azure ducally gorged or in its beak a pheon
argent   Mantle: Gules and ermine   Motto: In coelo quies
Skull and crossbones in base   Frame decorated with metal cherubs;
at top the letters I.S., and at the sides 17 & 92
For the Rev. John Sharp, Prebendary of Durham, 1768-1791, who m.
Mary, dau. of Heneage Dering, Dean of Ripon, and d. 1792.   (M.I.)

8. All black background
On a lozenge surmounted by a cherub's head
Qly, 1st and 4th, Argent on a bend cotised sable three stags' heads
cabossed or in sinister chief an escallop gules (Harland), 2nd and 3rd,
Qly sable and gules a double-headed eagle displayed argent within a
bordure invected counterchanged, a label of three points argent for
difference (Hoar), impaling, Azure a fess between three unicorns passant
or ermined sable (Wilkinson)

Mantling: Gules and argent   Skull and crossbones in base
For Anne (Wilkinson), who m. William Harland, and d. 16 Jan. 1842,
aged 82. He d. 16 Nov. 1833, aged 83.   (M.I.)

9. Dexter background black
Or three stags trippant azure (Wats), impaling, Gules a cross or (   )
Crest: A stag's head erased proper   Mantling: Gules and argent
Skull and crossbones in base   At top of frame W.W., and at sides 17
& 36
For the Rev. William Wats, Prebendary of Durham, who d. 9 Feb. 1736.
Mary, his widow, was buried 3 Aug. 1748.   (M.I.)

10. All black background
Vert on a fess or three lions rampant vert (Wheler), impaling, Vert three
cranes' heads erased argent (Higgons)
Crest: From a mural coronet argent a griffin's head erased or
Mantling: Gules and argent   Motto: Pax et charitas
Frame decorated with a cherub's head, skulls and crossbones
For the Rev. Sir George Wheler, Prebendary of Durham, 1648-1723,
who m. Grace, dau. of Sir Thomas Higgons, of Odiham, and d. 15 Jan.
1723/4, aged 74. She d. 1703.   (D.N.B.)
(All these ten hatchments have been, or are being, restored and reframed.
They are here recorded in their former state, for the original frames
were unusual in that all bore initials, dates, or emblems of mortality,
and in three instances metal cherubs and angels)

DURHAM Cathedral Library

1. All black background
Qly, 1st and 4th, England, 2nd, Scotland, 3rd, Ireland   In pretence:
tierced, 1st, Brunswick, 2nd, Luneberg, 3rd, Westphalia   On an
inescutcheon the crown of Charlemagne surmounted by the royal crown
of Hanover   The shield surrounded with the Garter
Crest: (above a crowned helm) A lion statant guardant or imperially
crowned proper   Motto: Dieu et mon droit   Supporters, Dexter
A lion rampant or   Sinister, A unicorn chained argent
Mantling: Or and ermine
Background actually dark purple surrounded by a wide border covered
in black felt
In dexter and sinister base W.R. and IV
For H.M. King William IV, d. 20 June 1837.
(This hatchment, recorded in 1953, is now missing)

DURHAM Castle

1.   Sinister background black
Azure a cross or between four lions rampant argent (See of Durham),
impaling, Gules two scythe blades saltireways points upwards argent
(Van Mildert)
Above shield is a coroneted mitre, and behind shield a crozier and sword
crossed in saltire
For William Van Mildert, Bishop of Durham, 1826-36, d. 21 Feb. 1836.
(Hunter Blair)

DURHAM, St Mary-the-Less

1.   All black background
Qly of six, 1st, Ermine three bows strung in pale gules (Bowes), 2nd,
Argent a cross flory between four martlets vert (Dalden), 3rd, Azure a
maunch or (Conyers), 4th, Conyers, with an annulet gules for difference,
5th, Barry of eight or and azure (Aske), 6th Azure five fusils in fess
argent (Dautrey)
Crest: A sheaf of six arrows in saltire, three and three, points downwards
or   Mantling: Gules and argent   Motto: Vivit post funera virtus
Skull and crossbones in base
Probably for Thomas Bowes, of Bradley Hall, who d. unm. 13 Mar.
1844, aged 86   (Memorial window)

EBCHESTER

1.   All black background
Ermine on a canton gules an orle argent (Surtees), impaling, Argent on
a chevron between three molets sable three escallops argent (Blackett)
Crest: From a ducal coronet three feathers or   Mantling: Gules and
or   Motto: Malo mori quam foedari   Skull and crossbones below
For Anthony Surtees, of Hamsterley Hall, who m. 1801, Alice, sister of
Christopher Blackett, of Wylam, and d. 5 Mar. 1838.   (B.L.G. 1937
ed.)

2.   All black background
Surtees, but orle or, impaling, Per fess gules and argent six martlets
counterchanged (Fenwick)
Crest: From a ducal coronet or three feathers argent
Mantling: Gules and argent   Motto: As 1.
For Robert Smith Surtees, of Hamsterley Hall, the famous sporting
novelist, who m. 1841, Elizabeth Jane, dau. and co-heir of Addison
Fenwick, of Bishop Wearmouth, and d. 16 Mar. 1864.   (B.L.G. 1937 ed.)

3. All black background
Surtees arms only, as 2.
Crest, mantling and motto: As 2.
For Anthony Surtees, of Hamsterley Hall, who d. unm. at Rome, 17
Mar. 1871.   (B.L.G. 1937 ed.)

EGGLESCLIFFE

1. Sinister background black
Azure a cross or between four lions rampant argent (See of Durham),
impaling, Or on a bend between in chief a lion rampant vert and in base
a cross formy gules three garbs or banded gules (Maltby)
On a shield surmounted by a Durham bishop's mitre, and flanked by
palm branches   Escallop below
For Edward Maltby, Bishop of Durham, who d. 3 July, 1859.
(Hunter Blair)

GAINFORD

1. Sinister background black
Qly, 1st and 4th, Argent on a chevron azure three garbs or (Cradock),
2nd and 3rd, Argent on a chevron gules three sheldrakes or on a canton
gules a rose argent (Sheldon), impaling, Per pale or and gules a lion
passant guardant per pale gules and argent (Place)
Crest: A bear's head argent muzzled gules   Mantling: Gules and argent
For Elizabeth, dau. of the Rev. Edward Place, Rector of Bedale, who m.
as his 1st wife, Sheldon Cradock, of Hartforth, d. and was buried at
Gainford, 11 Dec. 1742.   (B.L.G. 2nd ed.)

2. Sinister background black
Cradock   In pretence: Azure a fess or ermined sable between three
unicorns passant argent (Wilkinson)
Crest: A bear's head proper muzzled gules   Mantling: Gules and
argent   Motto: Virtus post funera vivit
Letters E and C in corners   The whole background is gutty argent
For Elizabeth, dau. of Christopher Wilkinson, of Thorpe-on-Tees, who
m. Sheldon Cradock (son of No. 1), and d. 25 Aug. 1812.
(B.L.G. 2nd ed.)

3. All black background
Azure three sinister gauntlets or a crescent argent for difference (Vane),
impaling, Argent three spears palewise two and one azure, on a chief
azure a lion passant guardant or (Lysaght)
Crest: A dexter gauntlet erect holding a sword proper pommel and hilt
or   Mantling: Gules and argent   Motto: In coelo quies

Skull and crossbones below
For the Hon. Frederick Vane, 2nd son of Henry, 1st Earl of Darlington,
who m. 2nd, Jane, eldest dau. of Arthur Lysaght, and d. 1801. She d.
7 Apr. 1813.   (B.P. 1875 ed.)   In view of background perhaps used
subsequently for his widow.

GIBSIDE Chapel

1.   Dexter background black
Argent a lion rampant azure within a double tressure flory counterflory
gules (Lyon), impaling, Per pale or and sable a chevron between three
horses' bits counterchanged (Milner)
Earl's coronet   Crest: Within a garland of bay leaves a lady to the
girdle richly habited holding in her dexter hand the royal thistle all
proper   Mantling: Gules and ermine   Motto: In te Domine
speravi   Supporters: Dexter, A unicorn argent armed, maned and
unguled or   Sinister, A lion rampant gules
For John, 10th Earl of Strathmore, who m. 2 July 1820, Mary, dau. of
J. Milner, of Staindrop, and d. 3 July 1820.   (B.P. 1949 ed.)

HAMSTERLEY (Nr Witton le Wear)

1.   All black background
Qly, 1st, Ermine on a canton gules an orle or (Surtees), 2nd, Azure on
a fess argent between three cross crosslets saltirewise or three choughs
proper (Crosier), 3rd, Argent a fess gules between three popinjays vert,
on the fess an annulet for difference (Lumley), 4th, Sable a chevron and
a chief indented argent (Thornton), impaling, Qly, 1st, Surtees, 2nd,
Sable on a fess between three lambs passant argent an annulet sable
(Lambton), 3rd, Gules three crescents ermine (Freville), 4th, Argent a
fess engrailed between three annulets gules (Eschalles)
Crest: From a ducal coronet or three feathers argent
Motto: Malo mori quam foedari
For Crosier Surtees, of Merryshields, who m. his cousin, Jane Surtees,
of Redworth, and d. 21 Dec. 1803.   (B.L.G. 2nd ed.; Hedley,
Northumberland Families)
(There is another hatchment for Crosier Surtees at Heighington)

HAUGHTON-LE-SKERNE

1.   Purple/black background
Per pale sable and argent a chevron counterchanged, on a chief per pale
argent and sable three cushions counterchanged (Alexander), impaling,
Azure a lion rampant and a chief or (Dixie)

Shield on a mantle gules and ermine   Motto: Ingenium vides superat
Skull and crossbones below   Above, on the frame E.A., below 90,
at sides 17 and 90
For Elizabeth Dixie, who m. William Alexander, M.D., and was bur. 27
Jan. 1790.   (Hunter Blair; Franks Cat. of Bookplates)

2. Dexter background black
Argent three bends enhanced gules (Byron), impaling, Argent a chevron
purpure between three lamps or flaming proper (Farmer)
Crest: A mermaid holding a mirror proper   Mantling: Gules and argent
Motto: In coelo quies   Cherub's head below
For the Rev. Richard Byron, Rector of Haughton, 3rd son of William,
4th Lord Byron, who m. 1768, Mary, dau. of Richard Farmer, and d. 5
Nov. 1811.   She d. 9 May 1827.   (B.P. 1949 ed.)

HEIGHINGTON

1. All brown background
Azure on a bend or between two swans argent a molet for difference
(Jenison), impaling, Ermine three longbows palewise gules in chief three
roundels gules (Bowes)
Crest: From a ducal coronet or a dragon's head azure langued gules
Mantling: Gules and argent   On a wood panel in frame decorated
with roses, leaves and acorns in gold, c. 2ft. x 2ft.
For Barbara, dau. of Henry Bowes of Thornton, who m. as his 1st wife,
Sir Ralf Jenison of Elswick and Walworth, and d. 1656.   (Hunter Blair)

2. All brown background
Jenison (no cadency mark), impaling, Argent on a bend sable between
three choughs proper three lions' heads erased or (Carr)
Crest and mantling: As 1.   A small hatchment in decorated frame, as 1.
Probably for Jane, dau. of Ralf Carr of Newcastle, who m. as his 2nd
wife, Sir Ralf Jenison, and d. 1699.   He d. 3 Apr. 1701. (Hunter Blair)

3. Identical to Hamsterley 1.
For Crosier Surtees of Merryshields, who m. his cousin, Jane Surtees, of
Redworth, and d. 21 Dec. 1803.   (B.L.G. 2nd ed.; Hedley, Northumber-
land Families)

4. Sinister background black
Ermine on a canton gules an orle argent (Surtees), impaling, Per pale
argent and gules two legs in armour in fess couped at the thigh counter-
changed (Cookson)
Crest: From a ducal coronet or three feathers argent   Mantling: Gules
Motto: Malo mori quam foedari

For Elizabeth, dau. of Isaac Cookson, of Whitehill, who m. 1811, as his
1st wife, Robert Surtees, of Redworth, and d. 8 May 1847.
(B.L.G. 1937 ed.)
(There is another hatchment for Elizabeth Surtees at Low Dinsdale)

5. All black background

Qly, 1st and 4th, Argent a cross sable between four choughs proper
(Aylmer), 2nd, Ermine a saltire gules (Fitzgerald), 3rd, Argent a bull
passant a bordure sable bezanty, on a canton azure a harp or (Cole)
In pretence: Qly, 1st and 4th, Azure a bezant between three demi-lions
rampant or (Harrison), 2nd and 3rd, Azure a fess and in chief three
molets of six points or (   )
Crest: From a ducal coronet or a chough wings expanded proper
Mantling: Gules and argent   Motto: Hallelujah
For Lieut. General Arthur Aylmer of Walworth, who m. 1807, Ann, dau.
and heir of John Harrison, of Walworth Castle, and d. 5 Feb. 1831.
(B.L.G. 5th ed.; bur. reg.)

6. All black background

Qly, 1st and 4th, Harrison, 2nd and 3rd, Azure a fess and in chief three
molets of six points or (   ), impaling, Sable a bend between six
goats passant argent (Garforth)
Crest: A demi-lion rampant or holding in its paws a chaplet vert
Mantling: Gules and or   On wide black border to hatchment, at top
J.H., below 1819, at sides 7 and 4
For John Harrison, of Walworth Castle, who was bur. 15 Dec. 1819.
(Sources, as 5.)

LANCHESTER

1. All black background

On a lozenge   Argent a bend engrailed between six martlets sable
(Tempest)
Motto: Mors iter ad vitam   Skull and crossbones below
Inscribed on frame, at top and bottom, E.T. & 83, to dexter and sinister,
17 & 90
For Elizabeth Tempest, of Hamsteels Hall, Lanchester, d. unm. 17 July
1790.   (Hunter Blair)

2. Dexter background black

Qly, 1st, Argent a chevron sable ermined argent between three griffins'
heads erased sable (Pemberton), 2nd, Or a chevron between three
dragons' heads erased gules (Pemberton), 3rd, Gules . . . (too worn to
identify, 4th, Or a lion rampant gules (Stote), in centre chief a crescent
sable for difference   In pretence: Or two lions addorsed rampant
gules (Rippon)

Crests: Dexter, A griffin's head sable beaked or   Sinister, A demi-
lion rampant gules holding a cross crosslet fitchy or
Mantling: Gules and argent   Motto: In coelo quies
Skull and crossbones below
For Ralph Stephen Pemberton, who m. Anne, dau. and heir of Thomas
Rippon, of Low Mill, and d. 27 Feb. 1847.   (Hunter Blair)

3. All black background
Qly or and gules a bend sable, in sinister chief the Badge of Ulster
(Clavering)
Crest: From a ducal coronet or a demi-lion rampant sable
Mantling: Gules and or
For Sir Thomas John Clavering, 8th Bt., who m. 1791, Clare, dau. of
John de Gallais, Count de la Sable, of Anjou, and d. 4 Nov. 1853.
(B.P. 1875 ed.; Hunter Blair)

LONG NEWTON

1. All black background
Two overlapping oval shields   Dexter, within collars of the Garter
and the Bath, Qly, 1st and 4th, Azure three gauntlets or (Vane), 2nd
and 3rd, Or a bend countercompony argent and azure between two
lions rampant gules (Stewart)   Sinister, as dexter, with in pretence,
Qly of twenty, 1st and 20th (1st obscured, but presumably both Vane),
2nd, Sable three horses' heads erased argent (Blayney), 3rd, Argent a
chevron engrailed between three roundels sable (De la Dene), 4th, Azure
a chief argent over all a lion rampant or crowned gules (De la Leke),
5th, Gules a cross argent in the first quarter an escutcheon or charged
with three chevronels gules (St Owen), 6th, partly obscured, but bend
and fleur-de-lys gules (Fitz Ellis), 7th, Qly i. & iv. Paly of six or and
gules, ii. & iii. Ermine; all within a bordure azure (Persall), 8th, Argent
a cross engrailed gules (Hawte), 9th, Argent three cinquefoils gules
(Darcy), 10th, Argent a fess between six oak leaves gules (Fitz Langley),
11th, Argent two battleaxes in saltire sable (Maddison), 12th Argent a
chevron between three martlets sable (Marley), 13th, Argent a cross
sable between four roundels sable each charged with a pheon argent
(Fletcher), 14th Argent a bend engrailed between six martlets sable
(Tempest), 15th, Gules a cinquefoil pierced argent between eight cross
crosslets or (Umfraville), 16th, Per chevron or and sable in chief two
molets and in base a heathcock counterchanged (Heath), 17th, Sable a
maunch argent (Wharton), 18th, Qly, i. Or a lion rampant gules, ii. Or
a dexter arm proper holding a cross crosslet fitchy azure, iii. Argent a
lymphad sable, iv. Per fess azure and vert a dolphin naiant proper
(McDonnell), 19th, Sable a bend and in chief a tower argent (Plunket),
20th, Azure three gauntlets or (Vane)
Marchioness's coronet

Crests: 1. An armed hand holding a sword proper pommel and hilt or
2. A dragon statant or   Motto: Metuenda corolla draconis
Supporters: Two hussars of 18th Light Dragoons, dexter on grey, sinister
on bay, horse
Eight decorations pendent below dexter shield and one below sinister
For Frances Anne Emily, only dau. and heiress of Sir Henry Vane-
Tempest, 2nd Bt., who m. as his 2nd wife, Charles William, 3rd Marquess
of Londonderry, K.G., and d. 20 Jan. 1865.   He d. 6 Mar. 1854.
(B.P. 1949 ed; Armorial Families, 4th ed.)
(Husband's hatchment is at Thorpe Thewles)

LOW DINSDALE

1. **Identical to Heighington 4.**
For Elizabeth, dau. of Isaac Cookson, of Whitehill, who m. 1811, as his
1st wife, Robert Surtees, of Redworth, and d. 8 May 1847. (B.L.G.
1937 ed.)

RYTON

1. **All black background**
Qly, 1st and 4th, Gules a fess between two lions passant or (Simpson),
2nd and 3rd, Argent three oak trees proper (Anderson), impaling,
Azure a lion rampant and in chief three escallops or (Clutterbuck)
Crest: A demi-lion rampant or   Mantling: Gules and argent
Skull and crossbones below
For John Simpson, of Bradley, who m. Anne, dau. of Richard Clutter-
buck, of Warkworth, and d. 24 Apr. 1786. She d. 4 Aug. 1783.
(Hunter Blair)

2. **Sinister background black**
Argent fretty gules on a chief gules three leopards' faces or in chief the
Badge of Ulster (Liddell)   In pretence: Qly, 1st and 4th, Gules a fess
between two lions passant guardant or (Simpson), 2nd and 3rd, Gules
three oak trees proper (Anderson)
Baroness's coronet   Crest: A lion rampant sable billetty and
crowned or   Motto: Fama semper vivit   Supporters: Two
leopards or semy of roundels and murally gorged purpure
Mantling: Gules and argent   Skull and crossbones below
On frame, above, M.S.R.; below, aged 73, 22nd Nov. 1845.
For Maria Susannah, dau. of John Simpson, who m. 1796, Sir Thomas
Henry Liddell, Bt., cr. Lord Ravensworth, 1821, and d. 22 Nov. 1845.
He d. 7 Mar. 1855.   (B.P. 1875 ed.)

STAINDROP

1. Sinister background black

Azure three dexter gauntlets or (Vane)   In pretence: Sable three
swords in pile points downwards argent pommels and hilts or (Powlett)
Countess's coronet   Supporters: Dexter, A griffin argent collared
azure thereon three gauntlets or   Sinister, An antelope or collared
azure thereon three martlets or   All on a mantle gules and ermine
For Katherine Margaret, 2nd dau. and co-heir of Harry, 6th and last
Duke of Bolton, who m. 1787, as his 1st wife, William Harry, 3rd Earl
of Darlington, later cr. Duke of Cleveland, and d. 17 June 1807.
(B.P. 1875 ed.)

2. Dexter background black

Two oval shields   Dexter, within the Order of the Garter, Qly, 1st
and 4th, Vane, 2nd and 3rd, qly i. & iv. France and England qly, ii.
Scotland, iii. Ireland, at centre point a baton sinister ermine (Fitzroy)
Sinister, Qly, 1st and 4th, Vane, 2nd and 3rd, Fitzroy, impaling to
dexter, Powlett, and to sinister, Or on a fess embattled counter-
embattled between three leopards' faces azure two molets argent
(Russell)
Duke's coronet   Crests: Dexter, A dexter gauntlet erect holding a
sword proper pommel and hilt or   Sinister, On a chapeau gules and
ermine a lion passant guardant or collared compony ermine and azure
ducally crowned azure   Motto: Nec temere nec timide
Supporters: Dexter, A lion rampant guardant or crowned azure collared
compony azure and ermine   Sinister, A greyhound argent collared
as dexter   All on a mantle gules and ermine
The George pendent below the shields
For William Harry, 1st Duke of Cleveland, K.G., who m. 1st, 1787,
Katharine Margaret, 2nd dau. and co-heir of Harry, 6th and last Duke
of Bolton, and 2nd, 1813, Elizabeth, dau. of Robert Russell, and d. 29
Jan. 1842.   She d. 31 Jan. 1861.   (B.P. 1875 ed.)

3. All black background

Two oval shields   Dexter, within the Order of the Garter, Vane
Sinister, within an ornamental wreath, Vane, impaling, Sable three
swords in pile points downwards argent pommels and hilts or (Poulett)
Duke's coronet   Crests: Dexter, as dexter of 2.   Sinister, On a
chapeau gules and ermine a lion passant guardant or ducally crowned
azure   Motto and supporters: As 2.   Skull and crossbones below
For Henry, 2nd Duke of Cleveland, K.G., who m. 1809, Sophia, eldest
dau. of John, 4th Earl Poulett, and d. 18 Jan. 1864.   She d. 9 Jan.
1859.   (B.P. 1875 ed.)

4. Dexter background black
Qly, 1st and 4th, Vane, 2nd and 3rd, Fitzroy, impaling, Or six annulets
azure (Lowther)
Duke's coronet   Crests, motto and supporters: As 2.
For William John Frederick, 3rd Duke of Cleveland, who m. 1815,
Caroline, 4th dau. of William, 1st Earl of Lonsdale, K.G., and d. 6 Sept.
1864.   (B.P. 1875 ed.)
(There is another hatchment for the 3rd Duke at Santon Downham,
Suffolk)

5. Dexter background black
Two oval shields   Dexter, within the Order of the Garter, Qly, 1st
and 4th, Powlett, 2nd, Vane, 3rd, Fitzroy   Sinister, within an
ornamental wreath, Qly ermine and gules (Stanhope)
Duke's coronet   Crest: A falcon rising belled or ducally gorged gules
Motto: Aymes loyaulté   Supporters: Dexter, A lion rampant
guardant or crowned azure collared counter-compony azure and
ermine   Sinister, A greyhound argent, collared as dexter
For Harry George, 4th and last Duke of Cleveland, K.G., who m. 1854,
Catherine Lucy Wilhelmina, Lady Dalmeny, only dau. of Philip Henry,
4th Earl Stanhope, and d. 21 Aug. 1891.   (B.P. 1875 ed.; Complete
Peerage)

6. All black background
On a lozenge   Azure three ducal coronets or a molet argent for
difference (Lee)   In pretence: Qly, 1st and 4th, Per pale gules and
azure a lion rampant argent between eight cross crosslets fitchy or
(Hutchinson), 2nd and 3rd, Ermine on a fess sable three pheons argent
(? Clagett)
Probably for Mary, widow of John Lee. She d. 17 Aug. 1812. He d.
5 Aug. 1793.   (M.I. by hatchment)
(Hatchments 1 to 5 were formerly at Raby Castle)

THORPE THEWLES

1. Dexter background black
Two oval shields, the dexter overlapping the sinister   Dexter, within
the Garter, Qly, 1st and 4th, Azure three gauntlets or in chief a trefoil
slipped or (Vane), 2nd and 3rd, Or a bend counter-compony argent and
azure between two lions rampant gules (Stewart)   Sinister, within an
ornamental wreath, as dexter, with in pretence, Qly of fifteen, 1st,
obscured but presumably Vane, 2nd, Argent a chevron engrailed between
three roundels sable (De la Dene), 3rd, Azure a chief argent over all a
lion rampant or crowned gules (De la Leke), 4th, Gules a cross or in the
first quarter an escutcheon or charged with two chevrons gules (St
Owen), 5th, Or a bend between six fleurs-de-lys gules (Fitz Ellis), 6th,

obscured, 7th, Or a cross engrailed gules (Hawte), 8th Or three cinquefoils gules (Darcy), 9th Or a fess between six oak leaves gules (Fitz
Langley), 10th, Or a battleaxe bendways sable (Maddison), 11th, A
bend sable, partly obscured (   ), 12th Or a cross engrailed sable
between four roundels sable each charged with a pheon argent (Fletcher),
13th, Or a bend engrailed between six martlets sable (Tempest), 14th,
Gules a cinquefoil between ten cross crosslets or (Umfraville), 15th,
Sable a maunch argent (Wharton)
Marquess's coronet   Crests: Dexter, A gauntlet proper charged with
a trefoil or holding aloft a sword proper pommel and hilt or   Sinister,
A dragon statant wings raised or charged on the breast with a crescent
sable   Motto: Metuenda corolla draconis
Supporters: Two hussars in full uniform of 18th Light Dragoons, dexter
on a grey, sinister on a bay horse
Five decorations pendent from dexter shield and four from sinister
For Charles William, 3rd Marquess of Londonderry, K.G., who m. 2nd,
Frances Anne Emily, only dau. and heiress of Sir Henry Vane-Tempest,
2nd Bt., and d. 6 Mar. 1854.   She d. 20 Jan. 1865.   (B.P. 1949 ed.;
Armorial Families, 4th ed.)
(Widow's hatchment is at Long Newton)

NORTHUMBERLAND

by

Alan and **Muriel Gardner**

Hexham 5: For Rt. Hon. Sir Percy Loraine, Bt., 1961
(*Photograph by Mrs. Anne Shields*)

INTRODUCTION

All the 50 funeral hatchments known in Northumberland have been inspected recently. Of these 45 are in parish churches and of the remaining five, four are in a private house (Bywell Hall), and one in a Youth Hostel (Rock Hall).

Forty-one of the hatchments are for the period 1790 to 1890. The earliest in the county was at first thought to be at Bywell St. Andrew for Christopher Hall who died in 1675, but it bears a long inscription and was clearly intended as a permanent memorial. However, we understand that it will be included in a later volume dealing with transitional examples and memorial boards. The earliest true hatchment is for Sir William Forster, who died in 1700. Both Sir William and his immediate forebears were extremely improvident and in 1704 the estates were purchased by Lord Crewe, Bishop of Durham, whose wife was of the family. The next chronologically is for Thomas Forster (died 1738) who was a Jacobite general in the '15. The latest hatchment is that in Hexham Abbey for Sir Percy Loraine who died in 1961.

In the great Victorian rebuilding programme many hatchments were destroyed or found their way into private hands. However, the pendulum has swung and modern opinion is to regard those that remain as worthy of preservation. But if they are to be preserved then they must be maintained in reasonable condition and it is pleasing to be able to congratulate Hexham Abbey on the cleaning of their hatchments and to compliment Whittingham (St. Bartholomew), Alnwick (St. Paul) and Dr. Charles Bosanquet at Rock on the restoration of theirs. The Alnwick hatchment was in a sorry state and badly cracked, having been rolled up for years; it is for Hugh Percy, 3rd Duke of Northumberland and it is the only hatchment in the county for a Knight of the Garter. The Order of the Bath is represented by a hatchment among the interesting collection in Seaton Delaval church for 'the gay Delavals'. It is for Sir Francis Blake Delaval, a notorious

18th-century dandy and amateur actor, who achieved the distinction of causing Parliament to adjourn on one occasion so that members might repair to Drury Lane to watch the Delavals perform 'Othello'!

There is a funeral board of carved wood in the keep of the Castle at Newcastle-upon-Tyne, which belongs to the Livery Company of Shipwrights and used to be displayed on the Sallyport Tower of the town walls of the city whenever a freeman of the Company died.

Little is generally known of the coach painters and undertakers who gradually usurped the rights of the heralds to provide for funeral obsequies, and so two books of drawings in the possession of the Antiquarian Society of Newcastle-upon-Tyne are of particular interest. These volumes contain drawings of coats of arms of Northumbrian gentry and are the work of Ralph Waters, father and son, house and coach painters in Newcastle, whose lives spanned the period from 1720 to 1817. The majority of the armorials in the books are remarkable for the care and accuracy of the heraldic details, particularly as regards the marshalling of arms and many of the drawings are so similar in style and treatment to some hatchments still surviving as to tempt one to think that if the hatchments were not actually produced by the Waters, at least they were painted from their drawings which may account for the general good standard of the funeral art in Northumberland.

The hatchment of Henry Collingwood at Cornhill is of particular interest as it shows the arms of all of his three wives marshalled in a remarkable manner. The arms of his first wife are impaled to the dexter, and of his second wife to the sinister, which is not unusual; but the arms of his third wife appear in the base of the shield, a form of marshalling which is certainly very rare and possibly unique.

Finally, we wish to express our thanks to Mr. Tom Brown, author of 'Coats of Arms in Cleveland' for his help in checking a number of hatchments we were unable to visit.

A. T. and M. Gardner,
100, The Links, Whitley Bay

ALNWICK

1. Dexter background black

Two oval shields   Dexter, within the Garter, Qly of six, 1st, qly i. & iv. Or a lion rampant azure (Percy), ii. & iii. Gules three lucies hauriant argent (Lucy), 2nd, Azure a fess indented or (Percy), 3rd, Barry or and azure a bend gules (Poynings), 4th, Gules three lions passant argent a bend azure (Fitzpayne), 5th, Or three piles azure (Bryan), 6th, Gules on a saltire argent an annulet sable (Neville)   Sinister, within an ornamental wreath, Qly 1st and 4th, Argent on a fess sable three molets or (Clive), 2nd and 3rd, Per pale azure and gules three lions rampant argent (Herbert)

Duke's coronet   Crest: On a chapeau gules and ermine a lion statant the tail extended azure   Motto: Esperance en Dieu

Badge (below motto): On a field per pale sable and gules a shacklebolt or within a crescent argent   Supporters: Dexter, A lion rampant azure   Sinister, A lion rampant crowned or collared compony azure and argent   Pendent below, on the dexter side, the George, and on the sinister, the Badge of the Order of St Patrick

For Hugh, 3rd Duke of Northumberland, K.G., who m. 1817, Charlotte Florentia, 2nd dau. of Edward, 1st Earl Powis, and d. 11 Feb. 1847. (B.P. 1949 ed.)

(There is another hatchment for the 3rd Duke at Syon House, Middlesex)

BAMBURGH

1. All black background

Gules a tilting spear fesswise to dexter or headed argent between two dexter arms embowed in armour couped at the shoulders proper elbowed and cuffed or hands extended proper (Armstrong)

Baron's coronet   Crest: A dexter arm embowed couped at the shoulder in armour proper and encircled by a wreath of oak leaves the hand grasping a hammer proper

Motto: Fortis in armis   Supporters: Two smiths each holding a hammer over his shoulder proper

Pendent below shield the Badge of the Order of the Bath

For William George, 1st Lord Armstrong, of Cragside, Northumberland, who m. 1835, Margaret, only dau. of William Ramshaw, of Bishop Auckland, and d.s.p. 27 Dec. 1900.   She d. 2 Sept. 1893, but her arms are not shown on hatchment.   (B.P. 1949 ed.)

2. Dexter background black
Argent a chevron vert between three buglehorns stringed sable, mouth-
pieces to dexter (Forster), impaling, Gules on a bend argent three
mascles gules (Pert)
Crest: A dexter arm in armour embowed proper grasping the shaft of a
broken tilting spear or   Mantling: Gules and argent
Motto (above crest): Sta saldo   Skull below
For William Forster, of Bamburgh Castle, who m. Elizabeth, dau. of
William Pert of Essex, and was buried 6 Sept. 1700. (Hunter Blair)

3. All black background
Forster arms only, as 2.
Crest: A stag's head erased proper   Mantling: Gules and vert
Motto: In caelo quies   Skull below
For Thomas Forster, of Adderston, who d. unm. at Boulogne, and was
buried at Bamburgh, 7 Dec. 1738.   (Hunter Blair)

4. All black background
Forster, with mouthpieces to sinister, impaling, Sable three salmon
hauriant two and one argent (Ord)
Crest: As 3.   Mantling: Gules, vert and argent ending in tassels
Mottoes: (above crest) In Caelo quies   (below shield) Memento mori
Skull and bone in base
Presumably, despite background, for John Forster, of Adderston, who
m. Isabella, dau. of William Ord of Sandy Bank, and was buried 3 July
1745.   She d. Nov. 1789.   (Hunter Blair)

BELSAY Castle

1. Sinister background black
Argent a chevron chequy or and sable between three leopards' heads
erased azure collared or, the Badge of Ulster (Monck), impaling, Or a
chevron gules between two lions passant guardant sable (Cooke)
Crest: On a mount vert a demi-griffin couchant couped argent
Motto: In coelo quies
For Louisa, 2nd dau. of Sir George Cooke, Bt., who m. 1804, as his 1st
wife, Sir Charles Miles Lambert Monck, 6th Bt., and d. 5 Dec. 1824.
(B.P. 1875 ed.)

2. All black background
Qly, 1st and 4th, Monck, 2nd and 3rd, Qly gules and or in the first and
fourth quarter a cross patonce argent (Middleton), over all the Badge of
Ulster, impaling, Qly, 1st and 4th, Gules a bezant between three demi-
lions rampant argent (Bennet), 2nd and 3rd, Gules a lion rampant
within a bordure engrailed argent (Grey)
Crest: A demi-griffin erased argent   Mantling: Gules and argent

For Sir Charles Miles Lambert Monck, 6th Bt., who m. 2nd, Mary Elizabeth, dau. of Charles, 4th Earl of Tankerville, and d. 20 July 1867.
(B.P. 1875 ed.)
(These two hatchments were sold in 1962 and their present whereabouts
is not known)

BYWELL ST ANDREW

1. Dexter background black

Gules a lion rampant within an orle of eight crescents argent (Beaumont),
impaling, Ermine a fess between three pheons sable (Atkinson)
Crest: A bull's head erased qly argent and gules   Mantling: Gules and or
Motto: Fide sed cui vide   Skull and crossbones in base
For Thomas Wentworth Beaumont of Bretton Hall, Yorks, and Bywell
Hall, Northumberland, who m. 1827, Henrietta, dau. and co-heir of
John Atkinson, of Maple Hayes, and d. 20 Dec. 1848.   (B.L.G. 5th
ed.; Hunter Blair)
(There is another hatchment for Thomas Wentworth Beaumont in
Bywell Hall)

2. Dexter background black

Ermine a boar passant azure armed or langued gules, on a chief or two
molets gules (Bacon), impaling, Gules a lion rampant within a bordure
engrailed argent a martlet for difference (Grey of Kyloe)
Crest: A demi-boar rampant reguardant in its mouth a spear argent
Mantling: Gules and argent   Motto: In coelo quies
For Charles Bacon Forster, of Adderston, who took the name and arms
of Bacon, m. Dorothy, sister and heiress of Marmaduke Grey, of Kyloe,
and d. 18 Sept. 1830.   She d. 1836.   (Hunter Blair)

BYWELL HALL

1. All black background

Qly, 1st and 4th, Sable a chevron between three leopards' faces or
(Wentworth), 2nd and 3rd, Argent on a chevron between three pierced
molets sable three escallops argent (Blackett), over all the Badge of
Ulster
Crest: A griffin passant argent ducally gorged or   Mantling: Gules and
argent   Motto: In coelo quies   Frame covered in black cloth
For Sir Thomas Wentworth, 5th Bt., who d. 10 July 1792.   (B.E.B.;
Hunter Blair)

2. Dexter background black

Qly, 1st and 4th, Gules a lion rampant within an orle of crescents argent,
a label for difference (Beaumont), 2nd and 3rd, Sable a fess or between

three asses argent (Ayscough)   In pretence: Sable a chevron between
three leopards' faces or a bordure compony argent and gules (Went-
worth)
Crests: Dexter, A bull's head erased qly argent and gules horned or
charged on the breast with a label and a crescent or   Sinister, A
griffin passant argent armed or   Mantling: Gules and argent
Motto: Fide sed qui vide   Frame covered in black cloth
For Thomas Richard Beaumont, of Bretton Hall, Yorks, and Hexham
Abbey, Northumberland, who m. Diana, sole heiress of Sir Thomas
Wentworth, Bt., and d. 31 July 1829.   (Hunter Blair)

3. All black background
On a lozenge surmounted with an escallop
Arms: As 2.
Frame covered in black cloth
For Diana, widow of Thomas Richard Beaumont. She d. 10 Aug. 1831.
(Hunter Blair)

4. Dexter background black
Qly, 1st and 4th, Gules a lion rampant within an orle of crescents argent
(Beaumont), 2nd, Ayscough, 3rd, Sable a chevron between three leopards'
faces or (Wentworth), impaling, Argent a double-headed eagle displayed
sable, on a chief or a cinquefoil between two martlets gules (Atkinson)
Crests: Dexter, A bull's head erased qly argent and gules   Sinister, A
griffin passant argent ducally gorged or   Mantling: Gules and argent
Motto: Fide sed qui vide   Frame covered in black cloth
For Thomas Wentworth Beaumont of Bretton Hall, Yorks, and Bywell
Hall, Northumberland, who m. 1827, Henrietta, dau. and co-heir of
John Atkinson, of Maple Hayes, and d. 20 Dec. 1848.   (Hunter Blair)
(There is another hatchment for Thomas Wentworth Beaumont in the
parish church, but with different arms for Atkinson)

CORNHILL

1. Dexter background black
Qly, 1st and 4th, Argent a chevron between three stags' heads erased
sable (Collingwood), 2nd, Azure a dexter arm embowed proper, sleeved
argent, holding a baton or (Clennell), 3rd, Ermine on a chevron
engrailed or three escallops sable in chief a lion passant or (Tolley),
impaling to the dexter, Barry of twelve argent and azure, over all six
escutcheons, three, two and one gules (Mills), impaling to the sinister,
Azure a fess between three unicorns passant or (Wilkinson), impaling
to the base, Gules three crescents two and one between three bars or in
chief two spears in saltire with broken points pendent or (Watson)
Crest: A stag statant in front of a holly bush proper
Mantling: Gules and argent   Motto: Ferar unus et idem

Skull and crossbones below
For Henry Collingwood, who m. 1st, Margaret Mills, of Glanton, and
2nd, 1793, Dorothy Wilkinson, of Cochoe, and 3rd, 1800, Mary Anne
(d. 17 Feb. 1852), younger dau. of the Rev. Samuel Watson, D.D., of
Rothbury, and d. 20 July 1827.   (B.L.G. 1937 ed.)

2. Dexter background black
Argent a chevron sable between three stags' heads erased proper
(Collingwood), impaling, Azure on a bend argent three billets sable
(Haggerston)
Crest and mantling: As 1.   Cherub's head below
For Henry John William Collingwood, who m. 1824, Frances Carnaby,
dau. of Thomas Haggerston, of Ellingham, and d. 14 Apr. 1840.
(B.L.G. 1937 ed.)

3. All black background
Collingwood arms only, as 1.
Crest and mantling: As 1.   Motto: In coelo quies
Probably for John Collingwood, of Lilburn Tower and Cornhill House,
who m. Miss Cornthwaite and was bur. 17 Aug. 1787.   (B.L.G. 1937
ed.; par.regs.)

CRAMLINGTON

1. Dexter background black
Qly, 1st and 4th, Argent two chevrons azure between three trefoils
slipped vert (de Cardonnel), 2nd, Argent two bars azure (Hilton), 3rd,
Argent a chevron between three martlets sable (Lawson)
Crests: Centre, A goldfinch proper, with the motto above, L'esperance
me console (de Cardonnel)   Dexter, On a chapeau gules and ermine
a molet of eight points or surmounted by a man's head affronté proper,
with the motto above, Tant que je puis (Hilton)   Sinister, Two arms
vambraced and embowed proper garnished or supporting in the hands a
sun in splendour proper, with the motto above, Rise and shine (Lawson)
Mantling: Gules and argent   Motto (below shield): In coelo quies
Probably for Adam Mansfeldt de Cardonnel-Lawson, who m. Mary
(d. 25 May 1830), dau. of General James Kidd, and was bur. at Cram-
lington, 14 June 1820, aged 73.   (Par. Regs.; MS pedigree of Lawson
family)

DALTON

1. Sinister background black
Argent a chevron between three stags' heads erased sable (Collingwood),
impaling, Per fess argent and ermine three lions passant guardant in
pale sable (Calcraft)

Three cherubs' heads above shield and skull and crossbones below
For Arabella, dau. of General Henry John Calcraft, of Cholderton,
Hants, who m. 1820, Edward Collingwood, of Dissington, and d. 31
May 1840.   (B.L.G. 1937 ed.; M.I.)

2. All black background
Arms: As 1.
Crest: In front of a fir tree a stag statant proper
Mantling: Gules and argent   Motto: Nil conscire sibi
For Edward Collingwood, who d. 4 Aug. 1866, aged 74.   (B.L.G.
1937 ed.)

EMBLETON

1. Sinister background black
Qly or and gules in the first quarter a raven proper (Craster, impaling,
Gules a double-headed eagle displayed argent, on a chief or a rose
between two martlets gules (Atkinson)
Motto: In coelo quies   Cherubs' heads above and at side of shield
For Isabella, dau. of Charles Atkinson, of Newcastle, who m. Shafto
Craster, of Craster, and d. Nov. 1831.   (B.L.G. 1937 ed.)

2. All black background
Arms: As 1.
Crest: A raven proper   Mantling: Gules and argent
Motto: Cum sanctis in coelo
For Shafto Craster, of Craster, who d. 7 May 1837.   (B.L.G. 1937 ed.)

HEBRON

1. Dexter background black
Qly, 1st and 4th, Argent a fess between three crescents gules (Ogle), 2nd
and 3rd, Azure an orle or (Bertram), impaling, Azure a wolf rampant
argent (Dunn)
Crest: From a ducal coronet or a bull's head sable armed or
Mantling: Gules and argent   Motto: Coelo quies
For Lt. Col. William Ogle Wallis Ogle, who m. Elizabeth, dau. of
Theophilus Dunn, of Morpeth, and was bur. at Hebburn, 18 Feb. 1804.
(Hodgson, History of Northumberland, part 2, vol. 2, p. 136)

HEXHAM

1. All black background

Argent on a bend gules between three roundels sable three swans argent
(Clarke)   In pretence: Gules a saltire or charged with another vert
(Andrewes)
Crest: A swan wings elevated proper resting the dexter claw on a roundel
sable   Mantling: Gules and argent   Motto: In coelo quies
Skull and crossbones in base   No frame
For the Rev. Sloughter Clarke, lecturer of Hexham Abbey, 1766-1801,
who m. Honor, dau. of Robert Andrewes, and d. 22 Apr. 1820. She d.
9 Mar. 1805.   (Hunter Blair)

2. Sinister background black

Qly, 1st and 4th, Clarke, 2nd and 3rd, Andrewes   In pretence: Gules
on a bend argent three molets azure (Shafto)
Three cherubs' heads above shield, skull and crossbones below, and background decorated with leafy boughs   No frame
For Martha, dau. of Charles Shafto, who m. the Rev. Robert Clarke,
lecturer of Hexham Abbey 1801-1824, and d. 1814.   (Hunter Blair)

3. All black background

Qly, 1st and 4th, Clarke, with a crescent gules charged with a label or
in 1st quarter for difference, 2nd and 3rd, Andrewes   In pretence:
Shafto
Crest and mantling: As 1.   Motto: Resurgam
For the Rev. Robert Clarke, who d. 20 Apr. 1824.   (Hunter Blair)
(There is another hatchment for the Rev. Robert Clarke at St Oswald-
at-Lee)

4. Dexter background black

Qly, 1st and 4th, Qly sable and gules an eagle displayed argent, on a
chief or three martlets gules (Sparke), 2nd and 3rd, Gules three herons
close argent (Heron)   In pretence: Gules on a bend argent three molets
azure (Shafto)
Crest: An eagle displayed ermine   Mantling: Gules and argent
No frame
For Isaac Sparke, of Summerods, Hexham, who m. Elizabeth Mary,
dau. and heiress of George Delaval Shafto of Carrycoats, and d. 1816.
She d. 1819.   (Hunter Blair)

5. All black background

Qly sable and argent a cross counterchanged, in dexter chief the Badge
of Ulster (Loraine)   The shield surrounded with the Collar of the
Order of St. Michael and St George and the motto of the Order

Crest: Out of a naval coronet or a naked'arm embowed encircled with a
laurel wreath proper the hand holding a trident or   Above the crest
the motto, Saevumque tridentum servamus   Below the arms the motto,
Lauro scutoque resurgo   Mantling: Sable and argent
Supporters: On either side a horse, the dexter sable, the sinister argent,
each bridled and resting the interior foreleg on the stump of a bay tree
eradicated and sprouting proper
For the Rt. Hon. Sir Percy Lyham Loraine, 12th Bt., P.C., G.C.M.G.,
who m. 1924, Louise Violet Beatrice, elder dau. of Major-General Hon.
Edward James Montagu-Stuart-Wortley, and d. 23 May 1961.   (B.P.
1949 ed.; Who was Who 1961-1970)
(Hatchment painted by Mr A. D. Cook)

LINDISFARNE

1. Dexter background black

Qly of eight, 1st, Sable a fess or between three asses passant argent a
martlet or for difference (Askew), 2nd, Gules two bars engrailed ermine,
on a chief or a lion passant guardant gules (Storrs), 3rd, Or a chevron
between three molets pierced azure (Crackenthorpe), 4th, Gules four
bars between three escallops argent (Rawlinson), 5th, Or five fusils
conjoined in fess azure (Pennington), 6th, Argent fretty gules a chief
azure (Curwen), 7th, Azure a lion rampant ermine (Monk), 8th, Sable
on a chevron argent between three cross crosslets or three roses gules
(Mottram)   In pretence: Qly, 1st and 4th, Argent on a chevron
engrailed sable between three martlets azure three crescents or (Watson),
2nd and 3rd, Qly or and gules in the first quarter a crow sable (Craster)
Crest: A dexter hand proper holding erect a dagger argent hilted or
transfixing a Saracen's head couped proper embrued gules, wreathed
about the temples argent and gules   On a scroll above crest: Fac et
spera   Mantling: Gules and argent
Motto: Patientia casus exuberat omnes   Winged skull below
For John Askew, of Pallinsburn, who m. 1770, Bridget, dau. and heir
of Thomas Watson, of Gostwick, Durham, and d. 28 Oct. 1794.
(B.L.G. 1937 ed.)

2. All black background

Barry of eight or and sable (Selby)   In pretence: Argent a fess
between a crescent in chief and a cinquefoil in base gules (Wilkie)
Crest: A Saracen's head and shoulders proper charged on the sinister
shoulder with a molet gules, wreathed at the temples sable and gules

Mantling: Gules and argent   Motto: Fort et loyale
For Henry Collingwood Selby, of Holy Island, who m. Frances, dau.
and heiress of Prideaux Wilkie, of Doddington, and d. 1839, aged 91.
She d. 1790, aged 36.   (Hunter Blair)

3. Dexter background black
Azure on a bend cotised argent three billets sable, on the bend the
Badge of Ulster (Haggerston), impaling, Sable three roses argent (Smythe)
Crest: A lion passant argent   Mantling: Sable and argent
Motto: In te Domine paravi   Skull and crossbones below
Frame covered in black material with rosettes at corners
For Sir Carnaby Haggerston, 5th Bt., who m. Frances, dau. of Walter
Smythe, and d. 3 Dec. 1831.   (B.P. 1949 ed.)

4. All black background
On a lozenge surmounted by three cherubs' heads
Arms: As 3.
Frame covered in black material with rosettes at corners
For Frances, widow of Sir Carnaby Haggerston, 5th Bt., d. 1836. (B.P.
1949 ed.)

ROCK Hall

1. Sinister background black
Qly, 1st and 4th, Or on a mount vert a tree proper, on a chief gules a
crescent between two molets or (Bosanquet), 2nd, Gules in dexter base
a buck's head cabossed argent attired or in sinister chief a castle or
(Dunster), 3rd, Per pale or and gules a fess between three hinds trippant
all counterchanged (Gardner), a crescent for difference over impalement
line, per pale or and gules, impaling, Qly, 1st, Argent a greyhound
passant sable (Holford), 2nd, Sable a lion passant argent, on a chief or
three molets sable (Stayner), 3rd, Per fess sable and ermine a pale
counterchanged and three pheons or (Nutt), 4th, Or a fess wavy between
three escallops or (Lade)
Motto: In coelo quies   Cherub's head above shield
For Charlotte Anne, dau. of Peter Holford, master in Chancery, who m.
Charles Bosanquet of London, and d. 15 Feb. 1839.   (Hunter Blair)

ROTHBURY

1. Identical to No. 1 at Bamburgh
For William George, 1st Lord Armstrong, who d.s.p. 27 Dec. 1900.
(B.P. 1949 ed.)

ST JOHN LEE

1.   All black background
Argent two bars and in chief three escallops azure (Errington)
Crest: A unicorn's head erased per pale argent and gules
Mantling: Gules and argent   Motto: Virtus   Skull and crossbones
below
Probably for John Errington, of Beaufront, who d. 28 June 1827.
(Hunter Blair)

2.   All black background
On a lozenge suspended from a lover's knot
Argent a cross engrailed gules between four molets azure, on a chief or
three roses gules (Allgood)   In pretence: Qly of six, 1st, Gules on a
chevron between three stags' heads erased or three hunting horns sable
(Hunter), 2nd, Argent a fess azure over all a lion rampant gules
(Whittingham), 3rd, Or a bend compony gules and or between two
roundels sable (Jaqueman), 4th, Argent a chevron between three
buntings azure (Bunting), 5th and 6th, Per pale argent and vert three
greyhounds courant in pale counterchanged, on a chief azure a sword
and garb in saltire or (Tomlinson)
For Elizabeth, 2nd dau. and co-heiress of John Hunter, of The Hermitage, who m. 1820, as his second wife, Robert Lancelot Allgood, of
Nunwick, and d. 7 Sept. 1864. He d. 25 May 1854.   (B.L.G. 1937
ed.)

3.   Dexter background black
Argent on a fess gules three cross crosslets fitchy argent (Cuthbert),
impaling, Qly, 1st and 4th, Per pale argent and gules two men's legs
couped at the thigh in armour counterchanged (Cookson), 2nd and 3rd,
Or a chevron chequy azure and gules between three cinquefoils gules
(Cooke)
Crest: A lion's head erased argent collared gules, the collar charged
with three cross crosslets fitchy argent   Mantling: Gules and argent
For William Cuthbert, of Beaufront Castle, who m. 1840, Mary, dau.
of Isaac Cookson, of Meldon, by Jane, dau. and heiress of Cooke of
Togstone, and d. 29 Nov. 1878. She d. 24 Apr. 1894.   (B.L.G. 1937
ed.)

ST OSWALD-AT-LEE

1.   Identical to Hexham No. 3
For the Rev. Robert Clarke, Lecturer of Hexham Abbey 1801-1824,
who m. Martha, dau. of Charles Shafto, and was bur. at Hexham, 2 May
1824.   (Hunter Blair)

SEATON DELAVAL

1. All black background

Two oval shields   Dexter, within Order of the Bath, Qly, 1st and 4th, Ermine two bars vert (Delaval), 2nd and 3rd, Argent a chevron between three garbs sable (Blake)   Sinister, two coats per fess, in chief, Sable three swords in pile argent pommels and hilts or (Paulet), in base, Delaval; both impaling, Sable an eagle displayed ermine a bordure argent (Tufton)

Crest: A ram's head erased argent armed or   Mantle: Gules and ermine
Motto: Dieu me conduise   Supporters: Dexter, A man bareheaded and in armour, a sash gules on his breast, in his right hand a scroll with seals attached, upon it Magna Charta, in his left hand a sword resting on top of the shield   Sinister, A man in like armour in his left hand a banner, Gules a lion passant within a bordure or, the banner resting on his right shoulder   Winged skull below

For Sir Francis Blake Delaval of Seaton Delaval, who m. Isabella, dau. of Thomas Tufton, Earl of Thanet, and widow of Lord Nassau Paulet, and d. 7 Aug. 1771.   (B.E.P.)

2. Dexter background black

Qly, 1st and 4th, Delaval, 2nd and 3rd, Or a cross vert (Hussey), impaling, Argent on a bend vert three crescents or a bordure engrailed gules (Scott)

Crest and motto: As 1.   Mantling: Gules and argent
For Edward Hussey Delaval, who m. 1808, Sarah, dau. of George Scott, of Methley, and d. 14 Aug. 1814.   (Hunter Blair)
(There is another hatchment for Edward Hussey Delaval in the parish church at Doddington, Lincs.)

3. Dexter background black

Qly, 1st and 4th, Delaval, 2nd and 3rd, Blake, over all the Badge of Ulster, impaling, Argent three bends gules, on a canton azure a spur rowel downwards or a bordure gules (Knight)

Baron's coronet   Crest, mantle, motto and supporters: As 1.
For John Hussey, 1st Baron Delaval, who m. 2nd, Susanna Elizabeth Knight, and d. 17 May 1808. She d. 20 Aug. 1822.   (B.E.P.; Hunter Blair)
(There is another hatchment for Lord Delaval in the parish church at Doddington, Lincs.)

4. All black background

Qly, 1st, Azure a pierced cinquefoil ermine a bordure engrailed or (Astley), 2nd, Argent a lion rampant gules crowned or (Constable), 3rd, Argent two lions passant gules (L'Estrange), 4th, Or a maunch gules (Hastings), over all the Badge of Ulster, impaling, Argent on a fess double cotised gules three griffins' heads erased or (Dashwood)

Baron's coronet   Crest: From a ducal coronet or five ostrich feathers
argent   Motto: Justitiae tenax   Supporters: Two lions rampant
gules ducally crowned and collared or, from the collar of each hangs an
escutcheon bearing the arms of Hastings, Or a maunch gules
For Sir Jacob Astley, 6th Bt., succeeded (barony called out of abeyance)
as 16th Baron Hastings, who m. 1819, Georgiana Carolina (d. 28 June
1835), 2nd dau. of Sir Henry Watkin Dashwood, Bt., and d. 27 Dec.
1859.   (B.P. 1949 ed.)

5. Dexter background black
Qly, as 4., impaling, blank (arabesque)
Coronet, crest, motto and supporters: As 4.   Mantle: Gules and ermine
For Jacob Henry Delaval, 17th Baron Hastings, who m. 1860, Frances,
dau. of T. Cosham, and d. 8 Mar. 1871.   (B.P. 1949 ed.)

6. All black background
Qly, as 4., impaling, Qly, 1st and 4th, Argent a canton sable (Sutton),
2nd and 3rd, Or two bars azure, a chief qly azure and gules on the first
and fourth two fleurs-de-lys or, on the second and third a lion passant
guardant or (Manners)
Coronet, crest, motto, supporters and mantle: As 5.
For the Rev. Delaval Loftus Astley, 18th Baron Hastings, who m. 1848,
Frances Diana, 2nd dau. of Charles, 1st Viscount Canterbury, and d.
28 Sept. 1872.   (B.P. 1949 ed.)

SIMONBURN

1. Dexter background black
Argent a cross engrailed gules between four molets azure, on a chief or
three roses gules (Allgood)   In pretence: Gules on a chevron between
three stags' heads or three hunting horns sable (Hunter)
Crest: Two arms embowed in armour proper holding a human heart
gules inflamed or charged with a tower triple-towered argent
Mantling: Gules and argent   Motto: Agi omne bonum
For Robert Lancelot Allgood, of Nunwick, who m. 2nd, 1820, Elizabeth
Elizabeth, 2nd dau. and co-heiress of John Hunter, of The Hermitage,
and d. 25 May 1854. She d. 7 Sept. 1864.   (B.L.G. 1937 ed.)
(The hatchment of Robert Lancelot Allgood's widow is at St John Lee)

2. Dexter background black
Allgood, impaling, Ermine on a fess sable a castle argent (Hill)
Crest and motto: As 1.
For Lancelot John Hunter Allgood, of Nunwick, who m. 1854, Louisa
Charlotte, 2nd dau. of Col. Sir Thomas Noel Hill, K.C.B., and d. 23
Jan. 1885.   (B.L.G. 1937 ed.)

TWEEDMOUTH

1. All black background
On a lozenge. Gules a fess between three padlocks or (Grieve), impaling,
Or a fess chequy argent and azure (Stewart)
Mottoes: (above) Resurgam (below) Hoc securior
For Hannah, dau. of John Stewart, of Lowick, who m. William Grieve,
of Ord House, and d. 1843. He d. 1827.   (Hunter Blair)

WHITTINGHAM

1. All black background
Ermine on a fess gules between three pheons or a lion passant or
(Atkinson)
Crest: A pheon or   Mantling: Gules and argent
Motto: In coelo quies   Skull and crossbones below
Frame decorated with poppies in relief made of woolly material
For Adam Atkinson, of Great Ryde, who d. at Lorbottle House, 1843.
(Hunter Blair)
(This hatchment was recorded by Hunter Blair and others with the fess
sable and without the lion. However, in 1975, Mr. Leonard Evetts
discovered on cleaning it that the fess had at some time been overpainted;
this was removed and the hatchment is now in its original condition)

2. Dexter background black
Qly, 1st and 4th, Azure a fess argent between three bucks courant or
(Hargrave), 2nd and 3rd, Gules a lion passant between three escallops
argent (Shield)   In pretence: Shield
Crest: A buck's head erased proper   Mantling: Gules and argent
Motto: In coelo quies   Skull in base
For William Hargrave, of Shawdon, who m. Catherine, dau. and co-
heiress of Samuel Shield, and d.s.p. 1817.   (Hunter Blair; B.L.G.
1937 ed.)

3. Dexter background black
Qly, 1st and 4th, Qly indented azure and gules on a fess ermine between
three bucks courant or three mascles azure (Hargrave), 2nd and 3rd,
Sable ermined argent two chevrons between three lions' gambs erased
or (Pawson), impaling, Argent on a chevron gules between three boars'
heads couped sable a molet argent (Trotter)
Crests: Dexter, A buck's head erased qly indented argent and gules,
upon it four roundels counterchanged   Sinister, On a mount vert a
roundel azure charged with a sun in splendour or
Mantling: Gules and argent   Motto: Favente Deo

For William Pawson Hargrave, grandson of John Pawson and Mary
Hargrave, assumed the additional name and arms of Hargrave, m. 1817,
Mary Ann, dau. of the Rev. Robert Trotter, of Morpeth, and d. 5 Jan.
1854.   (Sources, as 2.)

4. All black background
Argent fretty gules, on a chief gules three leopards' faces or (Liddell),
impaling, Or an anchor in pale sable between two lions passant gules
(Delmé)
Baron's coronet   Crest: A lion rampant sable billetty and crowned or
Supporters: Two leopards rampant or spotted sable each murally gorged
argent
Motto: Unus et idem   Winged skull below
For Sir Henry Liddell, 4th Bt., cr. Baron Ravensworth, 1747, m. 1737,
Anne, only dau. of Sir Peter Delmé, Lord Mayor of London, and d. 30
Jan. 1784, when the barony became extinct.   (B.P. 1949 ed.)

5. All black background
Liddell, with Badge of Ulster, impaling, Gules a bend compony ermine
and sable between two lions' heads erased or, on a chief azure three
billets or (Steele)
Crest: As 4.   Mantling: Gules and argent
Motto: Fama semper vivit
For Sir Henry George Liddell, 5th Bt., who m. 1773, Elizabeth, dau. of
Thomas Steele, of Hampsnet, Sussex, and d. 26 Nov. 1791.   (B.P. 1949
ed.)

6. All black background
Liddell, with Badge of Ulster   In pretence: Qly, 1st and 4th, Gules a
fess between two lions passant or (Simpson), 2nd and 3rd, Gules three
annulets interlaced or between three oak trees argent (Anderson)
Baron's coronet   Crest, mantling and motto: As 5.
Supporters: As 4.   Skull and crossbones below
On frame of hatchment: Top corner, Baron's coronet   Dexter corner,
March 7   Sinister corner, 1855   Bottom corner, Aged 80
For Sir Thomas Henry Liddell, 6th Bt., cr. Baron Ravensworth, 1821,
who m. 1796, Maria Susannah, dau. of John Simpson, of Bradley, and
d. 7 Mar. 1855.   (B.P. 1949 ed.)
(The hatchment of Lady Ravensworth is at Ryton, co. Durham)

LANCASHIRE

by

D. M. Hallowes

Bigland Hall: For Ralph Bigland, 1784
(*Photograph: Abbot Hall Art Gallery, Kendal*)

INTRODUCTION

Lancashire is well-known for its black and white heraldry and this is confirmed when we look through the blazons of the arms on the hatchments and see what a large number of them read, Argent a charge sable. The distribution of the hatchments is interesting. Most of them are in the south of the' county and most of these are in the rural areas between the centres of industry. There are comparatively few in the north of the county and almost all of these, for obvious reasons, lie outside the areas of the National Parks. There is a chain of hatchments along the Ribble valley, but of course some of these are in Yorkshire. None have been reported from the south-east of the county.

There seem to be no very old and no modern hatchments. As far as it is possible to date them, they all seem to be from the 18th or 19th centuries. Two hatchments deserve special mention. One is at Whalley and at first glance seems to be only a painting of the Royal Arms on a diamond shaped canvas, similar examples of which can be found in very many places, but in this case the motto 'Resurgam' seems to single it out as a funeral hatchment. The other, at Bigland Hall, is for a Garter King of Arms and shows the arms of Garter impaling Bigland. Also worth noting is the recent restoration of the †six hatchments at Hale, which are all for members of the same family and make a most pleasing display. There are many other Lancashire hatchments in need of a similar treatment. There are only two churches with more than six hatchments, Farnworth with seven, all for members of related families, including one with some interesting Polish heraldry, and Childwall with 12, an exceptionally large number for a church in the North of England.

We record here only 97 hatchments for the whole county including three at Wigan which disappeared between 1955 and 1965. One feels there ought to be more waiting to be

recorded and information about any that have been missed
will be welcomed.

Finally I must acknowledge the many people, too many
to name individually, who have helped in compiling this
survey. Although I have visited all those in the south of the
county and some in the north, at only four or five places
was I recording the details of the hatchments for the first
time. Elsewhere I was just checking the records of others,
although it must be admitted that in many cases the information originally received was full of errors.

D. M. Hallowes,
17, St. Albans Road, Halifax

†Destroyed, alas, by fire since this Introduction was written.

ACCRINGTON

1. Sinister background black

Argent three sheaves each of three arrows proper banded gules two and one, on a chief azure a bee volant or (Peel), impaling, Peel
Motto: Resurgam   Two cherubs' heads above shield
Perhaps for Anne, 3rd dau. of William Peel of Peele Fold, who m.
Robert Peel of Accrington and Hyndeburne, and d. 1827. He d. 1839.
(Foster)
(It is particularly difficult to give a firm identification of this hatchment as there have been at least eight local Peel/Peel marriages, but the above attribution seems more likely than most.)

ALTHAM

1. All black background

Qly azure and gules a castle argent, on a chief argent a bee volant between two mallets proper (Fort)
No helm   Crest: On a patch of grass proper a lion sejant gules semy of crescents and collared or holding a cross crosslet fitchy or
No mantling or motto
Perhaps for Richard Fort of Read Hall, who m. Anne (d. 1811), dau. of John Bulcock, and d. 1829. Or for John Fort of Read Hall, who m. Mary (d. 1865), dau. of James Kay, and d. 7 Apr. 1842, aged 49.
(B.L.G. 1937 ed.)

2. Dexter background black

Fort arms only
Crest: As 1.   Mantling: Gules and argent   Motto: Resurgam
Winged skull below
Perhaps for John Fort of Read Hall, who m. Mary (d. 1865), dau. of James Kay, and d. 7 Apr. 1842.   (B.L.G. 1937 ed.)

3. Dexter background black

Fort, with mallets sable, impaling, Azure two bars wavy ermine, on a chief or a demi-lion rampant issuant sable (Smith)
Crest: As 1., but double collared or, and cross crosslet fitchy sable
Mantling: Gules and argent   Motto: Fortis et audax
For Richard Fort, D.L., J.P., of Read Hall, who m. Margaret Ellen, dau. of Major Gen. John Smith, and d. 2 July 1868, aged 46.   (B.L.G. 1937 ed.; Whitaker, i., 41)

4. All black background
Qly, 1st, Per fess, in chief, Gules a lion passant guardant or, and in base,
paly of six ermine and azure (Walton), 2nd, Argent a cross patonce sable
(Banastre), 3rd, Argent a chevron gules between three hawks' heads
erased proper (Walton), 4th, Gules a quatrefoil or (Roe)
Crest: From a ducal coronet or a demi-lion or holding a rudder azure
Mantling (slight): Argent   Motto: Virtuti honores soli
Cherub's head on each side of shield   On wood panel
For Richard Thomas Roe Walton, who d. unm. Apr. 1845. (Whitaker,
ii., 270)

BIGLAND HALL, nr. Cartmel

1. Sinister background black
Argent a cross gules on a chief azure a ducal coronet enclosed in a
Garter between a lion passant guardant and a fleur-de-lys or (Garter
King of Arms), impaling, Qly, 1st, Azure two ears of big wheat or
(Bigland), 2nd, Argent two bars and in chief three escallops azure
(Errington), 3rd, Argent ten roundels, four, three, two and one gules
(Babington), 4th, Or a fret azure (Ward)
Above the shield a coronet of a King of Arms, and the shield is encircled
by a double chain or, pendent therefrom the badge of Garter King of
Arms
Crest: A lion passant reguardant gules holding in the dexter paw an ear
of big wheat or
Mottoes: (above crest) Gratitudo   (below shield) Garde l'honneur
The frame inscribed: Ralph Bigland Esq. Garter Principal King of Arms
Died March 27 1784   Buried in Gloucester Cathedral

BILLINGE

1. All black background
Qly, 1st and 4th, Sable a cross or between four fleurs-de-lys argent a
canton or (Bankes), 2nd and 3rd, Gules a lion rampant reguardant or
(Meredith), impaling, Argent a chevron between three goats' heads
erased sable armed or (Bunney)
Crest: A stork argent, legged, beaked and ducally gorged gules standing
on a tree stump couped with a sprig of leaves growing from its side
proper   Mantling: Gules and argent
Motto: In coelo quies   Winged skull below
For William Bankes, of Winstanley Hall, who m. Mary Anne (d. 1798),
dau. of Joseph Bunney of Leicester, and d.s.p. 1800.   (B.L.G. 5th
ed.)

BOLTON

1. Dexter background black

Qly, 1st and 4th, Argent three escallops in bend between two bendlets
sable (Bradshaw), 2nd and 3rd, Argent on a chevron sable between
three trefoils slipped vert three escallops argent (   ), impaling,
Qly, 1st and 4th, Gules an eagle displayed and crowned or (Greaves),
2nd and 3rd, Argent a lion rampant gules (Gilliam)   Also, in pretence,
over line of impalement, Argent three whales' heads erased lying fesswise two and one sable, langued gules, spouting water proper (Whalley)
Crest: A stag statant proper ducally gorged or in front of a tree on a
mound of grass proper   Mantling: Gules and argent
Motto: In coelo quies   Winged skull in base
For James Bradshaw, of Darcy Lever, who m. 1st, 1768, Ann (d. June
1778), dau. and co-heir of John Whalley, of Blackburn, and 2nd, 1779,
Jane, dau. of Edward Greaves of Culcheth-in-Newton, and d. 28 Feb.
1804, aged 66.   (J. C. Scholes, History of Bolton, 1892; Baines, iii.,
210; Whitaker, ii., 18)

2. All black background

Qly, 1st and 4th, Bradshaw, 2nd and 3rd, Argent a chevron engrailed
sable ermined argent between three trefoils slipped vert (   ),
impaling, Or a chevron cotised between three demi-griffins segreant
couped sable the two in chief respectant (Smith)
Crest: As 1., but stag also on mound   Mantling: Gules and argent
Motto: Non nobis solum nati sumus
For John Bradshaw, of Darcy Lever (son of 1.), who m. 1809, Charlotte
Mary Smith, and d. at Bath, 17 Jan. 1816, aged 33.   (Baines, iii., 210)

3. Sinister background black

Argent three horses' heads erased sable a chief gules (Slade), impaling,
Ermine on a bend engrailed between two cocks gules three molets or
(Law)
Mantling: Gules and argent   Three cherubs' heads above shield and
skull below
For Augusta, dau. of the Rt. Rev. George Henry Law, Bishop of Chester,
who m. 1812, as his 1st wife, the Rev. Canon James Slade, Vicar of
Bolton, and d. 5 May 1822. He d. 15 May 1860.   (Baines, iii., 179;
Alumni Cantab.; tablet below memorial window)

CARTMEL

1. Dexter background black

Or six annulets, three two and one sable, the Badge of Ulster (Lowther),
impaling, Sable three bucks' heads cabossed argent attired or
(Cavendish)

Crest: A dragon passant argent   Mantling: Gules and argent
For Sir Thomas Lowther, 2nd Bt., who m. 1723, Elizabeth (d. 7 Nov. 1747), dau. of William, 2nd Duke of Devonshire, and d. 23 Mar. 1745. (B.P. 1949 ed.)

2. All black background
On a lozenge   Lowther arms only
On a mantle gules and ermine, tasselled or   Skull and crossbones below
Probably for Catherine or Margaret, sisters of Sir Thomas Lowther, 2nd Bt.   (B.E.B.)

3. All black background
Cavendish, with crescent argent for cadency
Crest: A serpent nowed proper   Mantling: Gules and argent
Motto: Cavendo tutus   Cherub's head at each top corner of shield
Probably for Lord George Augustus Cavendish, of Holker, who d. unm. 2 May 1794.   (B.P. 1949 ed.)

4. Dexter background black
Cavendish, as 3.   In pretence: Sable a lion passant guardant or between three esquires' helms proper (Compton)
Earl's coronet   Crest and motto: As 3.
Supporters: Dexter, A buck proper wreathed round the neck with a chaplet of roses alternately argent and azure   Sinister, A dragon argent winged, collared and chained, the chain reflexed over the back or
For George Augustus Henry, 1st Earl of Burlington, who m. 1782, Elizabeth (d. 7 Apr. 1835), dau. and heir of Charles, 7th Earl of Northampton, and d. 9 May 1834.   (B.P. 1949 ed.)
(There is another hatchment for the first Earl of Burlington in the parish church at Eastbourne, Sussex, and also the hatchment of his widow)

5. All black background
Cavendish arms only, without crescent
Crest and motto: As 3.   Supporters: Two bucks proper each wreathed round the neck with a chaplet of roses alternately argent and azure   All on a mantle gules and ermine
Unidentified

CHILDWALL

1. Dexter background black
Argent on a fess engrailed between three crosses patonce gules three crescents argent (Hardman), impaling, Gules six gouttes or, on a chief or a griffin passant azure (Cockshutt)
Crest: An arm in armour embowed in the hand a millpick proper

Mantling: Gules and argent　　　　Dated, 1755
For John Hardman, of Allerton Hall, who m. Jane (d. 11 Apr. 1758),
dau. of John Cockshutt, and d. 6 Dec. 1755.　　　(R. Stewart-Brown,
History of Allerton, 1911; R. Stewart Brown, Notes on Childwall,
T.H.S.L.C., Vol. 65, p. 93)

2. All black background
Hardman arms only
Crest and mantling: As 1.
Probably for John Hardman (nephew of 1.), who d. unm. Mar. 1759,
aged 19.　　　(Sources, as 1.)

3. Sinister background black
On a cartouche surmounted by a cross
Argent a molet sable a canton gules (Ashton)　　　In pretence: Qly, 1st
and 4th, Gules a cross between four swords erect points upwards argent
(Philpot), 2nd and 3rd, Argent a bend sable ermined argent (Philpot)
Crest: A stag statant reguardant argent attired or wreathed about the
neck with leaves vert　　　Two eagles support the arms from behind
Roses take the place of mantling　　　Motto: So teach us to number
our days that we may apply our hearts unto wisdom
For Mary, only child of John Philpot, of Hefferston Grange, Cheshire,
who m. as his 1st wife, Nicholas Ashton, of Woolton Hall, Liverpool,
and d. 13 Mar. 1777.　　　(B.L.G. 1937 ed.)

4. Sinister background black
Ashton, impaling, Per chevron embattled or and azure three martlets
counterchanged (Hodgson)
Mantling: Gules and ermine　　　Motto: As 3.
Three cherubs' heads above shield
For Catherine, dau. of Thomas Hodgson, of Liverpool, who m. 1781, as
his 2nd wife, Nicholas Ashton, and d. May 1806.　　　(B.L.G.1937 ed.)

5. All black background
Ashton ˌ　　In pretence: Qly, 1st and 4th, Philpot, as 3., but swords
pommelled and hilted or, 2nd and 3rd, Argent a bend sable ermined
argent (Philpot)　　　Also impaling, Hodgson
Crest: A stag statant reguardant argent attired or collared vair
Mantling: Gules and argent　　　Motto: As 3.　　　Skull below
For Nicholas Ashton, who d. 23 Dec. 1833.　　　(B.L.G. 1937 ed.;
Notes on Childwall)

6. All black background
On a lozenge surmounted by a cherub's head
Qly, 1st and 4th, Argent on a pale sable a conger's head erect or (Gascoyne), 2nd and 3rd, Argent a pheon azure, on a chief azure a lion
passant or (Bamber)　　In pretence: Gules six fleurs-de-lys, three, two and
one argent (Ireland)

Skull below
For Mary, dau. and heir of Isaac Green, of Childwall, by Mary, dau. and
heir of Edward Aspinwall, by Eleanor, dau. and co-heir of John Ireland,
who m. Bamber Gascoyne, and d. 8 May 1799.   (M.I. in Hale church;
B.L.G. 2nd ed.)

7. Sinister background black

Qly, 1st and 4th, Gascoyne, 2nd and 3rd, Argent a pheon sable, on a
chief azure a lion passant argent (Bamber)   In pretence: Gules a
chevron between three spearheads argent (Price)
Motto: Raison pour guide   Three cherubs' heads above shield
For Sarah, dau. and heiress of Chase Price, M.P., who m. Bamber
Gascoyne, and d. 11 July 1820.   (B.L.G. 2nd ed.; Notes on Childwall)

8. All black background

Arms: As 7., but Price field azure
Crest: From a ducal coronet a conger's head couped and erect or
Mantling: Gules and argent   Motto: As 7
For Bamber Gascoyne, who d. 16 Jan. 1824.   (Sources, as 7.)

9. Sinister background black

Barry of ten argent and azure over all six escutcheons sable each charged
with a lion rampant argent, in chief a crescent gules for difference (Cecil)
In pretence: Qly, 1st and 4th, Gascoyne, 2nd and 3rd, Argent a pheon
sable, on a chief azure a lion passant or (Bamber)
Marchioness's coronet   Mantle: Gules and ermine
Supporters: Two lions ermine   An exceptionally large hatchment
For Frances Mary, dau. and heiress of Bamber Gascoyne, who m. 1821,
as his 1st wife, James, 2nd Marquess of Salisbury, and d. 15 Oct. 1839.
(B.P. 1939 ed.)

10. Sinister background black

Argent a fess gules between six choughs proper (Onslow), impaling, Or
on a pile gules between six fleurs-de-lys azure three lions of England
(Seymour Augmentation)
Mantling: Gules and argent   Motto: In coelo quies
Three cherubs' heads above shield and skull and crossbones below
For Arthur Onslow, who d. 26 Oct. 1807, aged 80.   (Notes on
Childwall, p. 94)

11. Dexter background black

Azure a cross moline quarterpierced or (Molyneux), impaling, Argent a
cross engrailed azure (Sinclair)
Crest: On a chapeau gules and ermine a plume of peacock feathers proper
Mantling: Gules and argent   Motto: Resurgam
For Edmund Molyneux, who m. Anne Machell Sinclair (d. 1867), and
d.s.p. 9 Mar. 1854.   (Notes on Childwall, p. 94)

12. All black background
Argent on a chevron gules between in chief two anvils and in base an
anchor sable a bee between two crescents argent (Walker), impaling,
Gules a chevron between three leopards' faces or (Parker)
Crest: A dove argent within a wreathed serpent or
Mantling: Gules and argent   Motto: Resurgam
For Joseph Need Walker, of Calderstone, Allerton, who m. Katherine,
dau. of Samuel Parker, of Scots House, Northumberland, and d. 15 Mar.
1865.   (B.L.G. 1937 ed.)

CLITHEROE

1. Dexter background black
Qly, 1st and 4th, Or a chevron between three griffins' heads erased
sable (Aspinall), 2nd and 3rd, Azure a fess between three suns in splendour or (   )   In pretence: Qly of six, 1st, Sable a chevron
between three gates argent (Yates), 2nd, Argent a balista azure (Maghull),
3rd, Argent a griffin segreant gules holding in its forepaws a shield azure
charged with a demi-griffin segreant argent (Trafford), 4th, Argent a
molet sable (Assheton), 5th, Or a fess dancetty sable (Vavasour), 6th,
Azure a cross moline or (Molyneux)
Crest: A demi-griffin segreant sable, beak, wings, claws and collar or
Mantling: Multi-coloured   To dexter of crest, the head and scythe of
Father Time   To sinister of crest, unidentifiable
Garlands at lower sides of shield, and cherub's head below
For John Aspinall, of Standen Hall, Lancs., who m. Maria, dau. of
Maghull Yates, by Elizabeth, dau. of Humphrey Trafford, and d. 1 Mar.
1784, aged 68.   (M.I.; Foster)

COLNE

1. All black background
Argent a cross engrailed sable between four roundels gules (Clayton)
In pretence: Argent on a fess sable a crescent argent, in chief three
molets sable (Townley)
Crest: A cock proper   Mantling: Gules and argent
Motto: Droyt   Skull in base
For John Clayton, of Little Harwood and Carr Hall, Barrowford, who
m. 1754, Margaret (d. 25 Apr. 1779), dau. and heir of Richard Townley,
of Barnside, and Carr Hall, and d. 17 Mar. 1803, aged 73.   (Whitaker,
ii., 256, 395)

2. All black background
Qly, 1st and 4th, Clayton, cross not engrailed, 2nd and 3rd, Townley,
impaling, Argent a shacklebolt sable (Nuttall)

Crest, mantling and motto: As 1.   Cherub's head at either side of
shield and skull and crossbones in base   On a wood panel
For Thomas Clayton, of Little Harwood and Carr Hall (son of 1.), who
m. 1788, Susan (d. 23 Dec. 1789), dau. of Robert Nuttall, of Bury, and
d.s.p. 12 Feb. 1835, aged 79.   (Source, as 1)

3. Dexter background black
Qly of nine, 1st and 3rd, Vert a chevron between three stags' heads
cabossed or (Parker), 2nd, Gules three cushions set lozengewise argent
(Redmayne), 4th, Argent a bend between six martlets sable (Tempest),
5th, Argent a fess between six martlets sable (Gilliot), 6th, Argent a
lion rampant gules within an orle of ten fleurs-de-lys azure (Thorpe),
7th, Gules a chevron vair between three cross crosslets fitchy argent
(Blakey), 8th, Vert a stag's head cabossed or between two flaunches
argent (Parker), 9th, Argent a cross between four martlets gules a canton
azure (Goulbourne), impaling, Argent a lion rampant sable (Barcroft)
Crests: Dexter, A stag trippant proper   Sinister, A cubit arm, vested
gules, cuffed argent, the hand holding a stag's antler argent
Mantling: Gules and argent   Motto: Resurgam
For Edward Parker, of Alkincoats, Colne, who m. 1816, Ellen, only
child of Ambrose William Barcroft, of Noyna, Lancs., and d. 22 May
1865.   (B.L.G. 1937 ed.; M.I.)

4. All white background
Sable three conies courant argent (Cunliffe), impaling, Sable a chevron
or between three owls argent, on a chief gules three roses argent (Old-
ham)
Crest: A greyhound sejant argent collared gules
Mantling: Gules and argent   Motto: Fideliter   Skull and cross-
bones in base, and a cherub's head in each of the other three corners
A very small hatchment
For Henry Owen Cunliffe, of Wycoller Hall, who m. Mary, dau. of
Adam Oldham, of Manchester, and d. 8 Nov. 1818, aged 66.
(J. Bentley, Portrait of Wycoller, 1975)

CROSTON

1. All black background
Argent a chevron gules between three chaplets or (Ashton)
Crest: From a ducal coronet or a demi-angel vested sable winged or
Mantling: Gules and argent   Motto: In coelis aeterna quies
Unidentified

DEANE

1. Dexter background black
Argent a lion rampant gules (Hulton), impaling, Argent two bars azure
over all a bend compony gules and azure (Leigh)
Crest: From a ducal coronet or a hart's head and neck argent attired or
between two branches of hawthorn proper
Mantling: Gules and argent   Skull and crossbones below
For William Hulton, who m. Mary, dau. and co-heir of William Leigh, of
Westhoughton, and d. Apr. 1741.   (B.L.G. 2nd ed.)

2. Dexter background black
Qly of six, 1st, Argent a lion rampant gules (Hulton), 2nd, Argent a
lion rampant doublequeued gules (Hulton), 3rd, Argent a lion rampant
gules crowned or (Hulton), 4th, Azure a chevron between three lozenges
or (Hyde), 5th, Or two bars and in chief three leopards' faces gules
(Jessop), 6th, Azure two bars argent over all a bend compony gules and
azure (Leigh)   In pretence: Azure a chevron sable masoned or between
three animals' heads erased or (Hall)
Crest and mantling: As 1.   Motto: Mens flecti nescia
For William Hulton, who m. 1759, Anne, dau. and heir of John Hall, of
Droylsden, and d. 1 Jan. 1773.   (B.L.G. 2nd ed.; Foster)

3. Dexter background black
Qly, 1st and 4th, Argent a lion rampant gules (Hulton), 2nd and 3rd,
Argent a lion rampant gules (Hulton), impaling, Or a cross engrailed per
pale sable and gules (Brooke)
Crest: A hart's head argent   Mantling: Gules and argent
Motto: As 2.
For William Hulton, who m. 1785, Jane, 3rd dau. of Peter Brooke, of
Mere, Chester, and d. 24 June 1800.   (B.L.G. 2nd ed.)

FARNWORTH, nr. Widnes

1. Dexter background black
Argent a griffin segreant sable (Bold), impaling, Azure a chevron
between three leopards' faces or (Wentworth)
Crest: From a ducal coronet gules a griffin's head sable between two
wings displayed or
Mantling: Gules and argent   Motto: Mors janua vitae
For Peter Bold, who m. Anna Maria, dau. of Godfrey Wentworth, and
d. 12 Sept. 1762.   (Burke's Commoners, Vol. III)

2. All black background
On a lozenge surmounted by two cherubs' heads
Argent a griffin segreant sable armed or (Bold), impaling, Wentworth

Motto: En Dieu est ma fiance   Winged skull below
For Anna Maria, widow of Peter Bold, bur. 4 Apr. 1792, aged 86.
(Musgrove's Obituary)

3. All black background
On a lozenge surmounted by three cherubs' heads
Bold arms only, as 2.
Motto: Spes mea in Deo   Skull below
Perhaps for Anna Maria, dau. of Peter Bold, d. 25 Nov. 1813.   (M.I.)

4. Dexter background black
Qly, 1st and 4th, Argent a griffin segreant sable armed or (Bold), 2nd
and 3rd, Lozengy ermine and sable a canton or (Patten), impaling,
Argent a chevron embattled between three stags' heads gules (Parker)
Crests: Dexter, From a ducal coronet gules a griffin's head sable beaked
or between two wings displayed or   Sinister, A griffin's head erased
sable beaked or
Mantling: Gules and argent   Motto: Resurgam   Skull below
For Peter Patten-Bold, M.P., son of Thomas Patten of Bank Hall, and
Dorothea, dau. of Peter Bold; he m. Mary, dau. of the Rev. John
Parker, of Astle, Cheshire, and d. 17 Oct. 1819.   (Foster; Commoners;
M.I.)

5. Sinister background black
Qly of nine, 1st, Gules a demi-arrow point upwards with two transverse
bars below the barb argent (Clas Lis, for Sapieha), 2nd, Azure three
fleurs-de-lys or (Kierdeja), 3rd, Gules an arm embowed in armour or
and sable in front of an arrow in pale argent (   ), 4th, Gules a
man on a white horse proper (Clan Pogon), 5th, hidden, 6th, Or a
centaur proper (Hippocenthaurus), 7th, Azure two demi-arrows con-
noined in pale the heads in chief and base argent (Clan Bogoria), 8th,
Gules the symbol of the columns argent (Jagello), 9th, Gules a column
argent crowned or (Clan Kolumna) In pretence: Qly, 1st and 4th,
Argent a griffin segreant sable (Bold), 2nd and 3rd, Lozengy ermine
and sable a canton gules (Patten)
The shield surmounted by a crown of the Holy Roman Empire
Motto: Resurgam   Supporters: Dexter, A fox reguardant proper
Sinister, An eagle reguardant argent   Cherub's head below
For Mary, dau. of Peter Patten-Bold, who m. 1823, Prince Eustace
Sapieha, a Polish nobleman, and d. 16 Dec. 1824.   (Foster;
M.I.; Par. regs.)

6. Sinister background black
Qly, 1st, qly i. & iv. Sable three bars argent (Hoghton), ii. & iii. Argent
a griffin segreant sable (Bold), 2nd, Argent three bars sable (Houghton),
3rd, Argent a molet sable (Ashton), 4th, Per chevron sable and argent,
on a canton or a sprig of oak proper (Aston), in chief the Badge of

Ulster   In pretence: Qly, 1st and 4th, Argent a griffin segreant sable
(Bold), 2nd and 3rd, Lozengy ermine and sable a canton or (Patten)
Motto: In Deo spes mea   Supporters: Two bulls argent
For Dorothea, 2nd dau. of Peter Patten-Bold, who m. 1820, as his 1st
wife, Sir Henry Bold-Hoghton, 8th Bt., and d. 7 Dec. 1840.   (B.P.
1949 ed.)

7. Sinister background black

Qly of six, 1st, Sable three bars argent on a canton or the rose of
England dimidiating the thistle of Scotland (Hoghton), 2nd, Argent
three bars sable (Houghton), 3rd, Per chevron sable and argent (Aston),
4th, Argent three estoiles in chevron between three boars' heads
couped and erect sable, langued gules (Booth), 5th, Or a cross engrailed
per pale gules and sable, a label and a crescent sable for difference
(Brooke), 6th, qly i. & iv. Argent a griffin segreant sable (Bold), ii. & iii.
Lozengy ermine and sable a canton gules (Patten), impaling, Qly, 1st
and 4th, Sable a chevron between three martlets argent (Jervis), 2nd
and 3rd, Gules a chevron vair between three lions rampant or (White)
Supporters: Two bulls argent each charged with a label sable
For Aline, 3rd dau. of Sir Henry Jervis White Jervis, 2nd Bt., who m.
1851, as his 2nd wife, Sir Henry de Hoghton, 9th Bt., and d. 29 Dec.
1852.   (Sources, as 6.)

GLASSON

1. Dexter background black

Qly, 1st and 4th, Argent a bend sable between six storks proper
(Starkie), 2nd and 3rd, Argent a chevron gules between three leopards'
faces sable (Farington), impaling, Gules an inescutcheon argent within
an orle of eight molets or (Chamberlain)
Crest: A stork proper   Mantling: Azure and argent
For Le Gendre Nicholas Starkie, D.L., J.P., of Huntroyde and Ashton
Hall, who m. 1827, Anne (d. 1888), dau. of Abraham Chamberlain, of
Rylstone, Yorks, and d. 15 May 1865.   (B.L.G. 5th ed.)

GOOSNARGH

1. All black background

Qly, 1st and 4th, Argent a chevron sable ermined argent a canton gules
(Shawe), 2nd and 3rd, Argent on a cross flory sable five molets pierced
argent (Rigby)
Crest: A falcon volant proper   No mantling or motto
A very small hatchment about 1½ft. x 1½ft.
For Townley Rigby Shawe, who d. unm. 11 Apr. 1843, aged 68, or his
brother, William Shawe who d. unm. 20 Jan. 1872, aged 89.   (Henry
Fishwick, The History of the Parish of Preston, 1900)

HABERGHAM, nr. Burnley

1.   Sinister background black
Qly, 1st and 4th, Argent three weavers' shuttles sable tipped or, furnished with quills of yarn the threads pendant sable, a canton argent
(Shuttleworth), 2nd and 3rd, Argent three ermine spots in bend
between two bendlets sable the whole between two crescents azure
(Kay), in centre chief the Badge of Ulster   In pretence: Qly, 1st and
4th, Argent three weavers' shuttles sable tipped or, furnished with quills
of yarn the threads pendant sable (Shuttleworth), 2nd and 3rd, Argent
three boars' heads couped gules (Barton)
Crests: Dexter, A cubit arm in armour proper grasping in the gauntlet a
shuttle sable, the arm charged with a bezant   Sinister, On a crescent
or a goldfinch proper
Mantling: Gules and argent   Motto: Kynd kynn knawne kepe
For Janet, only dau. and heir of Robert Shuttleworth, of Gawthorpe
Hall, who m. 1842, James Phillips Kay (assumed the name of Shuttleworth on his marriage, created a baronet 1849), and d. 14 Sept. 1872.
(B.P. 1963 ed.; Foster)

HALE

1.   Dexter background black
Qly, 1st, Argent a fess nebuly between three molets sable a label gules
for difference (Blackburne), 2nd, Qly argent and gules a fret or, on a
fess azure three estoiles or (Norris), 3rd, Argent two bends the upper
one engrailed sable (Lever), 4th, Argent a molet sable (Ashton)   In
pretence: Gules six fleurs-de-lys or (Ireland)
Crest: A cock argent combed gules standing on a trumpet fesswise or
Motto: Mors est inevitabilis'
For Thomas Blackburne, who m. 1752, Ireland, dau. and co-heir of
Isaac Green, of Childwall, by Mary, dau. and heir of Edward Aspinwall,
by Eleanor, sister and co-heir of Sir Gilbert Ireland, and d. 15 Jan.
1768.   (B.L.G. 1937 ed.; Foster)

2.   All black background
On a lozenge surmounted by three cherubs' heads
Arms: As 1., but in 2nd quarter the fess is sable
Motto: Resurgam
For Ireland, widow of Thomas Blackburne, d. 19 Aug. 1795.
(Sources, as 1.)

3.   Sinister background black
Qly, 1st and 4th, Argent a fess nebuly between three molets sable
(Blackburne), 2nd and 3rd, Ireland, impaling, Or on a chevron between
three bulls passant sable a pheon or (Rodbard)

Mantling: Gules and argent   Motto: In coelo quies
For Anne, dau. of Samuel Rodbard of Evercreech, who m. 1781, John
Blackburne, and d. 1823.   (Sources, as 1.)

4. All black background
Arms: As 3.
Crest: A cock proper standing on a trumpet fesswise or
Mantling: Gules and argent   Motto: Resurgam   Skull below
For John Blackburne, who d. 11 Apr. 1833.   (Sources, as 1.)

5. Sinister background black
Qly, 1st and 4th, Blackburne, as 3., 2nd and 3rd, Ireland   In pretence:
Or a fess engrailed gules (Bamford)
Motto: Resurgam   Shield suspended from a lover's knot
For Anne, dau. of William Bamford of Bamford, who m. 1811, John
Ireland Blackburne, and d. 20 July 1861.   (Sources, as 1.)

6. All black background
Arms: As 5.
Crests: Dexter, as 4.   Sinister, A dove with a sprig of laurel in its beak
proper
Mantling: Gules and argent   Motto: In solo Deo solus
For John Ireland Blackburne, who d. 27 Jan. 1874.   (Sources, as 1.;
M.I.)

HALEWOOD

1. Dexter background black
Azure two horses' heads erased ermine and in base an anchor with cable
or, on a chief wavy or three roundels azure each charged with a pheon
argent (Fletcher)
Crest: An arm embowed in armour proper in front of an anchor erect
or, the hand proper grasping an arrow or flighted argent
Mantling: Azure and argent   Motto: Nec quaerere nec spernere
honorem
On base of the frame a brass plate bearing the following inscription:
The escutcheon bearing the arms of the Fletcher family of Allerton
House, Liverpool, granted in 1802 was given to this Church for safe
keeping in 1962 by A. W. Fletcher. Family graves are in the churchyard.

HASLINGDEN

1. Dexter background black
Argent seven eagles displayed three, three and one gules (for Holden)
In pretence: Sable a fess between two chevrons ermine, between the

fess and upper chevron a covered cup or (Holden)   Also impaling,
Or a chevron between three griffins' heads erased sable (Aspinall)
Crests: Dexter, From a ducal coronet or a demi-pegasus gules winged or
Sinister, A moorcock sable winged argent
Mantling: Gules and argent   Motto: Nec temere nec timide
For John Greenwood, of Palace House, who assumed the surname of
Holden, m. 1821, Elizabeth, dau. of Henry Aspinall, of High Riley and
Reedley House, and d. 2 Oct. 1834.   (Foster; B.L.G. 5th ed.;
Whitaker, ii., 304)

2. All black background
On a lozenge surmounted by a cherub's head
Sable a fess between two chevrons ermine, between the fess and upper
chevron a covered cup or (Holden), impaling, Aspinall
For Elizabeth, widow of John Holden, d. 11 Jan. 1846. (Sources, as 1.)

3. Dexter background black
Ermine on a chevron gules between three anchors sable three escallops
or (Taylor)   In pretence: Qly, 1st and 4th, Holden as 2., 2nd and 3rd,
Argent a ?rose between six eagles displayed, three, two and one gules
(Holden)
Crest: A demi-lion rampant argent holding in its paws a rose gules
Mantling: Gules and argent   Motto: I trust in God   Skull below
For Hugh Taylor, of Rock House, Walton, who m. 1784, Frances (d.
6 May 1817), dau. and co-heir of Ralph Holden, and d. 14 Feb. 1811.
(Sources, as 1.)

HOOLE

1. All black background
Argent two chevronels engrailed sable each charged with three bezants
(Rothwell)
Crest: From a ducal coronet a stag's head or   Mantling: Gules and
argent   Motto: Virtuti fortuna comes   Skull in base
Unidentified

HORNBY

1. Dexter background black
Qly, 1st and 4th, Argent a cross formy between three cinquefoils azure
(Tatham), 2nd, Per chevron sable and ermine in chief two boars' heads
couped or (Sandford), 3rd, Gules a fess dancetty ermine between three
fleurs-de-lys or (Marsden), impaling, Or a fess wavy between three
cinquefoils gules (Davison)

Crests: Dexter, A goat passant argent   Sinister, A boar's head erect or
in the mouth a dagger proper
Mantle: Gules and ermine   Motto: Resurgam   Winged skull in base
For Admiral Sandford Tatham who d. 24 Jan. 1840, aged 84.
(Chippindall's History of the Township of Ireby, Chetham Soc., Vol.
95, 1935)

2. All black background
On a lozenge   Qly, as 1., impaling, Or a fess wavy between six
cinquefoils gules (Davison)
For the widow of Admiral Sandford Tatham.   She d. 1842.   (Source,
as 1.)

3. All black background
Gules a fess dancetty ermine between three fleurs-de-lys or (Marsden)
Crest: An arm embowed the hand holding a scimitar proper
Mantling: Gules and argent   Motto: Resurgam   Skull in base
For John Marsden, of Hornby, who d. 1826.   (V.C.H.L., viii. 196)

HORWICH

1. All black background
Qly, 1st and 4th, Or fretty sable (Willoughby), 2nd, Gules a chevron
ermine fimbriated or between three talbots' heads erased or (Whittle),
3rd, Argent a chevron between three cross crosslets fitchy sable a
crescent for difference (Davenport)
Baron's coronet   Crest: A man's head and shoulders proper ducally
crowned or   Mantling: Gules and argent   Motto: Verité sans
peur   Supporters: Dexter, An ostrich proper, legged or, in the beak
a horseshoe or   Sinister, A savage wreathed about the loins proper
For Hugh, 15th Baron Willoughby of Parham, who d. unm. 22 Jan.
1765.   (B.E.P.; Coat of Arms, No. 72, 283)

2. All black background
On a lozenge   Sable a pair of wings elevated and conjoined argent
(Ridgway), impaling, Azure a cross engrailed ermine (Wettenhall)
For Anna Maria, dau. of Peter Wettenhall, of Ravenscroft Hall, Cheshire,
who m. as his 2nd wife, Joseph Ridgway, of Ridgmont, J.P. and D.L.,
and d. 14 Nov. 1860. He was bur. at Horwich, 6 July 1842, aged 77.
(Par. Regs.; probate index; T. Hampson, History of Horwich, 1883)

MELLING

1. All black background
Gules a fess dancetty ermine between three fleurs-de-lys or (Marsden)
In pretence: Per chevron sable and ermine in chief two boars' heads
couped or (Sandford)

Crest: An arm embowed vested gules, the hand holding a scimitar
proper   Mantling: Gules and argent
For Henry Marsden, who m. Elizabeth, dau. and co-heir of William
Sandford, and d. 10 Oct. 1742.   (V.C.H.L., viii., 208)

2. Dexter background black

Azure three molets within a double tressure flory counter-flory or
(Murray), impaling, Per chevron argent and gules in chief two fleurs-de-
lys and in base an estoile all counterchanged (Smith of Wray)
Crest: A demi-man proper wreathed at the temples argent and azure, in
the dexter hand a sword and in the sinister a key proper
Mantling: Gules and argent   Motto: In coelo quies
Skull and crossbones in base
For David Murray, who m. Agnes Smith, and d. 3 Nov. 1822, aged 72.
She d. 21 Nov. 1840, aged 80.   (M.I. in church)

3. Dexter background black

Qly, 1st and 4th, Per chevron argent and gules in chief two fleurs-de-lys
azure and in base an estoile or (Smith of Wray), 2nd and 3rd, Azure a
fess argent, in chief two eagles' heads erased and in base a lion passant
argent (Skirrow), impaling, Ermine on a bend gules three annulets or, on
a chief azure three leopards' faces or (Addison)
Crest: From a mural coronet an ostrich's head argent
Mantling: Gules and argent   Motto: Fontes adire remotos
For Thomas Smith, of Wray, who m. Jane, and d. 24 Apr. 1831, aged
75. She d. 29 May 1837, aged 65.   (M.I. in church)

4. Dexter background black

Argent a crescent between three church bells azure, in chief three molets
of six points gules one and two, over all a chevron gules (Bell)
Crest: A dove volant in the beak a sprig of leaves proper
Mantling: Gules and argent   Motto: Praenuntia pacis
Probably for William Gillison Bell, of Melling Hall, who d. post 1871.
(B.L.G. 1871 ed.)

NEWTON-IN-MAKERFIELD, St. Peter

1. All black background

Qly, of seven, 1st, Gules a cross engrailed argent, over all on an
escutcheon sable semy of estoiles argent an arm in armour embowed
proper the hand holding a pennon argent (Legh), 2nd, qly, i. Azure
two bars argent a bend compony or and gules (Legh of Adlington), ii.
Or three lozenges azure (Baggiley), iii. Azure a chevron between three
ducal coronets or (Corona), iv. Azure a chevron between three covered
cups or (Butler), 3rd, qly i. & iv. Argent a pale fusilly sable (Danyers),
ii. & iii. Argent a cross botonny sable (Boydell of Grappenball), 4th,

qly i. & iv. Argent a cross and in dexter chief a fleur-de-lys sable
(Haydock), ii. Sable a chevron between three crosses patonce or
(Boydell of Pulcroft), iii. Argent a pierced molet sable, in dexter chief
a molet sable (Walton of Ulnes Walton), 5th, Chequy argent and sable
(Croft of Dalton), 6th, Sable on a bend argent three calves passant
gules (Calveley), 7th, qly i. & iv. Per pale nebuly or and azure six
martlets, two, two and two counterchanged (Fleetwood), ii. & iii.
Argent a cross formy sable (Banastre of Bank)
Crest: From a ducal coronet or a ram's head argent armed or, in the
mouth a laurel slip vert
Mantling: Gules and argent   Motto: Resurgam
Probably for Colonel Thomas Peter Legh, of Golborne Park, M.P. for
Newton from 1780 to 1797, who d.s.p.leg. at Peers Hill Barracks, near
Edinburgh, on 7 Aug. 1797, aged 44, and was buried at Winwick.
(Burke's Commoners, ii., 686)

ORMSKIRK

1. Dexter background black
Gules three molets in bend between two bendlets engrailed argent
(Scarisbrick), impaling, Qly, 1st and 4th, Or a chevron gules between
three leopards' faces proper (Farington), 2nd and 3rd, Gules three
cinquefoils or (Farington)
Crest: A dove sable, in its beak an olive branch proper
Mantling: Gules and argent   Motto: Resurgam   Skull below
For Thomas Scarisbrick, who m. Sybella Georgiana, dau. of William
ffarington, of Shaw Hall, and d.s.p. 11 July 1833.   (B.L.G. 2nd ed.)

2. All black background
Azure three fleurs-de-lys argent (   ), impaling, Azure three swords
points downwards argent, in fess point a .... argent (   )
Crest: A dove close argent   Mantling: Azure and or
Motto: Dea me judex
Charges almost formless and likely to be blazoned inaccurately
Unidentified

OVER KELLET

1. Dexter background black
Or an eagle displayed vert semy of molets and gorged with a plain collar
or a bordure azure charged with four fleurs-de-lys and four molets
alternately or (Booker)   In pretence: Qly, 1st and 4th, Argent a demi-
griffin sable beaked and membered gules in chief two towers sable
(   ), 2nd and 3rd, Per saltire ermine and gules two leopards' faces
in pale and two escallops in fess or (   )

Crest: On a mount vert a swan ermine collared and lined azure
Mantling: Gules and argent   Motto: In coelo quies
Skull and crossbones in base
Unidentified

POULTON-LE-FYLDE

1. No background, framed close
On a lozenge   Argent a double-headed eagle displayed sable (Hesketh),
impaling, Argent a griffin segreant sable (Bold)
Motto: I know that my Redeemer liveth
For Frances, dau. and co-heir of Peter Bold, of Bold Hall, who m. 1759,
Fleetwood Hesketh, and d. 9 Aug. 1809.   (B.L.G. 1937 ed.)

2. All black background
Qly, 1st and 4th, qly i. & iv. Argent a double-headed eagle displayed
gules (Hesketh), ii. & iii. Argent a griffin segreant sable (Bold), 2nd,
Argent on a bend sable three garbs or (Hesketh), 3rd, Per pale nebuly
azure and or six martlets, two, two and two, all counterchanged
(Fleetwood)
Crest: A garb or   Mantling: Gules and argent
Motto: My trust is in the Lord
Probably for Bold Fleetwood Hesketh, son of Fleetwood Hesketh and
Frances Bold who d. unm. 2 July 1819.   (B.L.G. 1937 ed.)

3. All black background
On a lozenge surmounted by a cherub's head
Qly, 1st and 4th, qly i. & iv. Hesketh, as 1., ii. & iii. Bold, 2nd, Argent
on a bend sable three garbs or (Hesketh), 3rd, Fleetwood, impaling,
Sable three swords in fess proper the centre point downwards, the outer
points upwards, a chief indented or (Rawlinson)
Motto: Lord Jesus receive my Spirit
For Maria, dau. of Henry Rawlinson, of Grass Yard Hall, who m. 1790,
Robert Hesketh (d. 22 Mar. 1824), and d. 3 July 1824.   (B.L.G. 1937
ed.)

4. Sinister background black
Qly of twelve, 1st and 12th, qly i. & iv. Fleetwood, ii. & iii. Argent on a
bend sable three garbs or, on a chief azure a double-headed eagle
displayed argent all within a bordure or ermined sable (Hesketh), 2nd,
Argent on a chevron qly gules and sable between three bustards gules
three bezants (Kitchin), 3rd, Sable three garbs or (Aughton), 4th,
Fleetwood with a canton argent within a bordure sable, 5th, Per fess
indented argent and sable three eagles' heads erased counterchanged
langued and crowned gules (Frances), 6th, Fleetwood, 7th, Argent on a
bend sable three calves or (Veale), 8th, Qly argent and gules in the

first quarter a molet gules (Massey), 9th, Argent on a bend sable three
covered cups argent (Rixton), 10th, Argent a squirrel sejant gules
(Horton), 11th, Bold   In pretence: Argent on a fess wavy gules
between three calves statant sable a dagger fessways proper (Metcalfe)
Motto: Blessed are the dead which die in the Lord   Two cherubs'
heads above shield
For Eliza Debonnaire, only child of Sir Theophilus John Metcalfe, Bt.,
who m. 1826, Peter Hesketh-Fleetwood, of Rossall, and d. 16 Jan.
1833.   (B.L.G. 17th ed.)

5. Dexter background black
Qly, 1st and 4th, Argent a chevron sable between three buglehorns
stringed gules (Hornby), 2nd and 3rd, Per pale argent and gules an
eagle displayed counterchanged (Winckley)
Crest: A buglehorn stringed gules   No mantling or motto
Unidentified

6. Dexter background black
Argent an eagle displayed gules, on a chief sable three molets pierced
argent (   )   In pretence: Or on a cross azure five pheons or
(Harrison)   Also impaling, Bendy of eight sable and argent a double-
headed eagle sable standing on a millrind or (Barlow)
Crest: A demi-eagle displayed gules   Mantling: Gules and argent
Motto: Resurgam
Unidentified

SEFTON

1. Dexter background black
Sable ten billets four, three, two and one argent (Blundell), impaling,
Sable a chevron between three molets argent (Langdale)
Crest: A demi-lion rampant sable holding a cross tau argent
Mantling: Gules and argent
For Nicholas Blundell, who m. Frances, dau. of Marmaduke, 2nd Lord
Langdale, and d. 1737.   (B.L.G. 1937 ed.)

2. All black background
Azure ten billets four, three, two and one or, on a canton or a rook
sable (Blundell), impaling, Per bend sinister emine and sable ermined
argent a lion rampant or (Mostyn)
Crest: A squirrel sejant cracking a nut proper
Mantling: Gules and ermine   Motto: Spes tutissima coelis
Skull in base
For Henry Blundell, who m. Elizabeth, dau. of Sir George Mostyn, 4th
Bt., and d. 1810.   (B.L.G. 1937 ed.; Foster)

3. Dexter background black
Azure a cross moline or (Molyneux), impaling, Paly of six argent and
vert (Hopwood)
Earl's coronet   Crest: On a chapeau gules and ermine a plume of
peacock's feathers proper   Mantling: Gules and ermine
Motto: Resurgam   Supporters: Two lions azure
For Charles William, 3rd Earl of Sefton, who m. 1834, Mary, only dau.
of Robert Gregge Hopwood, of Hopwood Hall, Lancs., and d. 2 Aug.
1855.   (B.P. 1949 ed.)

4. All black background
Argent two chevrons engrailed sable each charged with three bezants
(Rothwell)
Crest: From a ducal coronet a stag's head or   Mantling: Gules and
argent   Motto: Virtuti fortuna comes   Skull in base
Unidentified

5. All black background
Exactly as 4., but no helm or skull
Unidentified

SOUTHPORT, St Cuthbert

1. All black background
Qly of six, 1st and 6th, Argent a double-headed eagle displayed sable
(Hesketh), 2nd, Argent on a bend gules three garbs or (Hesketh), 3rd,
Argent a chevron sable between three trefoils slipped vert (   ),
4th Argent a chevron sable (   ), 5th, Per pale wavy gules and or
four martlets counterchanged (Fleetwood), impaling, Per pale argent
and gules an eagle displayed counterchanged (Winckley)
Crest: A garb or   Mantling: Gules and argent
On wood not canvas
For Roger Hesketh, of North Meols, who m. 2nd, Sarah, dau. of John
Winckley, of Preston, and d. 16 June 1791.   She d. 13 Nov. 1800.
(B.L.G. 1937 ed.; M.I.)
(in view of the background possibly used subsequently for his widow)

STANDISH

1. Dexter background black
Argent a cross engrailed between four roundels sable (Clayton),
impaling, Argent a saltire sable (Baldwin), the Badge of Ulster at fess
point over line of impalement
Crest: An arm embowed in armour grasping a dagger proper
No helm or mantling   Motto: Probitatem quam devitias

For Sir Robert Clayton, 2nd Bt., who m. 1786, Christophora, dau. of the Rev. Dr. Baldwin, Prebendary of Carlisle, and d.s.p. 10 Aug. 1839, aged 92.   (B.E.B.; Complete Baronetage)

2. All black background
Qly, 1st and 4th, Sable three standing dishes argent (Standish), 2nd and 3rd, Argent a fess and in chief three molets sable (Towneley), impaling, Argent a cross sable in the first quarter a fleur-de-lys or (Eccleston)
Crest: An owl proper   No helm or mantling   Motto: In coelo quies
For Edward Towneley-Standish, who m. Anne, dau. of Basil Thomas Eccleston, and d.s.p. 28 Mar. 1807.   (B.L.G. 2nd ed.; Foster)

3. Sinister background black
Qly, 1st, qly i. & iv. Standish, ii. & iii. Sable three escallops argent (Strickland), 2nd and 3rd, Strickland, 4th, Standish, impaling, Argent a chevron between three martlets sable (Lawson)
Motto: In coelo quies   Cherub's head above shield
For Anastasia, dau. and co-heir of Sir John Lawson, Bt., of Brough Hall, Yorks, who m. as his 1st wife, Thomas Strickland, of Sizergh (who assumed the name and arms of Standish), and d. 2 June 1807.
(Burke's Commoners; Foster)
(There is another hatchment for Anastasia Standish at Sizergh Castle, Westmorland)

4. Dexter background black
Qly, 1st and 4th, Standish, 2nd and 3rd, Strickland, impaling, Argent a saltire gules (Gerard)
Crests: Two, both indistinguishable   No mantling
Motto: In coelo quies
For Thomas Strickland Standish, who m. 2nd, Catherine Gerard, and d. 4 Dec. 1813.   (Sources, as 3.)

ULVERSTON

1. Dexter background black
Sable two swords in saltire points upwards argent hilts and pommels or between three fleurs-de-lys one in chief and two in flaunch and an anchor erect in base or, the Badge of Ulster (Barrow), impaling, Per pale or and sable in chief two estoiles and in base a roundel all counter-changed (Trüter)
Crest: A squirrel sejant cracking a nut proper charged on the shoulder with an anchor sable
Mantling: Gules and argent   Motto: Parum sufficit
For Sir John Barrow, 1st Bt., who m. 1798, Anna Maria, only dau. of Peter John Trüter, of the Cape of Good Hope, and d. 1848.   (B.P. 1949 ed.)

UPHOLLAND

1. All black background

Or two bars azure on a canton argent a chaplet gules and vert (Holme)
To dexter of main shield, Holme, impaling, Azure on a chevron argent
between three torches proper a fleur-de-lys between two martlets
sable (Meyrick) S.Bl.   To sinister of main shield, Holme, impaling,
Qly per fess indented or and gules (Leighton) A.Bl.
Crest: A griffin's head between two wings or
Mantling: Gules and argent   Motto: In Deo confido
Skull below shield
For the Rev. Thomas Holme, of Upholland House, father of Meyrick
Bankes (No. 3), who m. 1st, Mary, dau. of Richard Meyrick, and 2nd,
Anne, sister of Sir Baldwin Leighton, Bt., and d. 17 Aug. 1803. She d.
1820.   (B.L.G. 2nd ed.)
(In view of the background possibly used subsequently for his widow)

2. Sinister background black

Qly, 1st and 4th, Sable a cross between four fleurs-de-lys argent
(Bankes), 2nd and 3rd, Holme, impaling, Azure two lions rampant
argent supporting between them a tower argent (Lally)
Mantling: Gules and argent   Motto: In coelo quies
Cherub's head above
For Anne, dau. of the Rev. Edmund Lally, who m. as his 1st wife,
Meyrick Holme, of Winstanley Hall (who took the names of Bankes in
1804), and d. 31 Mar. 1809, aged 37.   (B.L.G. 1970 ed.; Gents. Mag.
1809, p. 388)

3. Dexter background black

Qly, as 2., impaling, Qly, 1st and 4th, Or a cross engrailed per pale gules
and sable (Brooke), 2nd and 3rd, Azure a sheldrake ambulant argent
(Langford)
Crests: Dexter, a stork, ducally gorged argent, on a log proper
Sinister, A demi-griffin argent   Mantling: Gules and argent
Motto: In coelo quies
For Meyrick Bankes, who m. 2nd, 1810, Maria Elizabeth, dau. of
Thomas Langford-Brooke, of Mere Hall, Cheshire, and d. 1 Mar. 1827.
(B.L.G. 2nd ed.)

4. All black background

Qly, 1st, Gules a cross argent between four lozenges ermine, the Badge
of Ulster (Leigh), 2nd, Argent on a bend engrailed sable three fleurs-de-
lys argent (Holt), 3rd, Argent a lion rampant and a canton sable (Owen),
4th, Gules a chevron embattled counterembattled between three lions'
heads erased argent, on a canton or a rose gules (Bispham)
Crest: A demi-lion gules holding a lozenge argent charged with a rose gules
Mantling: Gules and argent   Skull below

For Sir Robert Holt Leigh, Bt., M.P. for Wigan 1802-1825, cr. bt. 22
May 1815, and d. unm. at Hindley Hall, 21 Jan. 1843, aged 80.   (V.C.H.
Lancs., iv., 120)

WHALLEY

1.   All black background
Within the Garter, England quartering Scotland and Ireland, with an
escutcheon of Hanover
Crest and royal crown above, on either side of which are G.R. and IIII
Motto: Resurgam
A very small hatchment, 1¾ft. x 1¾ft.
For H.M. King George IV, who d. 26 June 1830.

WIGAN

1.   Sinister background black
Qly, 1st and 4th, Gules a fess chequy argent and azure (Lindsay), 2nd,
Argent two bendlets between two martlets sable (Bradshaw), 3rd, Or a
lion rampant gules over all a bend sable (Abernethy), impaling, Or five
fusils conjoined in fess azure (Pennington)
Countess's coronet   Crest: An ostrich argent in the beak a key or
Mantling: Gules and argent   Motto: Endure fort
Supporters: Two lions sejant guardant gules   An unusually small
hatchment
For Maria Margaret Frances, dau. of John, 1st Baron Muncaster, who m.
1811, James, 7th Earl of Balcarres and 24th Earl of Crawford, and d.
16 Nov. 1850.   (B.P. 1949 ed.)

2.   All black background
Qly, 1st and 4th, Lindsay, 2nd and 3rd, Abernethy, impaling,
Pennington
Earl's coronet   Crest and motto: As 1.
Supporters: Two lions rampant guardant gules
For James, 7th Earl of Balcarres and 24th Earl of Crawford, who d. 15
Dec. 1869.   (B.P. 1949 ed.)

3.   Dexter background black
Qly, 1st and 4th, qly i. & iv. Gules on a chief ermine two roundels
azure (Walmesley), ii. & iii. Argent a saltire gules (Gerard), 2nd and 3rd,
Sable a lion rampant between three scaling ladders or (Jeffreys),
impaling, Argent a griffin segreant gules holding in its claws an
escutcheon azure charged with a griffin segreant argent (de Trafford)
Crest: A lion passant guardant ermine ducally crowned gules
Mantling: Gules and argent   Motto: En Dieu est mon esperance

For William Gerard Walmesley, who m. 1838, Caroline, dau. of Sir
Thomas Joseph de Trafford, 1st Bt., and d. 11 Oct. 1868.   (B.L.G.
1937 ed.)
(This hatchment was recorded in 1954, but it has since disappeared)

4. All black background
On a lozenge   Qly, as 3., but with a crescent for difference on both
the Walmesley and Gerard coats, impaling, de Trafford with griffin or
For Caroline, widow of William Gerard Walmesley, d. 1883. (Source,
as 3.)
(This hatchment was recorded in 1954, but it has since disappeared)

5. Dexter background black
Qly, 1st and 4th, Walmesley as 3., 2nd and 3rd, Gerard as 3., impaling,
Sable three boars' heads couped or langued gules (Gordon)
Crest, mantling and motto: As 3.
For William Gerard Walmesley, who m. 1869, Augusta, youngest dau.
of Lord Henry Gordon, and d. 2 Jan. 1877.   (Source, as 3.)
(This hatchment was recorded in 1954, but it has since disappeared)

YORKSHIRE
by
D. M. Hallowes

Temple Newsam House: For Arthur, 3rd Viscount Irvine, 1702
(*Photograph by The Leeds City Art Galleries*)

INTRODUCTION

Yorkshire with its broad acres could be expected to have more hatchments than the average county, and we are not disappointed since we record more than three hundred, although the number per square mile is probably no higher than elsewhere. Their distribution over the county is fairly uniform except that, for obvious reasons, there are very few in the areas of the National Parks, and these few are near the edges of the parks. There are a surprising number in the traditionally industrial areas of the West Riding, but on closer inspection most of these are found to be in rural pockets between the centres of heavy industry.

Some indication of the value of the present survey can be gained by comparing the work of an earlier writer with the present position and so providing a measure of the rate of loss of hatchments. H. C. Bloom, writing about 100 years ago, described 115 hatchments in parts of the West Riding, but of these only 66 survive today. Happily there are signs that people in general nowadays value hatchments more highly, and there are many examples of repair and restoration in Yorkshire in recent years, notably at Ecclesfield, Fulford, Owston, Ravenfield and Thirsk; but, even so, through one accident or another six have been lost in the county since the present survey started in 1952.

There are in Yorkshire a number of armorial panels which might be mistaken by the uninformed for hatchments. Those at Saxton, Stonegrave and Worsborough are large, rectangular, with long inscriptions and could hardly be mistaken for hatchments. Again at Wensley there is an oval panel which does not look like a hatchment; indeed there is evidence that it relates to the raising of a body of volunteers during the Napoleonic Wars. Nearby at Grinton however there is an armorial canvas dated 1698 which has every appearance of being a hatchment but which disqualifies itself by including a long inscription commencing 'Here lyes ye body of Dorothy

Darcy . . .'. Similarly at Beverley there is an armorial panel
to the memory of Robert Hildyard dated 1685 which might
be taken for a hatchment but for an inscription containing
the words '. . . was buried here . . .'. At Sprotbrough there
is a rectangular board, divided into four, with paintings of
the arms of four members of the same family as that
commemorated by the hatchments. Rather more difficult
to classify, at Burton Fleming, there is a painting with the
same arms as Hunmanby (4.), but what is exceptional about
it is its shape which is rectangular with a semi-circular bay
on the top edge and it appears to be an old painting of the
Royal Arms reused. It is hoped sometime in the future to
publish a full account of these intermediate examples.

There are others about which doubt has been expressed,
but which finally have been included with the hatchments.
At Hemingbrough there is an inscription under the shield,
but since words like 'Here lieth' are not included it has been
accepted as a hatchment. At Hickleton there are two
achievements modelled in relief, but since one has a cherub's
head and the other has funeral mottoes they have been
included with the hatchments.

The churches with the largest number of hatchments are
Thornton Watlass and Hickleton with 11 each, followed by
Bridlington, 10, and Wragby, nine; and at each of these
churches, except Bridlington, most of the hatchments com-
memorate one family. The oldest hatchment in Yorkshire is
probably that at Tadcaster for Joceline, 11th Earl of
Northumberland who died in 1670. There are several other
hatchments from the 17th century, and a good number from
the 18th century, but of course most are from the 19th
century. There are 13 from the present century and the
newest is at Hickleton for the 2nd Viscount Halifax who
died in 1934. This hatchment was designed by Rowland
Bretton.

Compiling this survey and in particular identifying the
quarterings has resulted in the collecting of a far larger
amount of genealogical and other information than it is
possible to print here and enquiries are welcome. It would
be presumptuous to suppose that the following list of
hatchments is complete; two more turned up in the last

few months, and information about any that have been missed will be gratefully received. Yorkshire is far too vast an area for one person to cover single-handed, and although I have visited nearly all the hatchments and photographed many of them we must acknowledge our indebtedness to many people, too many to name individually, who have helped by notifying the existence of a hatchment initially or by checking its blazon or continued existence at a later stage.

D. M. Hallowes,
17, St. Albans Road, Halifax

ABERFORD

1. Dexter background black

Azure on a chief or a demi-lion rampant issuant gules (Markham),
impaling, Qly, 1st and 4th, Vert six escallops, three, two and one argent
(Holbech), 2nd and 3rd, Argent a lion rampant gules within a bordure
sable bezanty (Cornewall)

Crest: A winged lion passant, the dexter forepaw resting on a harp or
Mantling: Gules and argent   Motto: In coelo quies
For William Markham, of Becca Hall, Yorks, who m. 1828, Lucy Anne,
dau. of William Holbech of Farnborough Hall, Warwickshire, and d.
26 Jan. 1852.   (B.L.G. 1937 ed.)

2. All black background

Qly, 1st and 4th, Argent on a pale sable a conger's head couped and
erect or, a canton gules (Gascoigne), 2nd and 3rd, Or a chevron sable
between in chief two roundels sable and in base a fish naiant gules
(Oliver), impaling, Sable on a cross argent five fleurs-de-lys sable
(Turner)

Crests: Dexter, A conger's head erect or charged with a roundel sable
Sinister, A dexter arm, sleeved gules, cuffed argent, the hand grasping a
sprig of leaves proper   Mantling: Gules and argent
For Richard Oliver-Gascoigne, son of the Rt. Hon. Silver Oliver, M.P.,
of Castle Oliver, who m. Mary, dau. of Sir Charles Turner, 1st Bt., and
step-daughter of Sir Thomas Gascoigne, 8th Bt. He took the name and
arms of Gascoigne on succeeding to the estates, and d. 14 Apr. 1843.
(B.L.G. 1937 ed.)

ADEL

1. All black background

Gules a lion rampant within an orle of crescents argent (Beaumont)
In pretence, and impaling, Sable three eagles displayed or ermined sable
(Stringer)
Crest: A dove argent legs gules in its beak an olive branch proper
Mantling: Gules and argent   Motto: Fide sed cui vide
Frame decorated with skulls and crossbones   In poor condition,
showing bare canvas in places
For Richard Beaumont, who m. 1699, Katherine, dau. of Thomas
Stringer, of Charleston, and d. 27 June 1704.   (B.L.G. 2nd ed.)

2. Dexter background black

Sable a fess between three escallops argent (Arthington), impaling,
Gules a chevron between three lions' gambs erect and erased argent, on
a chief argent an eagle displayed sable, all within a bordure argent
(Browne)

Crest: A dove argent beak and legs gules in its beak an olive branch
proper   Mantling: Gules and argent
Frame decorated with skulls and crossbones
For Cyril Arthington, of Arthington, who m. Anne, dau. of Dr. Brown,
of London, and d. 28 Jan. 1730.   (Thoresby Society, Vol. V, Adel
Parish Registers)

ADWICK-LE-STREET

1. Dexter background black
Qly, 1st and 4th, Gules on a bordure sable eight estoiles argent, on a
canton argent a lion rampant gules (White), 2nd and 3rd, Vert a lion
rampant or (O'Farrell), impaling, Azure two bars and in chief three
cinquefoils argent (Denton)
Crests: Dexter, an ostrich argent   Sinister, A greyhound courant
argent   Mantling: Gules and argent
For John White, of Doncaster, son of Col. John White and Elizabeth,
dau. of Major-General O'Farrell, Governor of Minorca, who m. Matilda,
dau. of the Rev. Thomas Denton, Rector of Ashtead, Surrey, and d.
16 Aug. 1837, aged 76. She d. 1 Apr. 1854, aged 90.   (M.I. in church;
Bloom)

ALDBOROUGH

1. Dexter background black
Sable three horseshoes or in chief a label of three points ermine
(Smithson), impaling, Argent on a fess gules, between two chevrons
azure each charged with three escallops argent, three garbs or (Eden)
Crest: A horse's head argent bridle and reins or   Mantling: Gules and
argent   Two cherubs' heads above and skull and crossbones below
For Mark Smithson, of the parish of St. Bride's, London, who m. 1763,
Clare Eden of Aldborough, and d. 21 Nov. 1789, aged 57.   (Y.A.J.,
Vol. 9, 1885/6)

2. All black background
On a lozenge surmounted by a cherub's head
Arms: As 1.
For Clare, widow of Mark Smithson, who d. 20 June 1803, aged 72.
(Source, as 1.)

3. All black background
Qly, 1st and 4th, Azure a fess ermine between three unicorns passant
argent (Wilkinson), 2nd and 3rd, Gules in chief two helmets proper
garnished or, in base a garb or (Cholmley)
Crest: From a mural coronet gules a demi-unicorn ermine armed and crined
or

Mantling: Gules and argent
Probably for Charles Wilkinson, M.P. for Aldborough, 1774, who d.
unm. 1782, or for one of his bachelor brothers, Col. William, d. 1761,
Rev. James, Vicar of Sheffield, d. 1805, Capt. Thomas, d. 1773, or
George, d. 1761.   (Source, as 1.)

4. All black background
Arms: As 3., but the fess or ermined sable
Crest: As 3., but the demi-unicorn or ermined sable
Mantling: Gules and argent   Winged skull below
Identification, as for 3.

5. Dexter background black
Qly, 1st, Azure a fess ermine between three unicorns passant argent
(Wilkinson), 2nd, Argent two bars between nine molets, three, three
and three gules (Jessop of Broomhall), 3rd, Azure three bars gemel and
a chief or (Meynell), 4th, Azure three cinquefoils between eight cross
crosslets argent, in chief a fleur-de-lys or (Darcy), impaling, Qly, 1st, Or
a chevron vair between three stags statant sable (Swift), 2nd, Argent a
fess azure between three cinquefoils gules (Wickersley), 3rd, Cholmley,
4th, Paly of four argent and gules, on a chevron or three estoiles gules,
on a chief or a roundel sable charged with a demi-lion rampant argent
between two crescents sable each charged with three pearls proper
(Lawson)
Crest: As 3., but unicorn argent crined or   Mantling: Gules and argent
Probably for Capt. Andrew Wilkinson, who m. Dorothy, dau. of
Richard Lawson, and d.s.p. 24 May 1785, aged 58.   (Source, as 1.)

6. Dexter background black
Paly of four vert and gules, on a chevron or a greyhound's head erased
sable between two cinquefoils azure, on a chief or a roundel sable
charged with a demi-lion rampant argent between two crescents sable
each charged with three roundels argent (Lawson), impaling, Per fess
sable and azure a four-towered quadrangular castle, cornerwise, between
three martlets argent (Rawson)
Crest: A wolf's head sable, collared vert, charged on the neck with three
bezants   Mantling: Gules and argent   Motto: Loyal secret
For Andrew Sherlock Lawson, of Aldborough and Boroughbridge, who
m. 1889, Elinor Frances, eldest dau. of Henry, 14th Viscount Mount-
garret, and d. 20 Aug. 1914.   (B.L.G. 1937 ed.)

ALLERTON PARK

1. All black background (should be dexter black)
Qly, 1st, Sable a bend or between six fountains proper (Stourton), 2nd,
Gules on a bend between six cross crosslets fitchy argent the Augmen-

tation of Flodden (Howard), 3rd, Gules a lion rampant argent (Mowbray), 4th, Argent on a bend sable three owls argent, in sinister chief a crescent gules for difference (Savile), impaling, Azure a fess nebuly between three crescents ermine (Weld)

Baron's coronet   Crest: A demi-monk proper habited in russet, his girdle or and wielding in his dexter hand a scourge or thereon five knotted lashes   Motto: Loyal je serai durant ma vie

Supporters: Two sea-dogs sable scaled and finned or

For William Joseph, 18th Baron Stourton, who m. 1800, Catherine Winifred (d. 27 Dec. 1862), dau. of Thomas Weld of Lulworth Castle, Dorset, and d. 4 Dec. 1846.   (B.P. 1949 ed.)

ASKHAM BRYAN

1. Dexter background black

Argent two bars gules, on a canton gules a cinquefoil argent (Preston), impaling, Argent on a fess gules between three martlets sable three lions' faces argent (Consett)

Crest: On a tower a falcon rising argent   Mantle: Gules and argent, fringed, corded and tasselled or

For the Rev. John Preston, who m. 2nd, 1763, Jane, dau. of Peter Consett, of Brawith Hall, Thirsk, and d. 23 Sept. 1806.   (Par. Reg.; B.L.G. 1937 ed.; Foster; Col. Consett)

2. All black background

Preston, impaling, Gules on a fess or three spear heads erect in fess sable (Nares)

Crest: As 1.   Mantling: Gules and argent

On either side of the shield a flag, Argent a cross gules

For Admiral D'Arcy Preston, who m. Sophia, 4th dau. of Sir George Nares, and d. Jan. 1847. She d. Jan. 1833.   (B.L.G. 1937 ed.; Foster)

BAILDON

1. Dexter background black

Argent, the base vert, a wild man with white hair and beard, in his dexter hand a club resting on his dexter shoulder, ambulant between two oak trees all proper (Meyer)   In pretence: Per fess argent and sable a fess counter-embattled between three falcons counterchanged (Thompson)

Crest: A pelican in her piety proper   Mantling: Gules and argent

Motto: Sic transit gloria mundi

For Paul Meyer, of Baildon, who m. Jane, dau. and heir of Col. Francis Thompson, and d. 4 Jan. 1763, aged 28.   (M.I.; Foster; B.L.G. 2nd ed.)

2. All brown background
Tierced in pairle reversed, argent, gules and sable, a crescent in fess
point and another in centre chief both or (   )
Crest: An arm holding a spear sable   No helm or mantling
Mottoes (encircling the shield and crest): Resurgam, Libertas vita potior
A wood panel, c. 20 ins. x 20 ins.
Unidentified

BARDEN

1. Dexter ¾ black
Two oval shields   Dexter, within the Garter, Qly, 1st and 4th, Sable
three bucks' heads cabossed argent attired or (Cavendish), 2nd and 3rd,
Per bend embattled argent and gules (Boyle)   Sinister, Qly, 1st and
4th, Qly argent and gules a fret or, over all on a bend sable three
escallops argent (Spencer), 2nd and 3rd, Sable a lion rampant argent, on
a canton argent a cross gules (Churchill), impaling, Qly, 1st, Gules on a
bend argent three trefoils slipped vert (Hervey), 2nd, Gules three lions
passant guardant in pale or (England), 3rd, qly, i. Gules on a bend
between six cross crosslets fitchy argent the Augmentation of Flodden
(Howard), ii. Chequy or and azure (Warren), iii. Gules a lion rampant
argent (Fitzalan), iv. Qly or and azure an eagle or, over all on a bend
azure a fret between two martlets argent (Audley), 4th, Gules two lions
passant argent (Strange)
Duke's coronet   Crest: A knotted snake proper
Mantle: Gules and ermine   Motto: Cavendo tutis
Supporters: Two bucks proper, attired or, gorged with a chaplet of
white roses
For William, 5th Duke of Devonshire, K.G., who m. 1st, 1774, Georgiana,
dau. of John, Earl Spencer, and 2nd, 1809, Elizabeth, dau. of Frederick,
4th Earl of Bristol, and d. 29 July 1811.   (B.P. 1949 ed.)
(There is another hatchment for the 5th Duke at Ault Hucknall,
Derbyshire)

BARDSEY

1. All black background
On a lozenge surmounted by a cherub's head
Qly, 1st and 4th, Argent a lion rampant gules within a bordure sable, on
a canton azure a harp and in chief a royal crown or (Lane), 2nd and 3rd,
Argent a chevron between three foxes' heads erased gules (Fox),
impaling, Sable a fess chequy argent and azure between three bezants
(Pitt)
Motto: Inconcussa virtus
For Marcia Lucy, 3rd dau. of George, 1st Lord Rivers, who m. 1789, James
Fox, of Bramham Park, and d. 5 Aug. 1822.   (M.I. in Bramham church;
Foster)

2. Dexter background black
Dexter, as 1., but fox heads are proper, impaling, Azure a chevron
between three bulls' heads cabossed argent (Buckley)
Crests: Dexter, From a ducal coronet or a demi-griffin segreant sable
Sinister, On a ducal coronet or a fox passant proper
Mantling: Argent lined gules   Motto: As 1.
For George Lane-Fox, son and heir of James Fox, who m. 1814,
Georgiana Henrietta, dau. of Edward Pery Buckley, of Minstead Lodge,
Hants, and d. Nov. 1848.   (M.I. in Bramham church; Foster; B.P.
1949 ed.)

3. Dexter background black
Arms: As dexter of 1.
Knight's helm   Crests: As 2.   Mantling: Gules and argent
Motto: As 1.
Unidentified

BEAUCHIEF Abbey, Sheffield

1. All black background (should be dexter black)
Qly, 1st and 4th, Argent a chevron between three piles sable (Pegge),
2nd and 3rd, Paly of six sable and argent (Strelley), impaling, Argent
two bars gules, on a canton gules a cross argent (Broughton)
Crest: An old man's head proper   Mantling: Gules and argent
Motto: Mors janua vitae
For Strelley Pegge, who m. 2nd, Mary, dau. of Peter Broughton, of
Loudham, Notts, and d. 7 Apr. 1770, aged 60. She d. 4 Aug. 1774,
aged 52.   (Glover's History of Derbyshire)

BINGLEY

1. Sinister background black
Argent a chevron gules between three fleurs-de-lys vert (Busfeild),
impaling, Vert a buck's head couped or langued gules within a bordure
engrailed or (Fothergill)
Crest: A cubit arm in armour erect the hand proper holding a fleur-de-
lys or   Mantling: Gules and argent
Motto: Medio tutissimus ibis
Date at the side of the crest, A.D. 1726
For Elizabeth, dau. and co-heiress of Abraham Fothergill, of Chancery
Lane, who m. William Busfeild, of Gray's Inn and Ryshworth, and d. 24
Apr. 1726   (B.L.G. 5th ed.; Foster)

2. All black background
Identical to 1., but with the date, A.D. 1729
For William Busfeild, who d. 21 Mar. 1729.   (Sources, as 1.)

BISHOP BURTON

1. All black background (should be dexter black)
Qly, 1st, Per pale or and azure a fess nebuly between four fleurs-de-lys
all counterchanged (Watt), 2nd, Per chevron gules and argent three
talbots' heads erased counterchanged (Hall), 3rd, Per pale gules and
azure a cross patonce or (Wainman), 4th, Argent a chevron sable
(Bradley), impaling, Qly argent and sable on a bend gules three molets
argent (Cayley)
Crest: A greyhound sejant argent semy-de-lys azure, the dexter forepaw
resting on two arrows in saltire points downwards proper
Mantling: Azure and or   Motto: Viguer de dessus
For Ernest Richard Bradley Hall Watt, who m. 1891, Julia Philadelphia,
2nd dau. of Digby Cayley, of Malton, and d. 8 July 1908. She d. 29
Apr. 1923.   (B.L.G. 1937 ed.; M.I.)

2. All black background
Gules a sword in bend argent pommel and hilt or (Gee)
Crest: A mailed fist proper holding a short sword argent, pommel and
hilt or   Mantling: Gules and argent
Unidentified

BISHOPTHORPE

1. All black background
Gules two keys in saltire argent in chief a royal crown proper (See of
York), impaling, Qly, 1st and 4th, Gules two bars or (Harcourt), 2nd
and 3rd, qly i. & iv. Azure two bars argent (Venables), ii. Argent a fret
sable (Vernon), iii. Or on a fess azure three garbs or (Vernon)
A gold mitre of an archbishop above shield, with coronet at its base
Motto: Le bon temps viendra   In a narrow wood frame
For the Rt. Hon. Most Rev. Edward Vernon-Harcourt, Archbishop of
York, who d. 5 Nov. 1847.   (B.P. 1949 ed.)
(There is another hatchment for the Archbishop at Nuneham Courtenay,
Oxon.)

2. All black background
Almost identical to 1., but different draughtsmanship, very much
smaller, and without a frame
(This hatchment is no longer present in the church, having been stolen)

3. Background black behind sinister half of sinister shield only
Two shields, the dexter overlapping the sinister   Dexter, surmounted
by a mitre, arms as 1.   Sinister, suspended from a lover's knot, as
sinister of 1., impaling, Qly, 1st and 4th, Barry of eight argent and gules,

over all a cross flory sable (Gower), 2nd and 3rd, Azure three laurel
leaves or (Leveson)
Cherub's head below   In a narrow wood frame
For Anne, dau. of George, 1st Marquess of Stafford, K.G., who m.
1784, Edward Vernon-Harcourt, Archbishop of York, and d. 16 Nov.
1832.   (B.P. 1949 ed.)
(This hatchment is in the Palace; there is an almost identical hatchment
at Nuneham Courtenay, Oxon.)

BOLTON Abbey

1. All black background
Qly, 1st and 4th, Sable three bucks' heads cabossed argent (Cavendish),
2nd, Per bend embattled argent and gules (Boyle), 3rd, Chequy argent
and azure a fess gules (Clifford)
Shield within the Garter and surmounted by a duke's coronet
Motto: Cavendo tutus   Supporters: Two bucks proper
The George and stars of two other Orders pendent below
All on a mantle gules and ermine
Probably for William Spencer, 6th Duke of Devonshire, K.G., who d.
unm. 17 Jan. 1858.   (B.P. 1949 ed.)
(There is another hatchment for the 6th Duke at Hardwick Hall,
Derbyshire)

BOLTON-BY-BOWLAND

1. Dexter background black
Qly, 1st and 4th, Azure on a bend engrailed argent three daws sable
(Dawson), 2nd and 3rd, Vert a chevron between three pierced molets or
(Pudsey), impaling, Argent on a chevron sable three helmets proper
(Scott)
Crest: A cat's head erased at the neck affronté proper, murally gorged
or, holding in its mouth a rat proper   Mantling: Gules and argent
Motto: O Lord in Thee have I trusted   Skull below shield
For Pudsey Dawson, of Langcliffe Hall, and Bolton, who m. 1774,
Elizabeth Anne, dau. of James Scott of Amsterdam, and d. 19 Apr.
1816.   (B.L.G. 1937 ed.)

2. All black background
On a lozenge in ornamental gold frame, surmounted by a cherub's head
Qly, 1st and 4th, Argent a lion passant gules, on a chief azure three
cross crosslets argent (Littledale), 2nd, Per pale argent and or three
chevrons gules (Langton), 3rd, Or a fess between three greyhounds
courant sable (Patrickson), impaling, Qly of twenty, 1st, Azure on a
bend engrailed argent three daws sable (Dawson), 2nd, Vert a chevron

between three pierced molets or (Pudsey), 3rd, Gules a chevron between
three molets argent, in chief two bird-bolts palewise points downwards
or (Bolton), 4th Argent a fess engrailed between six cross crosslets
fitchy sable (Laton), 5th, Paly engrailed of eight or and sable, on a
canton qly argent and gules a bend sable (Atholl, Eure on the canton),
6th, Gules three lions passant guardant or debruised by a bend sinister
per bend sinister argent and sable (   ), 7th, Gules three garbs
within a double tressure flory counter-flory or (Comyn), 8th, Or a lion
rampant within a double tressure flory counter-flory gules (Scotland),
9th, Gules an orle argent (Balioll), 10th, Azure a lion rampant argent
crowned or (Galloway), 11th, Or three piles in point gules (Scot), 12th,
Azure a cross patonce between four martlets or (   ), 13th, Argent
a lion rampant sable a chief gules (   ), 14th, Azure a wolf's head
erased argent (Lupus), 15th, Barry of ten argent and azure (   ),
16th, Argent on a chief azure three crosses formy fitchy at the foot
argent (Strongbow), 17th, Argent a cross patonce voided gules
(Pilkington), 18th, Azure a bend or (Scrope), 19th, Per chevron sable
and ermine in chief two boars' heads couped or (Sandford), 20th,
Argent two bars, on a canton gules a lion passant guardant or (Lancaster)
Motto: Fac et spera
For Mary, eldest dau. of Pudsey Dawson of Bolton Hall, who m. 1809,
Anthony Littledale, of Everton House, Lancs, and d. 3 Nov. 1855.
(B.L.G. 1937 ed.)

3. Dexter background black

Qly, as dexter of 2., impaling, Qly of twenty, 1st and 20th, Gules a
lion's head erased between three cross crosslets argent (Armytage), 2nd,
Sable a chevron between three leopards' heads or (Wentworth), 3rd,
Argent a cross with each arm of three steps sable (Woodhouse), 4th,
Gules three fleurs-de-lys argent (Rotherfield), 5th, Sable a fess between
two chevrons or (De L'Isle), 6th Paly of six argent and gules a bend
counterchanged (Pollington), 7th, Argent on a bend sable three towers
argent (Ashburne), 8th, Argent a cross formy sable (Hoton), 9th, Gules
ten cross crosslets, four, three, two and one or (?Fernland), 10th, Argent
three bars sable (   ), 11th, Azure a fess between three fleurs-de-lys
or (Skelton), 12th, Argent a chevron between three foxes' heads erased
gules (Tynslow), 13th, Argent a lion rampant gules a bordure ermine
(Dundas), 14th, as 10th, 15th, Azure a fess argent between fifteen billets,
five, four, three, two and one or (Brett), 16th, as 9th, 17th, as 10th,
18th, Azure on a bend or three roundels gules (Whitley), 19th, Argent
three pallets wavy gules (Downes)
Crest: A demi-lion rampant gules gorged with a collar gemel and holding
in its dexter paw a cross crosslet argent
Mantling: Gules and argent   Motto: Fac et spera
For Henry Anthony Littledale, of Bolton Hall, eldest son of Anthony
Littledale and Mary Dawson, who m. 1845, Mary Elizabeth, dau. of John,
eldest son of Sir George Armytage, Bart., and d. 6 July 1859.
(B.L.G. 5th ed.)

4. Dexter background black
Qly, as dexter of 2., impaling, Or a cross gules, in dexter chief a lion
rampant sable (Burke)
Knight's helm   Crest, mantling and motto: As 3.
Unidentified

BRANDSBY

1. All black background
Gules in chief two esquires' helmets proper garnished or, in base a garb
or, in chief a fleur-de-lys or issuant from a crescent ermine (Cholmeley),
impaling, Qly, 1st and 4th, Sable six horseshoes three, two and one or
(Ferrers), 2nd and 3rd, Gules nine mascles conjoined five, three and one
argent, a canton ermine (Ferrers)
Crest: A demi-griffin segreant sable, wings, legs and beak or holding a
helmet as in the arms
Mantling: Gules and argent   Motto: Cassis tutissima virtus
For Francis Cholmeley, who m. Mary, dau. of Edward Ferrers, of
Baddesley Clinton, Warwickshire, and d. 26 Apr. 1780.   (Foster;
B.L.G. 1937 ed.)

2. Dexter background black
Cholmeley, as 1., but no fleur-de-lys or crescent, impaling, Gules two
bars argent, on a chief or a lion passant azure (Englefield)
Crest, mantling and motto: As 1.
For Francis Cholmeley, who m. 1782, Teresa Ann, dau. and co-heir of
Sir Henry Englefield, Bt., of White Knights, Berkshire, and d. 27 Jan.
1808.   (Sources, as 1.)

3. All black background
On a rococo lozenge with a cherub's head at each corner
Arms: As 2.
For Teresa Ann, widow of Francis Cholmeley, who d. 1810.   (Sources,
as 1.)

BRIDLINGTON Priory

1. All black background
Qly, 1st and 4th, Per fess argent a gules a pale counterchanged, three
rooks sable (Creyke), 2nd, Gules on a cross fleuretty argent five eaglets
displayed gules (Eggington), 3rd, Paly of six or and gules, on a chief
argent three lozenges gules (Arden), impaling, Paly of eight argent and
vert (Langley)
Crest: On a garb fesswise or a rook proper   Mantling: Gules and argent
Motto: Resurgam   Skull in base

CENTRE
for OXFORDSHIRE
STUDIES

For Ralph Creyke, of Marton, who m. 1772, Jane (d. 31 Dec. 1794), dau.
of Richard Langley, of Wykeham Abbey, and d. 24 May 1826.
(B.L.G. 1937 ed.; Foster)

2. Dexter background black
Creyke, impaling, Qly, 1st and 4th, Argent a bend between in chief a
unicorn's head erased and in base a cross crosslet fitchy gules (Denison),
2nd and 3rd, Per pale argent and azure three lions passant in pale
counterchanged (Sunderland)
Crest, mantling and motto: As 1.   Skull in base
For Ralph Creyke, of Marton and Rawcliffe, who m. 1807, Frances
(d. 1840), dau. of Robert Denison, of Kilnwick Percy, and d. 7 June
1828.   (Sources, as 1.)

3. Dexter background black
Qly, 1st and 4th, Creyke, 2nd, Gules a cross botonny argent (Egginton),
3rd, Paly of six or and gules, on a chief argent three lozenges gules
(Arden), impaling, Qly indented or ermined sable and gules, in the first
quarter a lion passant guardant sable (Croft)
Crest, mantling and motto: As 1.
For Ralph Creyke, who m. 1846, Louisa Frances (d. 20 July 1890),
dau. of Col. Croft of Stillington, and d. 7 Feb. 1858.   (Sources, as 1.
and Church Notes)

4. All black background
On an ornamental lozenge with a cherub's head at each corner, except
at the sinister where there are two
Argent two pallets azure, on a canton or a pierced molet sable
(Hebblethwaite)
Possibly for Adriana Hebblethwaite, b. 12 Aug. 1756, d. 22 June 1761.
(M.I.)

5. All black background
On a lozenge surrounded with decorative scrollwork
Hebblethwaite arms only
Skull below
Possibly for Harriet Hebblethwaite, d. unm. 7 Apr. 1827, aged 64.
(M.I.)

6. All black background
Hebblethwaite arms only
Crest: From a ducal coronet or a demi-wolf issuant argent
Mantling: Gules and argent   Motto: Christo salus nostra
Probably for James Hebblethwaite, d. 11 Nov. 1773.   (M.I.)

7. Dexter background black/sinister red
Per chevron embattled or and azure three martlets counterchanged
(Hudson), impaling, Sable a wolf rampant, in chief three estoiles or (Wilson)

Crest: A martlet or, winged azure   Mantling: Gules and argent
Probably for Benjamin Hudson, of Burlingtŏn, who m. Elizabeth, dau.
of Thomas Wilson, of Burlington, and d.   (B.G.A. 1884 ed.)

8. All black background
On a lozenge surrounded by decorative scrollwork, with a cherub's head
at the top and bottom
Arms: As 7.
Probably for Elizabeth, widow of Benjamin Hudson d.
(Source, as 7)

9. All black background
Or on a cross quarter pierced azure four mascles or (Prickett), impaling,
Azure a bend between two bucks trippant argent (Buck)
Crest: A stag statant proper   Mantling: Gules and argent
Motto: In coelo quies
For Marmaduke Prickett, who m. Frances, dau. of the Rev. William
Buck, vicar of Church Fenton, and d. 21 Oct. 1809.   She d. 21 Feb.
1805.   (M.I.; B.L.G. 1937 ed.)

10. All black background
Prickett, impaling, Prickett
Crest and mantling: As 9.   Motto: Resurgam
For Marmaduke Prickett, of Bridlington, who m. 1803, Elizabeth (d. 17
Jan. 1816), dau. of Paul Prickett, of London, and d. 5 June 1837.
(Sources, as 9.)

BROUGH-BY-CATTERICK

1. Sinister background black
Argent a chevron between three martlets sable, the Badge of Ulster
(Lawson), impaling, Lawson
Grey-green mantle behind shield and cherub's head above
For Clarinda Catherine, only dau. and heir of John Lawson, M.D. of
York, who m. Sir William (Wright) Lawson, 1st Bt., son of John Wright
of Kelvedon and Elizabeth Lawson, and d. 10 Jan. 1861.   (B.P.
1949 ed.)

2. All black background
Arms: As 1.
Crest: On a chapeau gules and ermine a martlet sable
Mantling: Sable and argent   Motto: (very worn) Leve et reluis
Skull below
For Sir William Lawson, 1st Bt., who d. 22 June 1865.   (B.P. 1949
ed.)

3. Sinister background black

Lawson, with Badge of Ulster on the chevron, impaling, Argent a saltire gules (Gerard)
Mantling: Gules and argent   Cherub's head above shield
For Mary Anne, dau. of Frederick Sewallis Gerard, who m. 1856, as his 1st wife, Sir John Lawson, 2nd Bt., and d. 5 Nov. 1868.   (B.P. 1949 ed.)

BROUGHTON Hall, nr. Skipton

1. All black background

Qly of six, 1st, Argent a bend between six martlets sable, in dexter chief the Badge of Ulster (Tempest), 2nd, Argent a fess sable between three lions' heads erased gules (Fermor), 3rd, Gules on a saltire argent an annulet gules (Nevil), 4th, Qly gules and or in the first quarter a molet or (De Vere), 5th, Gules a bend argent between six cross crosslets fitchy or (Howard), 6th, Azure six escallops, three, two and one argent
(   )
No helm   Crest: A griffin's head erased per pale argent and sable
Motto: Love as thou finds
Probably for Sir Charles Robert Tempest, 1st Bt. of Broughton Hall, and of Coleby Hall, Lincs, who d. unm. 8 Dec. 1865.   (B.P. 1949 ed.)

BUBWITH

1. Dexter background black

Qly of eight, 1st, Or on a fess dancetty sable a fleur-de-lys argent, in cheif the Badge of Ulster (Vavasour), 2nd, Argent a demi-lion rampant sable charged on the shoulder with a fleur-de-lys or (Mervyn), 3rd, Sable a fess between three ducks argent (Sheldon), 4th, Argent on a bend between two lions rampant sable a wyvern argent (Ruding), 5th, Argent three lions' heads erased sable a chief gules (   ), 6th, Gules three battle-axes argent (   ), 7th, Azure ten roundels, four, three, two and one argent (   ), 8th, Azure a chevron between three molets of six points argent (   )   In pretence, Qly of six, 1st, Per fess sable and ermine, on a fess nebuly between three gates, three goats' heads all counterchanged (Yates), 2nd, Argent a griffin segreant gules (Trafford), 3rd, Argent a pierced molet sable (Assheton), 4th, Or on a fess dancetty sable a fleur-de-lys argent (Vavasour), 5th, Argent three escallops in bend gules between two bendlets sable (de la Haye), 6th, Gules three covered cups within a bordure engrailed or (Butler)
Crest: A cockerel gules   Mantling: Gules and argent
For Sir Henry Vavasour, 1st Bt. (formerly Nooth), who m. Ann Assheton, dau. and co-heir of Mail Yates, of Mail, Lancs, took the name and arms of Vavasour on his wife succeeding to the Spaldington estate, and d. 15 Mar. 1813.   (Foster)

BURNSALL

1. Dexter background black
Argent a fess between six cross crosslets fitchy gules (Craven), impaling,
Argent on a fess sable three pierced molets of six points or, in dexter
chief an ermine spot sable (Grimston)
Earl's coronet   Crest: On a chapeau gules and ermine, a griffin statant
wings elevated ermine   Motto: Virtus in actione consistit
Supporters: Two griffins wings elevated ermine
For William, 2nd Earl of Craven, who m. 1835, Emily Mary, 2nd dau.
of James Walter, 1st Earl of Verulam, and d. 25 Aug. 1866.   (B.P. 1949
ed.)

BURTON AGNES

1. Dexter background black
Or a fess between three crescents gules, in fess point the Badge of Ulster
(Boynton), impaling, Argent two pallets azure, on a canton sable a molet
or (Heblethwayte)
Crest: A goat trippant sable, gutty argent, horns and hooves or
Mantling: Gules and argent   Mottoes: Il tempo passa, and, Resurgam
For Sir Griffith Boynton, 6th Bt., who m. 2nd, 1768, Mary (d. 13 May
1815), dau. of James Heblethwayte, and d. 6 Jan. 1778.   (B.P. 1949
ed.; Foster; M.I.)

2. Sinister background black
Qly of nine, 1st, Or a fess between three crescents gules (Boynton), 2nd,
Or on a cross sable five bulls' heads couped argent (Aton), 3rd, Gules a
cross moline or (Monceaux), 4th, Argent a chevron between three roses
gules (Rossels), 5th, Azure two bars wavy argent (Del See), 6th, Sable a
bend flory counter-flory argent (?Highlord), 7th, Gules on a fess dancetty
argent between six lions rampant or three martlets sable (Griffith), 8th
Azure crusilly fitchy three eagles displayed or (Somerville), 9th, Argent
five barrulets gules, on a bordure azure ten martlets or (Merley), impaling,
Gules a chevron or between three crosses formy argent, on a canton
ermine a stag's head erased sable (Strickland)
Crest and mantling: As 1.   Motto: Il tempo passa
Cherub's head below
For Louisa, dau. of Walter Strickland, of Cokethorpe Park, Oxon, who
m. 1833, as his 1st wife, Sir Henry Boynton, 10th Bt., and d. 1841.
(Foster; B.P. 1949 ed.)

3. Dexter background black
Boynton, in chief the Badge of Ulster, impaling two coats per fess, in
chief, Strickland, and in base, Barry of six or and gules on a bend sable
three escallops argent (Lightfoot)

Crest, mantling and mottoes: As 1.
For Sir Henry Boynton, 10th Bt., who m. 1st, Louisa (d. 1841), dau. of
Walter Strickland, and 2nd, 1843, Harriet (d. 13 Sept. 1889), dau. of
Thomas Lightfoot of Sevenoaks, Kent, and d. 25 June 1869.   (Sources,
as 2.)

4.   Sinister background black

Azure on a chevron argent three millrinds sable, on a canton or a trefoil
slipped sable (Milnes)   In pretence: Qly, 1st, Gules on each of two
bars argent three mascles gules, on a canton or a leopard's face sable
(Gery), 2nd, Sable two spearheads palewise in fess, in dexter chief a
crescent, in sinister chief a boar's head couped argent (   ), 3rd,
Sable a fess between three boars' heads couped or (   ), 4th, Vairy
argent and sable on a chief or three pierced molets sable (Benyon)
Motto: Resurgam
For Eleanor, dau. of William Gery of Bushmead, Beds, who m. the Rev.
Thomas Milnes, Rector of Burton Agnes, and d.   He d. 1833.
(B.L.G. 2nd ed.; M.I.)

CARLTON Towers, nr. Selby

1.   Dexter two-thirds background black

Qly, 1st and 4th, Argent a lion rampant sable (Stapleton), 2nd and 3rd,
Argent two bars and in chief three escallops azure (Errington), impaling,
to the dexter, Or a bend gules between three eagles close sable (Witham),
and to the sinister, Qly argent and gules (Tuite)
Crest: A Saracen's head proper, wreathed argent and sable
Mantling: Gules and argent   Motto: Meulx serra
At each upper corner of shield a cherub's head, and winged skull in base
For Thomas Stapleton, of Carlton, who m. 1st, Catherine, dau. of
Henry Witham of Cliffe, and 2nd, Anne, dau. of Nicholas Tuite, and d.
25 Apr. 1821, aged 83.   (Foster; B.P. 1949 ed.)

2.   Dexter two-thirds background black

Qly, as 1., impaling to the dexter, Argent a saltire gules (Gerard), and to
the sinister, Ermine a saltire sable (Anster)
Crest and motto: As 1.
A strangely marshalled hatchment; the arms as a whole are on a lozenge,
but Stapleton quartering Errington is on a rectangular panel, the crest
occupies the apex of the lozenge, and the motto overlaps its base
For Thomas Stapleton, who m. 1st, 1802, Maria Juliana (d. 9 Feb.
1827), dau. of Sir Robert Cansfield Gerard, Bt., and 2nd, 1829,
Henrietta Lavinia (d. 14 Nov. 1858), dau. of Richard Fitzgerald Anster,
and d. 6 July 1839.   (Sources, as 1.)

3. Dexter background black

Qly, 1st, Qly, as 1., but in fess point of Errington a crescent gules for difference, 2nd, Gules three bars nebuly or (Lovel), 3rd, Azure semy-de-lys a lion rampant or (Beaumont), 4th, Azure three cinquefoils or (Bardolf), impaling, Sable three lions passant in bend between two double cotises argent (Browne)
Baron's coronet   Crest and motto: As 1.
Supporters: Two talbots argent
For Miles Thomas, 8th Baron Beaumont, who m. 1844, Isabella Anne, dau. of Lord Kilmaine, and d. 10 Aug. 1854.   (Sources, as 1.)

4. Identical to 3., heraldically, but there are some differences in the style of painting.

Presumably also for Miles Thomas, 8th Baron Beaumont, d. 10 Aug. 1854.

CATTERICK

1. All black background

Argent a chevron between three martlets sable, in fess point the Badge of Ulster (Lawson), impaling, Argent a three masted ship, rigging and sails furled, red flags, on a sea in base all proper (Maire)
Crest: Two cubit arms, hands proper, sleeved sable ermined argent, cuffed argent, holding an annulet within which a sun in splendour or
Motto: Leve et reluis
For Sir Henry Lawson, 4th Bt., of Brough Hall, who m. 1742, Anastasia, dau. of Thomas Maire, of Dartington Hall, Yorks, and d. 1 Oct. 1781. (B.P. 1949 ed.)

2. Dexter and top sinister background black, and all background gutty argent

Qly of six, 1st, Lawson, 2nd, Argent on a fess sable three bezants (Brough), 3rd, Gules a saltire argent (Nevill), 4th, Argent on a saltire sable five swans argent (Brough), 5th, Azure a cross flory or (   ), 6th, Argent a fess engrailed between six fleurs-de-lys sable (   ), impaling two coats per fess, in chief, Gules three molets in bend between two bendlets engrailed argent (Scarisbrick), and in base, Argent a lion rampant sable (Stapleton)
Crest: On a chapeau gules and ermine a martlet sable
Mantling: Gules and argent   Motto: Leve et reluis   Skull below
For Sir John Lawson, 5th Bt., who m. 1st, 1768, Elizabeth (d. 1801), dau. of William Scarisbrick, and 2nd, 1803, Monica, dau. of Miles Stapleton, of Drax, and d. 27 June 1811.   (B.P. 1949 ed.)

3. Sinister background black

Lawson, impaling, Argent a fess sable between three lions' heads erased gules (Fermor)

Cherub's head above shield
For Catherine, dau. of Henry Fermor, of Worcs, who m. 1801, as his
2nd wife, Sir Henry Lawson, 6th Bt., and d. 13 Sept. 1824.   (B.P.
1949 ed.; M.I.)

4. All black background
Lawson, impaling two coats per fess, in chief, Argent a lion rampant
sable (Stapleton), and in base, Argent a fess sable between three lions'
heads erased gules (Fermor)
Crest, mantling and motto: As 2.   Skull below
For Sir Henry Lawson, 6th Bt., who m. 1st, 1773, Monica (d. 1800),
dau. of Nicolas Stapleton, of Carlton, Yorks, and 2nd, 1801, Catherine
(d. 1824), dau. of Henry Fermor, and d. 9 Jan. 1834.   (Sources, as 3.)

NORTH CAVE

1. Dexter background black
Azure a fess between three talbots' heads erased or (Burton)
Crest: A beacon or   Mantling: Gules and argent
In wide frame decorated with skulls and crossbones
Possibly for Richard Burton, of Hull Bank, who d. 1 Oct. 1784, aged
26.   (M.I.)

2. All black background
Qly, 1st and 4th, Azure a fess or ermined sable between three talbots'
heads erased or (Burton), 2nd and 3rd, Argent a saltire between four
molets sable (Christie), over all a fess or ermined sable, impaling, Argent
a chevron between three crescents azure (   )
Crests (on two helms): Dexter, A beacon sable flammant or
Sinister, A bird argent in its beak a spray of leaves proper
Mantle: Gules and ermine   Mottoes: above, Quis separabit
below, Tria juncta in uno
In top corner winged and crowned skull and in bottom corner skull and
crossbones
For Robert Burton, of Hotham, and North Cave, M.P. who d. 13 Apr.
1822, aged 37.   (M.I.)

CHERRY BURTON

1. Dexter background black
Argent on a chevron between three fleurs-de-lys sable three rams' heads
argent (Ramsden), impaling, Azure a chevron ermine between three
swans argent (Swan)
Crest: A mailed cubit arm erect the hand holding a fleur-de-lys sable
Mantling: Gules and argent   Motto: Audaces fortuna juvet

For Henry Ramsden, Rector of Cherry Burton, who m. 1821, Mary,
dau. of Robert Swann, of Askham Bryan, and d. 2 June 1837.
(Foster)

COLLINGHAM

1. All black background

Sable a chevron invected between in chief two dexter gauntlets erect,
clenched, and in base a stag's head erased or (Gunter), impaling, Qly,
1st and 4th, Per chevron or and gules three gates counterchanged (Yates),
2nd and 3rd, Vairy argent and sable, on a chief or three molets sable, a
sinister canton azure (Benyon), in fess point of shield the Badge of
Ulster

Crests: Dexter, A dexter gauntlet clenched fesswise, the fist to the
dexter or, surmounted by a stag's head erased or   Sinister, On a
grass plot a griffin sejant vert, collared vairy argent and sable
Motto: Deus noster refugium
For Sir Robert Gunter, 1st Bt., of Wetherby Grange, who m. 1862,
Jane Marguerite (d. 10 May 1907), dau. of Thomas Benyon of Gledhow
Hall, Yorks, and d. 18 Sept. 1905.   (B.P. 1949 ed.)
(In view of the background perhaps also used subsequently for his
widow)

SOUTH COWTON

1. All black background

Qly, 1st, Gules three cross crosslets fitchy and a chief or (Arden), 2nd,
Sable a chevron between three buckles argent (Mallet), 3rd, Argent two
bars azure, over all on a bend gules three arrows or (Done), 4th, Barry
of six or and gules on a sinister canton gules a Tudor rose argent (Pepper)
Crest: Out of a ducal coronet or a panache of five ostrich feathers
argent banded vert
Mantling: Gules, or and argent   Motto: Patientia vinces
Possibly for John Arden (brother of Richard Pepper, 1st Baron Alvanley),
who d.   (B.E.P.)

COXWOLD

1. Sinister background black

Qly, 1st and 4th, Argent a chevron gules between three fleurs-de-lys
azure (Belasyse), 2nd and 3rd, Argent a pale engrailed between two
pallets sable (Belasyse)   In pretence: Qly, 1st and 4th, Argent a
chevron between three boars passant sable (Betham), 2nd and 3rd,
Ermine on a quarter gules an owl or (Barton)

Countess's coronet   Motto: Bonne et belle assez
Supporters: Dexter, A stag holding in its mouth a sprig of oak fructed
proper   Sinister, A unicorn azure, mane, tufts, horn and hooves or
For Catherine, dau. and heiress of John Betham, of Rowington, Warws,
who m. 1726, Thomas, 1st Earl Fauconberg, and d. 30 May 1760.
(B.E.P.)

2. All black background
Arms: As 1.
Earl's coronet   Crest: A lion couchant guardant azure
Mantling: Gules and argent   Motto and supporters: As 1.
For Thomas, 1st Earl Fauconberg, who d. 4 Feb. 1774.   (B.E.P.)

CRAMBE

1. Dexter background black
Azure a saltire between two molets in pale and an increscent and a
decrescent in fess argent (Haigh), impaling, Argent a cross between four
fleurs-de-lys sable (Fenton)
Crest: A talbot's head erased gules   Mantling: Gules and argent
For Joseph Haigh, of Whitwell Hall and Springwood, who m. Emilia
(Fenton), and d. 4 Aug. 1835, aged 70.   (M.I.)

2. Dexter background black
Haigh, as 1., but estoiles instead of molets, impaling, Argent a cross
patonce between four fleurs-de-lys gules (Ward)
Crest and mantling: As 1.
For John Haigh, of Whitwell Hall, who m. Anna Maria, dau. of James
Ward, of Willey, Surrey, and d. 6 Sept. 1837, aged 32.   (M.I.;
B.L.G. 2nd ed.)

CROFTON

1. Dexter background black
Qly, 1st and 4th, Sable a wolf salient or charged on the breast with a
mascle gules, in chief an estoile or between two estoiles argent (Wilson),
2nd and 3rd, Argent three bars gemel gules, on a chief azure three
leopards' faces or, a canton ermine (Wright), impaling, Qly, 1st and 4th,
qly i. & iv. Or a saltire and a chief gules, on a canton argent a lion
rampant azure (Bruce), ii. & iii. Argent a chevron gules between three
chapeaux azure (Brudenell), 2nd and 3rd, Wright, with canton or
ermined sable
Crests: Dexter, A demi-wolf salient or   Sinister, From a mural coronet
chequy argent and gules a dragon's head vert
Mantling: Gules and argent   Motto: Res non verba

For Sir Henry Wright Wilson, of Crofton Hall, who m. 2nd, Frances
Elizabeth, youngest dau. of Thomas, 1st Earl of Ailesbury, and d. 3
Dec. 1832, aged 73.   (B.P. 1949 ed.; M.I.)
(There is another hatchment for Sir Henry Wright Wilson at Barton
Stacey, Hampshire)

2. All black background
On a lozenge surmounted by a cherub's head
Arms: As 1.
For Frances Elizabeth, widow of Sir Henry Wright Wilson, who d. 7
Feb. 1836.   (Sources, as 1.)
(There is another hatchment for Lady Frances Wilson at Barton Stacey,
Hampshire)

CUSWORTH Hall

1. All black background
On a lozenge surmounted by an escallop and surrounded by rococo
scrollwork
Qly, 1st and 4th, Sable a chevron argent between three goats statant
argent each charged on the flank with a pale gules, on a chief or a demi-
wildman affronté couped with a club on his right shoulder between two
quatrefoils gules (Battie), 2nd and 3rd, Or a fess counter-compony
argent and azure between three griffins' heads erased azure (Wrightson)
In pretence: Qly, 1st and 4th, Wrightson, 2nd and 3rd, Per fess gules
and argent six martlets three and three counterchanged (Fenwick)
Motto: In coelo quies
For Isabella, only child and heiress of William Wrightson, of Cusworth,
who m. 1748, John Battie (d. 1766) of Warmsworth (who assumed the
name and arms of Wrightson), and d. 1784.   (B.L.G. 1937 ed.;
Foster)

2. Sinister background black
Or a fess counter-compony argent and azure between three griffins'
heads erased azure (Wrightson)   In pretence: Argent on a bend sable
three pheons points downwards argent (Bland)
Cherub's head above and palm fronds flanking shield
For Barbara, dau. and sole heiress of James Bland, of Hurworth,
Durham, who m. as his 1st wife, William Wrightson, of Cusworth, and
d. 1782.   (Sources, as 1.)

3. Sinister background black
Or a fess counter-compony argent and gules between three griffins'
heads erased gules (Wrightson)   In pretence: Bland   Also in pretence
(surmounting the last): Per fess gules and sable a lion rampant and in
dexter chief an estoile or (Heber)

Mantling: Gules and argent   Cherub's head above
For Henrietta, dau. and co-heiress of Richard Heber, of Marton, who m.
1787, as his 2nd wife, William Wrightson, of Cusworth, and d. May
1820.   (Sources, as 1.)

4. All black background
Arms: As 3.
Crest: A unicorn rampant argent crined and armed or
Mantling: Gules and argent   Motto: Resurgam
For William Wrightson, of Cusworth, who m. 1st, Barbara, dau. of
James Bland, and 2nd, Henrietta, dau. of Richard Heber, and d. 26 Dec.
1827.   (Sources, as 1.)

5. Dexter background black
Qly, 1st and 4th, Or a fess engrailed counter-compony azure and argent
between four griffins' heads erased azure three in chief and one in base
(Wrightson), 2nd and 3rd, Sable a chevron argent between three goats
statant argent, on the flank of each two pallets gules, on a chief or a
demi-wildman affronté issuant with a club over his right shoulder
between two cinquefoils gules (Battie), impaling, Barry of ten argent
and azure six escutcheons sable each charged with a lion rampant argent
(Cecil)
Crests: Dexter, On stony ground proper a unicorn rampant argent, the
lower forehoof resting on a shield or, thereon a griffin's head erased
azure   Sinister, A stork argent beaked and legged gules, in its beak
a fish argent
Mantling: Azure and or   Motto: Battez contre le viz
For William Henry Battie-Wrightson, of Cusworth, who m. 1884,
Isabella (d. 1917), eldest dau. of William, 3rd Marquess of Exeter, and
d. 28 Apr. 1903.   (Sources, as 1.)

NORTH DALTON

1. All black background
Argent a bear rampant sable (   )
Crest: A bear's head erased sable (very difficult to see and may not be
correct)   Mantling: Gules and argent
Motto: Morior ut vivam
Frame decorated with skulls and crossbones
Unidentified

SOUTH DALTON

1. Dexter background black

Barry of ten argent and azure, on a canton or a chough proper, in fess
point the Badge of Ulster (Hotham), impaling, Sable an estoile or
between two flaunches ermine (Hobart)
Shield surrounded with the motto of the Order of the Bath
Crest: A demi-man naked issuant from water holding in the dexter hand
a sword and on the sinister arm a shield with the arms of Hotham
Mantle: Gules and ermine   Motto: Certum pete finem
Supporters: Dexter, A lion or charged on the shoulder with a fleur-de-
lys or on a roundel azure   Sinister, A stag reguardant proper collar
and chain or
For Sir Charles Hotham-Thompson, K.B., 8th Bt., who m. Dorothy,
dau. of John, 1st Earl of Buckinghamshire, and d. 26 Jan. 1794.
(B.P. 1949 ed.)

2. Sinister background black

Azure a bishop seated with mitre and staff or (See of Clogher), impaling,
Hotham, with Ulster Badge in fess point
Bishop's mitre above shield   Motto: As 1.
For the Rt. Rev. Sir John Hotham, 9th Bt., Bishop of Clogher, who d.
3 Nov. 1795.   (B.P. 1949 ed.)

3. Dexter background black

Hotham, with Ulster Badge in fess point, impaling, Sable on a chevron
between three staves raguly argent inflamed gules a fleur-de-lys gules
between two choughs proper (Meyrick)
Crest: As 1.   Mantling: Gules and argent
Motto: Resurgam   Skull in base
For Sir Charles Hotham, 10th Bt., who m. 1804 Elizabeth, dau. of
Owen M. Meyrick, and d. July 1811.   (Foster)

4. All black background

Hotham arms only, with Badge of Ulster in fess point
Baron's coronet   Crest: A demi-man naked, in his dexter hand a
sword, blade wavy, and on sinister arm a shield charged, Sable an estoile
argent   Mantle: Gules and ermine   Motto: In coelo quies
Supporters: Two sailors proper each outer hand resting on a cutlass
Skull in base
Probably for Admiral Sir William Hotham, 1st Baron Hotham, who d.
unm. 2 May 1813.   (B.P. 1949 ed.; Foster)

5. All black background

Hotham, no Badge of Ulster, impaling, Per pale gules and azure a lion
rampant or (for Hankey)
Baron's coronet   Crest, mantle, motto and supporters: As 4.

Skull in base
For Beaumont, 2nd Baron Hotham, who m. 1767, Susannah, dau. of
Sir Thomas Hankey, and d. 4 Mar. 1814.   (B.P. 1949 ed.)

6.   All black background
Hotham arms only, with no Badge of Ulster
Baron's coronet   Crest: As 1.   Mottoes: Lead on   Resurgam
Supporters: As 4.
Probably for Beaumont, 3rd Baron Hotham, who d. unm. 12 Dec. 1780,
or his brother Charles, 4th Baron Hotham, who d. unm. 29 May 1872.
(B.P. 1949 ed.)

DENTON

1.   Dexter background black
Gules on a bend cotised argent between two fleeces or three escallops
gules (Ibbetson), impaling, Gules an arrow palewise point downwards
argent between two garbs or, on a chief argent a cherub's head proper
between two estoiles or (Thackeray), in centre chief the Badge of Ulster
Crest: A unicorn's head erased per fess argent and gules
Mantling: Grey (?Gules and argent badly faded)
Motto: Vixi liber et moriar
For Sir Charles Henry Ibbetson, 5th Bt., of Denton Park, who m. 1847,
Eden, dau. of J. T. Thackeray, and d. 6 July 1861.   (B.P. 1875 ed.;
Foster)

DINNINGTON Hall

1.   Dexter background black
Qly, 1st and 4th, Azure a cock argent comb   gules (Boucherett), 2nd
and 3rd, Sable a fess argent between three asses passant proper
(Ayscough), impaling, Argent a chevron between in chief two molets of
six points and in base a crescent gules (?Crokatt)
No helm   Crest: A cockatrice sable, legs beak and tip of tail or,
wings comb and wattle gules   Mantle: Gules and ermine
Motto: Resurgam
Probably for Ayscoghe Boucherett, of Willingham, Lincs, who m. 1789,
Emilia, dau. of Charles Crokatt, of Luxborough Hall, Essex, and d. 15
Sept. 1815.   (B.L.G. 2nd ed.)

DOWNHOLME

1.   All black background
Gules on a fess between three cushions, set lozengewise, fringed and
tasselled or three fleurs-de-lys gules (Hutton), impaling, Per bend

indented argent and azure three cinquefoils counterchanged (Chaytor)
Crest: A cushion gules, set lozengewise, fringed and tasselled or, charged
with an open book argent, edged gold, inscribed Odor Vitae
Mantling: Brown and argent   Motto: Resurgam
For Timothy Hutton, of Clifton Castle and Marske Hall, who m. 1804,
Elizabeth, dau. of William Chaytor, of Croft and Spennithorne, and d.
1864.   (Foster; B.L.G. 1937 ed.)
(There is another hatchment for Timothy Hutton at Thornton Watlass)

2. Dexter background black
Hutton, as 1. but cushions set squarewise, impaling, Argent a chevron
engrailed gules between three lambs passant sable (Lamb)
Crest: As 1.   Mantling: Gules and argent
Motto: Spiritus gladius
For John Timothy D'Arcy Hutton, of Marske and Aldborough Hall,
who m. 1845, Emma Rebecca, only dau. of Thomas March Lamb, of
Middleham, and d. Oct. 1874.   (Sources, as 1.)

EASBY

1. Dexter background black
Sable a chevron between three cronels, in chief a molet argent (Yeoman),
impaling, Vert a lion rampant between two piles engrailed argent within
a bordure engrailed argent semy of popinjays vert beaks and legs gules
(Home)
Crest: A mailed arm, the bare hand holding a broken tilting spear proper
Mantling: Gules and argent   Motto: Resurgam
For Capt. Bernard Yeoman, R.N., who m. 1826, Charlotte, dau. of Sir
Everard Home, Bt., and d. 9 May 1836.   (B.L.G. 5th ed.; M.I.)
(This hatchment was recorded in 1962, but is now missing; for other
hatchments formerly in church, see under Richmond Museum)

ECCLESALL, Sheffield

1. All black background
Qly, 1st and 4th, Azure three molets argent within a double tressure
flory counter-flory or (Murray), 2nd and 3rd, qly i. & iv. Paly of six or
and sable (Athol), ii. & iii. Or a fess chequy azure and argent (Stuart)
In pretence: Qly, 1st and 4th, Gules a lion rampant between eight cross
crosslets fitchy in pale argent (Dalton), 2nd and 3rd, Per pale azure and
gules a bend or between two molets argent (Bright)
Crest: A demi-savage proper, wreathed about the head and loins, in the
dexter hand a sword erect proper, in the sinister hand a key or
Mantling: Gules and argent   Motto: Furth fortune and fill the fetters

Supporters: Dexter, A savage proper wreathed about the loins and
fettered with a chain held in the dexter hand proper   Sinister, A lion
rampant gules, gorged with a collar azure charged with three molets
argent
For Lord John Murray, of Banner Cross Hall, son of John, 1st Duke of
Atholl, by his 2nd marriage, who m. 1758, Mary, daù. and heiress of
Richard Dalton and Mary Bright, and d. 26 May 1787.   She d. 21 May
1765.   (B.P. 1875 ed.; Foster; Hunter's Hallamshire, p. 353)

2.   All black background
Arms: Qly, as 1.
Crest, mantling and motto: As 1.   Supporters: As 1., but savage
wreathed about the head as well as the loins
Perhaps also for Lord John Murray (see 1.)

ECCLESFIELD

1.   All black background
Or a fess between three greyhounds' heads erased sable collared and
ringed gules (Shiercliffe)
Crest: A scimitar erect transfixing a leopard's head or
Mantling: Gules and argent   Motto: Mors janua vitae
Possibly for Thomas Shiercliffe, of Ecclesfield Hall, who d. unm. 25
Dec. 1779, during the lifetime of his father and was buried in Ecclesfield
Church.   (Hunter's Hallamshire, p. 446)

2.   All black background
Sable a bend between six escallops or (Foljambe), impaling, Azure a fess
wavy ermine between six seamews' heads erased argent beaked gules
(Spencer)
Crest: A mailed leg with spur qly or and sable
Mantling: Gules and argent   Motto: Soyez ferme
Supporters (but depicted as if crests): Dexter, An antelope couchant
qly or and sable   Sinister, A Bengal tiger couchant proper
For Thomas Foljambe, of Aldwarke, who m. Sarah, dau. of William
Spencer, of Bramley Grange, and d. 28 Mar. 1758, buried in the family
vault at Ecclesfield.   (Foster; Bloom; B.L.G. 1937 ed.)

3.   Dexter background black
Foljambe, impaling, Argent a fess gules between three popinjays vert,
beaked legged and collared gules (Lumley)
Crest: A mailed leg qly or and sable spurred or lined gules
Mantling: Gules and or   Motto: Resurgam   Skull and wings below
For Francis Ferrand Foljambe, who m. 2nd, 1792, Mary (d. 1817), dau.
of Richard, 4th Earl of Scarbrough, and d. 13 Nov. 1814.   (Foster;
Hunter: B.L.G. 1937 ed.)
(This hatchment, when seen in 1974, was in rags)

4. Dexter and upper half of sinister background black

Per pale azure and gules a bend engrailed between two roundels argent,
on a chief argent a rose between two roundels gules (Dixon)
Crest: A dexter arm embowed, sleeved azure semy of roundels argent,
cuffed argent, the hand grasping a chaplet of three red roses proper
Mantling: Or   Motto: Fide et constantia
For James Dixon, of Page Hall, Sheffield, who m. 1st, 1797, Hannah
Cooper, of Burslem, and 2nd, 1806, Ann (d. 1861), dau. of Thomas
Nowill, and d. 17 Oct. 1852.   (Foster; Bloom; Pedigree by A. Willis-
Dixon, 1920; M.I.)

5. All black background

Argent two bars gemel wavy azure, on a chief sable a square tower
argent (Parkin), impaling, to the dexter, Argent a cross moline sable
(Copley), and to the sinister, Azure a cross patonce or (Warde)
Crest: A four-towered castle set cornerwise argent
Mantling: Gules and argent   Motto: Beatus ante obitum nemo
On back of frame, a piece of parchment inscribed, Late Mr. Parkin,
Mortomley Hall, obt 1758.
For William Parkin, of Mortomley, who m. 1st, Mary (d. 1736), dau. of
Lionel Copley, of Sprotbrough, and 2nd, Catherine (d. 1761), dau. of
Patience Warde, of Hooton Pagnell, and d.s.p. 2 May 1757.   (Hunter,
p. 437; Eastwood's History of Ecclesfield, p. 432; Hunter's Fam. Min.
Gent. IV, 1275)

6. All white background

Argent three lozenges sable (Freeman), impaling, Argent a fess or
between in chief a goat's head erased and in base three escallops, two
and one, argent (Warham)
Crest: A goat's head erased argent   Mantling: Gules and argent
Unidentified

EGTON

1. Dexter background black

Per chevron azure and argent a chevron paly of eight argent and gules
between in chief a sun in splendour between two bugle horns stringed
or and in base a bugle horn stringed or (Foster), impaling, Gules on a
fess or between three boars' heads erased argent langued gules three
lions rampant sable langued gules (Hudson)
Motto: Spes mea in Deo
A small hatchment of true lozenge shape, c. 2½ft. x 2ft.
For John Foster, of Egton, who m. 1865, Fanny Elizabeth (d. 24 Feb.
1928), dau. of Robert Hudson, of Roundhay, Yorks, and d. 8 Feb.
1910.   (B.L.G. 1937 ed.)

2.   Dexter background black

Foster, as 1., but per chevron azure and ermine, impaling, Azure a
chevron ermine between three billets or (Ussher)
Crest: A stag's head erased proper gutty or transfixed through the head
by an arrow palewise or headed and flighted argent
Motto: Justum perficito nihil timeto
A small hatchment of true lozenge shape, c. 2ft. x 1½ft.
For John Kenneth Foster, of Egton, who m. 1896, Mary, only dau. of
John Ussher, of The Dene, Great Budworth, and d. 2 Mar. 1930.
(B.L.G. 1937 ed.)

FIRBECK

1.   All black background

On an ornamental lozenge pendent from a lover's knot
Qly, 1st and 4th, Azure a chevron ermine between three lozenges argent
each charged with a fleur-de-lys sable (Miles), 2nd and 3rd, Per fess
azure and gules a leopard rampant argent spotted sable, on a canton or
a tower port open sable (More of Peachey), impaling, Qly, 1st, Qly vert
and or in the first quarter a hawk close, in the fourth a lure, argent
(Jebb), 2nd, Vert three greyhounds courant two and one argent (De
Witt), 3rd, Ermine a chief azure, over all on a bend gules a sword argent
pommel and hilt or (Gladwin), 4th, Gules three cinquefoils in pale or
between two flaunches argent each charged with a griffin sable (Du
Keyne)
Two palm branches below the lozenge
For Frances Harriott, dau. of Joshua Jebb, of Bramfield Hall, who m.
1829, William Miles, of Clifton, Glos., and d.s.p. Oct. 1877.   (B.L.G.
1937 ed.)

2.   All black background

Qly, 1st and 4th, Azure fretty argent a chief or (St Leger), 2nd and 3rd,
Argent three covered cups in bend between two bendlets engrailed sable
(Butler)
Crest: A griffin passant or   Mantling: Gules and argent
Motto: Haut et bon
Supporters: Two griffins or wings elevated azure fretty argent
For Col. Anthony Francis Butler St Leger, who d. 31 Oct. 1862.
(B.L.G. 1937 ed.)

3.   All black background

On a lozenge   Qly, 1st and 4th, Gules on a chevron or between in
chief two pierced molets of six points and in base a cock argent, armed
or, a chain of nine links sable (Gally), 2nd and 3rd, Or on a chief sable
three griffins segreant or (Knight), impaling, Gules three lions rampant
or (Fitzherbert)

Motto: In coelo quies
For Selina, dau. of William Fitzherbert, of Tissington, Derbyshire, who
m. Henry Gally-Knight, of Langold, and d. 2 Jan. 1823.   He d. 1808.
(B.L.G. 1852 ed.; Hunter's South Yorkshire, i. 299)

4. Dexter background black
Qly, 1st and 4th, Knight, 2nd and 3rd, Gules on a chevron or between
in chief two estoiles of eight rays and in base a cock argent a chain of
nine links sable (Gally), impaling, Argent on a chevron sable three
quatrefoils or (Eyre)
Crests: Dexter, From a viscount's coronet proper a cock argent, wattled
and combed or (Gally)   Sinister, From a ducal coronet or an eagle
displayed ermine (Knight)   Mantling: Gules and argent
Motto: Tout jour prêt
For Henry Gally-Knight, of Firbeck Hall, who m. 1828, Henrietta, 3rd
dau. of Anthony Hardolph Eyre, of Grove, Notts, and d. 9 Feb. 1846.
(B.L.G. 2nd ed.; Bloom)

FULFORD, St. Oswald, York

1. Dexter background black
Azure a saltire engrailed argent between four cross crosslets fitchy or
(Oates), impaling, Argent three bears' paws erased and erect sable armed
gules (Bedford)
Crest: From a ducal coronet or a cross crosslet fitchy sable
Mantling: Gules and argent
Frame decorated with skulls and crossbones
For Robert Oates, of Water Fulford Hall, who m. Isabella Bedford, of
Gainsborough, and d. 27 July 1739, aged 76.   (M.I.)

2. Dexter background black
Sable on a chief argent three bears' heads erased sable ermined argent
(Richardson), impaling, Per pale nebuly argent and azure two molets in
fess counterchanged (Athorpe)
Crest: A bear's head erased sable ermined argent langued gules
Mantling: Gules and argent
For William Richardson, who m. 1784, Elizabeth Athorpe, and d. at
Fulford House, 6 Oct. 1816.   (Church notes)

FYLINGDALES, Old Church

1. All black background
On a lozenge surmounted by a cherub's head
Qly, 1st and 4th, Argent on a chevron engrailed azure between three
martlets sable three crescents or (Watson), 2nd and 3rd, Gules a fess or

between three bezants (Farsyde), impaling, Argent a cross gules and
in the dexter chief a martlet sable (Hartley)
For Hannah, dau. of the Rev. James Hartley, of Staveley, who m. John
Farsyde, son of John Farsyde, of Fylingdales, and Mary Watson (who
assumed the surname of Watson), and d. 1847. He d. 1810.
(B.L.G. 2nd ed.)

GARTON

1. Dexter background black
Qly of eight, 1st, Argent on a fess sable three molets or pierced gules
(Grimston), 2nd, Or six roundels gules each charged with a pierced
molet or (Goodmadam), 3rd, Argent a lion rampant sable (?Stapleton),
4th, Argent five lozenges in cross gules (Flynton), 5th, Gules on a bend
argent three choughs proper (Portington), 6th Barry of six argent and
azure on a chief azure three lions' faces or (Newarke), 7th, Argent on a
fess sable between three fleurs-de-lys gules three bezants (Thwaites),
8th, Vert three garbs or (Close), impaling, Argent on a bend between
six molets gules a cross formy argent (Legard)
Crest: A stag's head proper   Mantling: Gules and argent
Motto: Faitz proverount   Skull in base
For Thomas Grimston, of Grimston and Kilnwick, who m. 1780,
Frances, dau. of Sir Digby Legard, 5th Bt., and d. 2 May 1821. (Foster;
B.L.G. 1937 ed.)

2. Dexter background black
Grimston, Qly as 1., impaling, Argent a lion passant guardant gules
between three fleurs-de-lys azure, on a chief azure a sun or (Trench)
Crest: A stag's head proper collared or
Mantling: Gules and argent   Motto: Resurgam
For Charles Grimston, of Grimston Garth and Kilnwick, who m. 1823,
Jane, dau. of the Very Rev. Thomas Trench, Dean of Kildare, and d. 21
Mar. 1859.   (B.L.G. 1937 ed.; Foster)
(There is an almost identical hatchment for Charles Grimston at Kilnwick)

GIGGLESWICK

1. All black background
Azure on a bend engrailed argent three daws sable (Dawson), impaling,
Vert a chevron between three molets pierced or (Pudsey)
Crest: A cat's head affronté erased, murally gorged or
Mantling: Brown and argent   Motto: Resurgam
For William Dawson, of Langcliffe, who m. 1st, 1705, Jane (d. 1708), dau.
of Ambrose Pudsey, of Bolton, and 2nd, Elizabeth (d. 1752), dau. of
Henry Marsden, and d. 17 June 1762, aged 82.   (B.L.G. 1937 ed.)

GISBURN

1. All black background

Ermine on a fess sable three molets or, in chief a crescent or for difference (Lister)   In pretence: Argent on a chevron azure between in
chief two eagles' heads and in base a horse passant gules a cinquefoil
between two anchors or (Fielding)
Baron's coronet   Crest: A stag's head or
Motto: Retinens vestigia famae   Supporters: Dexter, A stag
reguardant sable, attired, gorged with a collar of SS, and charged on the
body with an eagle displayed or   Sinister, A horse, bridled and
saddled proper, the saddle cloth or, supporting a guidon or inscribed
Y.L.   All on a mantle gules and ermine
D.
For Thomas, 1st Baron Ribblesdale, of Gisburn Park, who m. Rebecca
(d. 1816), dau. and co-heir of Joseph Fielding of Ireland, and d. 22
Sept. 1826.   (B.P. 1875 ed.; B.L.G.; Foster)

2. Dexter background black

Qly, 1st and 4th, Ermine on a fess sable three molets or (Lister), 2nd
and 3rd, Fielding, impaling, Lister
Baron's coronet   Crest, motto, supporters and mantle: As 1.
For Thomas, 2nd Baron Ribblesdale, who m. 1826, Adelaide (d. 1838),
dau. of Thomas Lister of Armitage Park, and d. 10 Dec. 1832.
(B.P. 1875 ed.; Foster)

3. Dexter background black

Lister, as 2., impaling, Argent on a fess azure three molets or within a
bordure engrailed gules (Mure)
Baron's coronet   Crest: A stag's head erased per fess proper and
gules charged with a crescent argent
Supporters: As 1. except the stag is also unguled or, the horse has no
saddle cloth, and the guidon is azure incribed Y.L.D. in gold
Motto: As 1.
For Thomas, 3rd Baron Ribblesdale, who m. 1853, Emma (d. 1911),
dau. of Col. William Mure, of Caldwell, Scotland, and d. 25 Aug. 1876.
(Sources, as 2.)

4. Dexter background black

Lister, as 2., impaling, Argent two crescents in fess sable, on a chief
gules a boar's head couped argent langued azure, within a bordure
compony sable and argent (Tennant)
Baron's coronet   Crest: A stag's head proper parted per fess and
charged with a crescent gules
Motto: As 1.
Supporters: As 1., but guidon or, fringed or, gules and sable
All on a mantle gules and ermine

For Thomas, 4th Baron Ribblesdale, who m. 1st, 1877, Charlotte
Monckton (d.1911), dau. of Sir Charles Tennant, Bt., and 2nd, 1919,
Ava, dau. of Edward Willings, and d. 21 Oct. 1925.   (B.P. 1939 ed.)
(N.B. Background has sinister half white since his 2nd wife survived
him, but the impaled arms are those of his 1st wife)

GUISELEY

1. Dexter background black
Vert three goats passant argent (Stansfield)   In pretence: Argent on
a chief gules two crosses patonce argent (Ferrand)
Crest: A lion's head erased gules   Mantling: Gules and argent
Motto: Medio tutissimus ibis
For Robert Stansfield, of Esholt, who m. Jane, dau. and co-heir of
Richardson Ferrand, of Harden, and d. 14 Sept. 1772, aged 44.   (M.I.;
Burke's Commoners, Vol. III)

2. All black background
On a lozenge surmounted by a cherub's head
Vert three goats passant argent horns and hoofs or (Stansfield)   In
pretence: Argent on a chief gules two crosses flory argent (Ferrand)
Motto: In coelo quies
For Jane, widow of Robert Stansfield, who d. 18 June 1796, aged 65.
(Sources, as 1.)

3. Dexter background black
Argent a fess between three rooks sable (Rookes)   In pretence: Stans-
field, as 2., but goats ermine
Crest: A garb or lying on its side, standing thereon and pecking thereat
a rook proper
Mantling: Gules and argent   Motto: In caelo quies
For William Rookes, last male of the ancient family of Rookes of Roydes
Hall, who m. Ann, only surviving sister and heiress of Robert Stansfield,
and d. 24 Oct. 1789, aged 70.   (Sources, as 1.)

4. All black background
On a lozenge surmounted by a cherub's head
Arms: As 3., but goats argent
Motto: In caelo quies
For Ann, widow of William Rookes, who d. 12 Feb. 1798, aged 68.
(Sources, as 1.)

5. Sinister background black
Vert on a bend cotised argent between two covered cups or a lion
passant gules, on a chief or three pheons sable (Crompton)   In pretence:
Qly, 1st and 4th, Rookes, 2nd and 3rd, Stansfield, as 2.

Decorative surround to shield which is surmounted by a cherub's head
For Anna Maria, eldest dau. and co-heiress of William and Ann Rookes,
who m. 1786, Joshua Crompton, of York, and d. 5 June 1819, aged 56.
(M.I.; B.L.G. 5th ed.)

6. All black background
Vert on a bend argent double cotised ermine between two covered cups
or a lion passant gules, on a chief azure three pheons or (Crompton)
In pretence: As 5.
Crest: A demi-horse rampant sable pierced in the chest by an arrow
argent
Mantling: Gules and argent   Motto: Love and Loyalty
For Joshua Crompton, of York, who d. 13 Feb. 1832.   (M.I.;
B.L.G. 5th ed.; Foster)
(There is another hatchment for Joshua Crompton at Holy Trinity,
York)

HALIFAX, Shibden Hall

1. All black background
Ermine on a fess sable three molets or a canton gules (Lister)   In
pretence: Argent three battleaxes two and one sable (?Battle)
Crest: A stag's head erased proper charged on the neck with a trefoil
slipped gules
Mantling: Gules and argent   Motto: Resurgam
Probably for Capt. Jeremy Lister, who m. 1788, Rebecca (d. 1817),
dau. and co-heiress of William Battle, of Welton, Yorks, and d. 3 Apr.
1836.   (R. Bretton, Halifax Ant. Soc. Trans. 1952, p. 46)

2. All black background
On a lozenge surrounded with decoration in the form of mantling, gules
and argent, with branches of palm and laurel at sides
Lister arms only
Probably for Anne Lister, who d. 22 Sept. 1840, or her aunt, Anne
Lister, who d. 10 Oct. 1836.   (Source, as 1., and Pedigree of Lister,
H.A.S.T. 1956, p. 15)

3. All black background
On a lozenge surrounded with decorative scrollwork and surmounted by
a cherub's head
Lister arms only
Probably for Anne Lister, who d. 22 Sept. 1840, or her aunt, Anne
Lister, who d. 10 Oct. 1836.   (Sources, as 2)

HAMPOLE, Priory Restaurant

1. Dexter background black

Qly of six, 1st and 3rd, Or a fess counter-compony argent and azure
between three griffins' heads erased azure langued gules (Wrightson),
2nd Sable a chevron between three goats passant argent each charged
on the flank with an annulet gules, on a chief or issuant a demi-wildman
affronté with a club over his right shoulder between two cinquefoils
gules, wreathed about the loins vert (Battie), 4th, Per fess gules and
argent six martlets, three and three counterchanged (Fenwick), 5th, Per
fess sable and gules a lion rampant or, in dexter chief a cinquefoil argent
(Heber), 6th, Sable a fess dancetty between six cross crosslets fitchy
argent (Barnardiston)   In pretence: Azure a ducal coronet between
three cross crosslets fitchy or, on a canton argent three lions rampant
gules and a chief sable (Peirse with a canton of Thomas)
Crests: Dexter, A unicorn rampant qly argent and azure, hoofed,
horned, maned and tufted or   Sinister, A heron argent, beaked and
legged or, holding in its beak a fish proper
Mantling: Gules and argent   Motto: Battez contre le viz
For William Battie Wrightson, of Cusworth, who m. 1821, Georgiana,
only surviving dau. of Inigo Thomas of Ratton, Sussex, by Charlotte,
his wife, dau. and co-heir of Henry Peirse of Bedale, and d. 10 Feb.
1879.   (B.L.G. 1900 ed.; Foster)

HARTHILL

1. Sinister background black

Qly of eight, 1st, Qly ermine and azure a cross or (Osborne), 2nd, Argent
two bars gules, on a canton gules a cross argent (Broughton), 3rd, Argent
a chevron sable between three annulets gules (   ), 4th, Vert on a
fess cotised flory or between three talbots argent langued gules three
herons proper (   ), 5th, Gules a chevron between three owls argent
(Hewit), 6th, Gules on a chief ermine two roundels azure (Walmesley),
7th, Gules a chevron between three pierced molets of six points or
(Danvers), 8th, Gules a saltire argent charged with a roundel sable
(Nevill), impaling, Qly of six, 1st and 6th, Argent three battering rams
barwise in pale proper headed and garnished azure (Bertie), 2nd, Or
fretty azure (Willoughby of Eresby), 3rd, Gules a cross moline argent
(Beke), 4th, Sable a cross engrailed or (Willoughby of Parham), 5th,
Qly gules and or in the first quarter a molet argent (De Vere)
Duchess's coronet   Motto: Pax in bello
Supporters: Dexter, A griffin or ducally gorged sable   Sinister, A
savage proper, wreathed about the waist and temples
For Bridget, dau. of Montagu, 2nd Earl of Lindsey, who m. Thomas, 1st
Duke of Leeds, and d. 7 July 1704.   He d. 26 July 1712.   (B.P.
1949 ed.; Bloom)

2. Sinister background black
Two shields   Dexter, within the Garter, Qly ermine and azure a cross
or (Osborne)   Sinister, Gules a double-headed eagle displayed between
three. fleurs-de-lys argent (Godolphin)
Duchess's coronet   Motto: As 1.   Supporters: Dexter, as 1.
Sinister, An eagle argent   Cherub's head below
For Mary, dau. and heiress of Francis, Earl of Godolphin, who m. 1740,
Thomas, 4th Duke of Leeds, K.G., and d. 3 Aug. 1764.   (B.P. 1949 ed.)

3. All black background
Osborne arms only, within the Garter
Duke's coronet   Motto: As 1.   Supporters: Dexter, as 1.
Sinister, A heraldic tyger or ducally gorged sable
Probably for Thomas, 4th Duke of Leeds, K.G., who d. 23 Mar. 1789.
(B.P. 1949 ed.)
(In very poor condition, 1974, torn and with bits missing)

HATFIELD

1. Dexter background black
Qly of eight, 1st, Per fess indented argent and sable, a pale counterchanged, three goats' heads erased, two and one vert, and three crosses
formy fitchy, one and two argent (Gossip), 2nd, Gules a chevron vair
between three eagles displayed or (Wilmer), 3rd, Argent a chevron gules
between three popinjays vert collared gules (Thwenge), 4th, Azure a
lion rampant or (   ), 5th, Argent a lion rampant azure (Bruce),
6th, Gules three arches of masonry argent (Arches), 7th, as 5th, 8th,
Argent two bars gules, on a canton gules a lion passant guardant
crowned or (Lancaster)   In pretence: Qly, 1st and 4th, qly i. & iv.
Ermine on a chevron sable three cinquefoils or a canton gules (Hatfeild),
ii. & iii. Gules three crescents within a bordure engrailed or (Hallows),
2nd and 3rd, Ermine on a canton or a chevron gules (Middleton)
Crest: Two goats' heads erased addorsed, the dexter vert, the sinister
argent   Mantling: Gules and argent   Motto: Prospice respice
No frame
For William Gossip, of Hatfield, who m. 1787, Anne (d. 1833), dau.
and heiress of John Hatfeild, of Hatfield, and d. 26 Mar. 1830. (Foster)

HAUXWELL

1. All black background
On a lozenge   Qly, 1st and 4th, Azure on a fess between three saltires
argent three lions' heads erased azure (Gale), 2nd, Azure crusilly or a
lion rampant guardant argent a chief barry nebuly argent and sable
(Dalton), 3rd, Per pale azure and gules three saltires argent (Lane)

Inscription under hatchment: Mrs. Gale (Born Mary Dalton of Hauxwell Hall) who died 1845 ae 95.
Despite inscription more probably for a daughter of Mrs. Gale; for Catherine, d. 16 Sept. 1864, aged 80; or for Anne, d. 12 Nov. 1877, aged 88.   (M.I.)

HEMINGBROUGH

1. Dexter two-thirds black
Three coats per pale   Azure three demi-lions rampant erased or (Harrison), impaling to the dexter, Ermine three bezants (Smith), and to the sinister, Argent a cross patonce voided gules (Pilkington)
Baronet's helm   Crest: A reaper with scythe, vested bendy argent and sable, hose gules   Mantling: Gules and argent
Under the shield the inscription, 'Dame Lenox Pilkington, Sole daughter and heiress of Cuthbert Harrison of Acaster Selby Esq., Dyed the 17th day of July AD 1706'
Frame decorated with skulls and crossbones
For Lennox, only child and heiress of Cuthbert Harrison of Acaster Selby, who m. 1st, 1674, George (d. 1681), son of Sir Jeremiah Smith, of Osgodby, and 2nd, 1700, Sir Lyon Pilkington, 3rd Bt., and d. 17 July 1706. He d. 7 Aug. 1714.   (B.P. 1949 ed.; Burton and Raine, History of Hemingbrough)

HEPTONSTALL

1.   All black background
Qly, 1st and 4th, Sable a chevron ermine cotised or between three swans wings endorsed and inverted argent (Eastwood), 2nd and 3rd, Or on a fess gules three lozenge buckles or (Shackleton)
Crest: A sinister arm embowed elbow to sinister, vested gules cuffed ermine, the hand holding a staff with pheon head point upwards proper
Mantling: Gules and argent   Motto: Hoc tenemus
Probably for Robert Shackleton Eastwood, J.P., Barrister, who d. 1858, aged 40.   (R. Bretton, Halifax Ant. Soc. Trans. 1952, p. 44)

2.   Sinister background black
Arms: As 1.
Mantling: Gules and argent   Motto: Resurgam
Cherub's head above and lover's knot below
Unidentified

HICKLETON

1. Sinister background black
Qly, 1st, Azure three savages ambulant in fess proper, in the dexter
hand of each a shield argent charged with a cross gules, in the sinister a
club resting on the shoulder proper, on a canton ermine three lozenges
in fess sable (Wood), 2nd, Barry of ten or and sable a bend gules
(Barker), 3rd, Qly per fess indented ermine and azure, in the second
quarter a wolf's head erased or (Lacon), 4th, Per fess argent and sable a
fess per fess embattled counter-embattled between three falcons counterchanged (Thompson), in centre chief the Badge of Ulster   In pretence:
Qly, 1st and 4th, Paly bendy of eight or and azure a canton ermine
(Buck), 2nd and 3rd, Sable three swans' heads couped argent (Squire)
Lover's knot above shield, palm branches at sides and cherub's head
below
For Anne, dau. and co-heiress of Samuel Buck, of New Grange, Leeds,
who m. 1798, Sir Francis Lindley Wood, 2nd Bt. of Bowling Hall and
Hemsworth, and d. 11 Jan. 1841.   (B.P. 1949 ed.)

2. All black background
Arms: As 1.
Crest: A savage as in the arms, but with shield sable charged with a
griffin's head erased argent   Mantling: Azure and argent
Motto: Deus misereatur
For Sir Francis Lindley Wood, 2nd Bt., who d. 31 Dec. 1846.
(B.P. 1949 ed.)

3. All black background
Arms: As 1.
Crest and mantling: As 2.   Motto: Perseverando
Also for Sir Francis Lindley Wood, 2nd Bt., who d. 31 Dec. 1846.

4. Sinister background black
Two shields   Dexter, within the Collar of the Order of the Bath, and
with Badge of Order pendent below, Qly, 1st and 4th, Wood, 2nd and
3rd, Buck   Sinister, within an ornamental wreath, as dexter shield,
impaling Qly, 1st and 4th, Gules a lion rampant and a bordure argent
(Grey), 2nd and 3rd, Barry of six argent and azure a bend gules (Grey)
Viscountess's coronet   Mantle: Gules and ermine
Supporters: Two griffins sable winged argent gorged with a collar and
pendent therefrom a portcullis or
For Mary, dau. of Charles, 2nd Earl Grey, who m. 1829, Charles, 1st
Viscount Halifax, and d. 6 July 1884.   (B.P. 1949 ed.)

5. All black background
Arms: As 4.
Viscount's coronet   Crest: A savage as in the arms

Motto: Perseverando   Mantle and supporters: As 4.
For Charles, 1st Viscount Halifax, who d. 8 Aug. 1885. (B.P. 1949 ed.)

6. Sinister background black
Qly of six, 1st, Wood, 2nd, Lacon, 3rd, Barker, 4th, Thompson, 5th,
Buck, 6th, Squire   In pretence: Qly, 1st and 4th, Or three roundels
gules a label azure (Courtenay), 2nd and 3rd, Or a lion rampant azure
(Redvers)
Viscountess's coronet   Mantle: Gules and ermine   Supporters: As 4.
For Agnes Elizabeth, dau. of William, 11th Earl of Devon, who m. 1869,
Charles, 2nd Viscount Halifax, and d. 4 July 1919.   (B.P. 1949 ed.)

7. All black background
Arms: As 6.
Viscount's coronet   Crest: As 2.   Mantle: Gules and ermine
Supporters: As 4.   Motto: I like my choice
For Charles, 2nd Viscount Halifax, who d. 19 Jan. 1934. (B.P. 1949 ed.)

8. Dexter background black
Qly, 1st, Vairy argent and sable (Meynell), 2nd, Ermine on a fess gules
three escallops or (Ingram), 3rd, Argent three bars gules (Romilly), 4th,
Argent a chevron between three escallops sable (Lyttleton), impaling,
Qly, 1st and 4th, Wood, 2nd, Buck, 3rd, Squire
Crests: Dexter, A cock or   Sinister, A horse's head erased argent
Mantling: Azure and argent   Motto: Un Dieu un Roi
For Hugo Francis Meynell Ingram, M.P., of Hoar Cross, Staffs, who m.
1863, Emily Charlotte (d. 1904), eldest dau. of Charles, 1st Viscount
Halifax, and d. 26 May 1871.   (B.P. 1949 ed.)

9. All black background
Qly, 1st and 4th, Ingram, 2nd and 3rd, Meynell
Crests: As 8.   Mantling: Gules and argent   Motto: As 8
Possibly for Henry Meynell Ingram, brother of Hugo (8.), d.

10. All red background
An octagonal wooden panel modelled in relief
Two shields   Dexter, Qly Wood and Buck   Sinister, Grey qly as 4.
Viscount's coronet   Crest: As 2.   Mantling: Azure and argent
Mottoes: Requiem aeternam dona vis & Vix perpetua luceat vis
Supporters: As 4. Pendent below sinister shield badge with monogram
VRI
For Charles, 1st Viscount Halifax, who m. Mary, dau. of Charles, 2nd
Earl Grey, and d. 8 Aug. 1885.   (B.P. 1949 ed.)

11. All red background
Modelled in relief
Qly, 1st and 4th, Gules on a fess between three sheldrakes argent a
crescent gules (Jackson), 2nd and 3rd, Azure a chevron counter-
compony argent and gules (Wilkinson), impaling, Qly, 1st, Argent on a
bend sable three owls argent (Savile), 2nd, Gules a cross formy or
(Golcar), 3rd, Argent a bend between an eagle displayed and a cross
crosslet sable (Rishworth), 4th, Argent a cross moline sable (Copley)
Crests (each on separate helm): Dexter, A sheldrake or   Sinister, An
owl argent   Mantling: Dexter, Gules and argent   Sinister, Sable
and argent
Cherub's head above   A very small hatchment
Unidentified

HOOTON PAGNELL

1. All black background
Argent a cross patonce or (Warde), impaling, Argent two annulets linked
in pale gules between three crosses formy sable (Thornhaugh)
Crest: An eagle's head erased or   Mantling: Gules and argent
Two cherubs' heads above shield and winged skull below
For Patientius Warde, who m. Frances, dau. of St. Andrew Thornhaugh,
of Fenton and Osberton, Notts, and d. 30 July 1786.   (B.L.G. 1937
ed.)

2. Sinister background black
Warde, impaling, Or a chevron gules between two lions passant sable
(Cooke)
Mantling: Gules and argent   Escallop in place of crest
For Mary Ann, dau. of Anthony Cooke, of Owston, who m. St. Andrew
Warde, only son and heir of Patientius Warde, and d.   He d. Mar.
1822.   (B.L.G. 1937 ed.)

HORBURY

1. Dexter background black
Per pale gules and azure, on a chevron embattled argent three estoiles
sable, in chief a martlet argent for difference (Carr), impaling, Gules a
fess dancetty ermine between three fleurs-de-lys argent (Marsden)
Crest: A stag's head issuant from a circlet of red roses holding in its
mouth a red rose   Mantling: Gules and argent
Two branches of palm at base of shield
For John Carr, attorney, who m. 1785, Hannah Maria Marsden, and d.
28 Mar. 1824.   (J. W. Walker, Yorkshire Pedigrees, Harl. Soc. vol.
94)

HOWDEN

1.   All black background
On a lozenge   Argent three pierced cinquefoils between nine cross crosslets gules (Saltmarshe), impaling, Per fess azure and sable a four-towered castle argent (Rawson)

For Elizabeth, dau. of Christopher Rawson, of Stony Royd, near Halifax, who m. 1779, Philip Saltmarshe, 16th of Saltmarshe, and d. 1834.   (B.L.G. 1937 ed.; Foster)

2.   Dexter background black
Saltmarshe, impaling, Qly, 1st and 4th, Argent a bend between in chief a unicorn's head erased and in base a cross crosslet fitchy gules (Denison), 2nd and 3rd, Per pale argent and azure three lions passant in pale counterchanged (Sunderland)

Crest: A ship's rudder or   Mantling: Gules and argent
Motto: Resurgam

For Philip Saltmarshe, 17th of Saltmarshe, who m. 1824, Harriet, dau. of Robert Denison, of Kilnwick Percy, Yorks, and d. 28 Nov. 1846. (Sources, as 1.)

3.   Dexter background black
Saltmarshe, impaling, Vert fretty or (Whitmore)
Crest, mantling and motto: As 2.

For Christopher Saltmarshe, who m. 2nd, Elizabeth, dau. of William Whitmore, and d. 15 Oct. 1852.   (B.L.G. 2nd ed.; Foster)

4.   Dexter background black
Saltmarshe, impaling, Azure a savage wreathed about the loins, sinister hand resting on a club, bearing in the dexter hand a telescope, all argent, pointing to a star in dexter chief or (Oswald)

Crest: As 2.   Mantling: Argent   Motto: As 2.

For Arthur Saltmarshe, 2nd son of Philip 16th, and brother of Philip 17th, and Christopher, who m. Caroline, dau. of Alexander Oswald, and d. 1864.   (B.L.G. 1852 ed.; M.I.)

HUNMANBY

1.   Dexter two-thirds background black (including first two wives), sinister one-third red
Argent a mascle between three roundels and in chief a martlet sable (Osbaldeston)   In pretence: Or a fess gules between three elephants' heads erased sable tusked argent (Fountain)   Also impaling three coats per pale, 1. Gules a chevron or between three crosses formy argent, on a canton ermine a buck's head erased sable (Strickland), 2. Fountain, 3. Vert three snakes erect wavy in fess argent (Hassel)

Crest: A knight in armour on a white horse, holding in his dexter hand
a sword proper and on his sinister arm a shield, Argent a mascle between
three roundels sable   Mantling: Gules and argent
Motto: Virtus certe sempiterna   Cherub's head below
For Sir Richard Osbaldeston, who m. 1st, Frances (d. 11 Oct. 1682),
dau. of Sir Thomas Strickland of Boynton, 2nd, Elizabeth (d. 25 July
1697), dau. and co-heiress of John Fountayne, of Melton, and 3rd,
Catherine (d. Feb. 1735), dau. of Samuel Hassel of Hutton, E. Yorks,
and d. 24 Dec. 1728, aged 74.   (B.L.G. 1937 ed.; Foster)

2. All black background
Argent a mascle between three roundels sable (Osbaldeston)
Crest and mantling: As 1.   Motto: Virtus sempiterna certe
For William Osbaldeston, who d. unm. 6 Sept. 1765.   (B.L.G. 1937 ed.)

3. All black background
Arms: As 2.
Crest, mantling and motto: As 2.
For Fountayne Wentworth Osbaldeston, who d. unm. 10 June 1770.
(B.L.G. 1937 ed.)

4. All black background
Osbaldeston, as 2., impaling, Or five fusils in fess azure (Pennington)
Crest: As 1.   Mantle: Gules and argent   Motto: In coelo quies
For Humphrey Brooke Osbaldeston, who m. 1772, Catherine, dau. of
Sir John Pennington, 4th Bt., of Muncaster Castle, Cumberland, and d.
1835, aged 90.   (B.L.G. 1937 ed.)

5. Dexter background black
Qly of six, 1st, Argent a fess between three moles proper (Mitford), 2nd,
Argent a pierced molet sable (Ashton), 3rd, Argent a mascle between
three roundels sable (Osbaldeston), 4th, Sable a chevron between three
lions' faces or (Wentworth), 5th, Or a fess gules between three
elephants' heads erased proper (Fountain), 6th, Sable on a chevron
between three martlets or three molets sable (Monckton), impaling,
Azure three garbs or banded sable (Dunsmore)
Crest: Two cubit arms couped proper supporting a sword in pale argent,
hilt and pommel or, pierced through a boar's head couped sable tusked
argent langued gules
Mantling: Grey   Motto: God caryth for us
For Admiral Robert Mitford, who m. 1830, Margaret, dau. of James
Dunsmure, M.D. of Edinburgh, and d. 18 June 1870.   (B.L.G. 1852
ed. & 1937 ed.)

6. Dexter background black
Qly, 1st and 4th, Mitford, 2nd and 3rd, Osbaldeston, as 2., impaling,
Mitford

Crests: Dexter, Mitford   Sinister, Osbaldeston
Mantling: Gules and argent   Motto: In coelo quies
Branches in leaf below shield
Frame covered with pleated cloth with rosettes at corners
For Colonel John Philip Osbaldeston-Mitford, who m. 1844, his cousin
Fanny (d. 9 Dec. 1901), only dau. of Charles Mitford, of Pitshill, Sussex,
and d. 27 Nov. 1895.   (Sources, as 5.)

INGLEBY GREENHOW

1. Dexter background black
Argent three laurel leaves erect vert, in chief the Badge of Ulster
(Foulis)   In pretence: Vert a chevron between three stags trippant or
(Robinson)
Crest: Out of a crescent argent a cross formy fitchy sable
Mantling: Gules and argent
For Sir William Foulis, 6th Bt., of Ingleby, who m. 1758, Hannah, only
dau. and heiress of John Robinson of Buckton, Yorks, and d. Feb.
1780.   (B.P. 1875 ed.; Foster)

2. Dexter background black
Foulis with Badge of Ulster in fess point, impaling, Sable ermined argent
on a cross quarter pierced argent four millrinds sable (Turner)
Crest and mantling: As 1.   Motto: Mors janua vitae
For Sir William Foulis, 7th Bt., of Ingleby, who m. 1789, Mary Anne
(d. 18 Oct. 1831), dau. of Edmund Turner, of Panton House, Lincs. and
d. 5 Sept. 1802.   (Sources, as 1.)

KILHAM

1. All black background
Per fess argent a.id sable a fess per fess embattled counter-embattled
between three hawks counterchanged ringed and belled gules (Thompson)
No helm   Crest: A mailed arm proper the hand grasping a tilting
spear or   Motto: Je veux de bonne guerre
Possibly for William Henry Thompson, d. 1861, aged 75.   (Foster)

KILNWICK

1. Dexter background black
Qly of eight, 1st, Argent on a fess sable three molets of six points or
pierced gules (Grimston), 2nd, Or six roundels, three two and one gules,
each charged with a molet or pierced gules (Goodmadam), 3rd, Argent
a lion rampant sable (   ), 4th, Argent five lozenges conjoined in

cross gules (Flynton), 5th, Gules on a bend argent three blackbirds
proper (Portington), 6th, Barry of six argent and azure, on a chief azure
three lions' faces or (Newarke), 7th, Argent on a fess sable between
three fleurs-de-lys gules three molets of six points or pierced gules
(Thwaites), 8th, Vert three garbs or (Close), impaling, Argent a lion
passant gules between three fleurs-de-lys azure, on a chief azure a sun's
face or (Trench)
Crest: A stag's head argent attired or   Mantling: Gules and or
Motto: Resurgam
For Charles Grimston, of Grimston Garth and Kilnwick, who m. 1823,
Jane, dau. of the Very Rev. Thomas Trench, Dean of Kildare, and d. 21
Mar. 1859.   (B.L.G. 1937 ed.; Foster)
(There is an almost identical hatchment for Charles Grimston at Garton)

KIRKHEATON

1. All black background
On a curvilinear lozenge surmounted by two cherubs' heads
Gules a lion rampant within an orle of crescents argent (Beaumont)
In pretence: Argent on a bend engrailed sable three fleurs-de-lys argent
(Holt)
For Elizabeth, dau. and heiress of William Holt, of Grizzlehurst and
Little Mitton, Lancs, who m. 1747, as his 2nd wife, Richard Beaumont,
of Whitley Beaumont, and d. 18 Aug. 1791.   (Tolson, History of
Kirkheaton; Bloom; B.L.G. 2nd ed.)

2. All black background
Qly, 1st and 4th, Beaumont, 2nd and 3rd, Holt
Crest: A bull's head erased qly argent and gules
Mantling: Gules and argent   Motto: Fide sed cui vide
For Richard Henry Beaumont, eldest son of Richard Beaumont, who
d. unm. 22 Nov. 1810.   (B.L.G. 2nd ed.)

3. All black background
Arms: As 2.
Crest and mantling: As 2.
Perhaps also for Richard Henry Beaumont, who d. unm. 22 Nov. 1810.

4. Dexter background black
Beaumont, impaling, Argent on a chevron sable between three quatrefoils
slipped (each foil in fess per fess or and vert, and in pale per pale gules
and vert) three bezants (Wiggins)
Crest, mantling and motto: As 2.
For Richard Henry Beaumont, who m. 1831, Catherine, dau. of Timothy
Wiggin, of U.S.A., and d. 1857.   (B.L.G. 2nd ed.)

5. Dexter background black

Per fess gules and sable a fess ermine between in chief two lions' heads erased or and in base a dolphin embowed argent (Senior), impaling, Sable a wolf salient or, in chief three molets of six points argent (Wilson)

Crest: A leopard couchant guardant crowned or

Mantling: Gules and argent   Motto: Sola salus servire Deo

For John Senior, of Dalton Lodge, Kirkheaton, who d. 31 July 1854.
(Leigh Tolson, History of Kirkheaton, 1929; Bloom)

KIRKLEATHAM

1. Dexter background black

Qly, 1st and 4th, Argent a lion's head erased sable between three crescents gules (Newcomen), 2nd and 3rd, Argent a fess of five fusils gules (   )   In pretence: Ermine an eagle displayed sable, on a chief gules a ducal coronet between two crosses formy or (Vansittart)

No helm   Crest: A lion's gamb erased sable

Motto: Stet honos et gratia vivax

For Arthur Newcomen, R.H.A., who m. 1841, Teresa (d. 29 Apr. 1887), only dau. and heiress of Henry Vansittart, of Foxley and Kirkleatham, and d. 17 Dec. 1848.   (B.L.G. 1937 ed.)

KIRKLINGTON

1. Dexter background black

Qly of six, 1st, Or a lion rampant double-tailed azure (Wandesforde), 2nd, Argent a bend and a bordure engrailed gules (Musters), 3rd, Or a fess gules and in chief three roundels gules (Colville), 4th, Azure a maunch argent (Conyers), 5th, Argent a cross moline sable (Fulthorpe), 6th, Argent on a bend sable three pheons argent (Bland), in fess point the Badge of Ulster, impaling, Or six annulets, three, two and one sable (Lowther)

Crest: A church with spire proper   Mantling: Gules and argent

Motto: Tout pour l'Eglise

Frame decorated with skulls and crossbones

For Sir Christopher Wandesforde, 1st Bt., who m. Eleanor, dau. of Sir John Lowther, Bt., of Lowther Hall, Westmorland, and d. Feb. 1686.
(B.E.B.)

KNARESBOROUGH

1. All black background

Qly, 1st and 4th, Gules a chevron between in chief two leopards' faces and in base a hunting horn argent (Scriven), 2nd and 3rd, Argent a

griffin segreant sable over all a bar gules (Slingsby), in fess point the
Badge of a baronet of Nova Scotia
Crest: A lion passant vert   Mantling: Gules and argent
Motto: Fax mentis honestae gloria   Supporters: Dexter, A unicorn
argent, armed, collared and chained or   Sinister, A savage wreathed
about the loins proper
For a baronet of the Slingsby family who d. unm. There is a similar
hatchment at Moor Monkton, but without supporters.   (B.P. 1859 ed.)

2. All black background
Arms: As 1.
Crest, mantling and supporters: As 1.   Motto: Veritas liberavit
Skull below
For a baronet of the Slingsby family (see 1.)
(B.P. 1859 ed.)

3. Dexter background black
Argent on a chevron engrailed azure between three martlets sable three
crescents or (Watson), impaling, Or two bars and in chief a lion passant
azure (Gregory)
Crest: A griffin's head erased sable, langued gules, ducally gorged or
Mantling: Gules and argent   Motto: Gloria fides
Skull below   No frame
Unidentified

4. Dexter background black
Qly, 1st and 4th, Watson, 2nd and 3rd, Gules a fess or between three
bezants (Farside), impaling, Argent a chevron gules between three
popinjays vert within a bordure azure bezanty (White)
Crest and mantling: As 3.   Mottoes: As 3. & Ferthe and feare
nought   No frame
For John Farside-Watson, of Bilton Park, who m. 1830, Georgina White,
and d. 1 Apr. 1831.   (B.L.G. 1852 ed.; M.I.)

LEEDS, St. Peter

1. All black background
Gules a fess between three boars' heads couped or ermined sable, in
chief a crescent or for difference (Beckett)
Crest: A boar's head couped pierced by a cross formy fitchy erect or
Mantling: Gules and argent   Motto: Resurgam   Skull below
For Christopher Beckett, 2nd son of Sir John Beckett, 1st Bt., Mayor
of Leeds, 1819 and 1829, d. unm. 5 Mar. 1847.   (M.I.; Foster;
Rusby, History of St. Peter's)

LEEDS, St. Saviour

1. All black background

Qly, 1st and 4th, Sable three bars argent (Pusey), 2nd and 3rd, Per fess
or and argent a double-headed eagle displayed bearing an escutcheon,
or a bend vair (Bouverie), impaling, Qly, 1st and 4th, Sable five escallops
in cross or (Barker), 2nd and 3rd, Sable a chevron between three eagles
displayed argent, on a chief argent three martlets sable (Raymond)
This hatchment is unusually small, c. 2ft. x 2ft. and is remarkable in
that the arms are painted on a wooden shield, backed by a wood panel
covered with black cloth.
For the Rev. Edward Pusey, D.D., Canon of Christ Church, who m.
1828, Maria Catherine, youngest dau. of John Raymond Barker, of
Fairford Park, Gloucester, and d. 16 Sept. 1882.   (B.L.G. 1937 ed.)
(There are five more Pusey hatchments at Pusey, Berkshire)

LOVERSALL

1. All black background

Sable on a cross between in the first and fourth quarters a fleur-de-lys
and in the second and third an eagle's head erased or, three roundels in
fess sable (Banks)
Crest: An eagle's head erased sable between two fleurs-de-lys argent
Mantling: Gules and argent   Motto: Suivez raison
For George Banks, b. 14 Aug. 1777, who d. 14 Dec. 1843.   (M.I.)

MAPPLETON

1. All black background

On a lozenge surmounted by a cherub's head
Qly, 1st and 4th, Sable three foxes rampant in fess, in chief three
crescents argent (   ), 2nd, Argent five lozenges in cross gules
(Flynton), 3rd, Argent on a bend sable three dexter hands couped
proper (   ), impaling, Paly of six or and sable a bend counter-
changed (Calvert)
Skull below
Unidentified

MARRICK Priory

1. All black background

Sable three swords in pile points in base argent pommels and hilts or
(Paulet)

Marquess's coronet   Crest: None recorded
Motto: Aymes loyaulté
Supporters: Two hinds proper
For a Marquess of Winchester
(This hatchment is painted on the back of a William III royal arms, and
on the same canvas; it is now invisible as the royal achievement is
firmly bolted to the wall)

MARSKE-BY-THE-SEA

There are three hatchments in the church, and these are, with only
minor differences, duplicates of those at Richmond Museum, 2, 4
& 5. A fourth hatchment was recorded in 1953, which was a duplicate
of 3. at Richmond, but this is now missing.

EAST MARTON

1. All black background
Or a fess gules between three olive branches proper (Roundell)
Crest: A dagger erect argent, pommel and guard or, handle gules
Mantling: Gules and argent   Motto: Resurgam
Probably for Richard Henry Roundell, of Gledstone and Scriven, who
d. unm. 26 Aug. 1851.   (B.L.G. 1937 ed.; Foster)

2. Sinister background black
Or ermined sable a fess gules between three olive branches proper
(Roundell), impaling, Argent three laurel leaves vert (Foulis)
Motto: Resurgam   Knotted blue ribon above and below shield,
sprays of leaves at sides, with shield hanging from upper ribbon by a
gold ring
For Hannah, eldest dau. of Sir William Foulis, 7th Bt., of Ingleby
Manor, who m. 1815, Danson Richardson Roundell, of Gledstone, and
d. 1869.   (Sources, as 1.)

3. All black background
Arms: As 2.
Motto and decorations: As 2.
For Danson Richardson Roundell, who d. 10 Mar. 1873.
(Sources, as 1.)

4. Dexter background black
Roundell, as 1., impaling, Sable three piles in point gules, on a chief
gules a lion passant guardant or (Hacket)
Crest: A dagger erect argent, pommel, handle and guard or
Mantling: Gules and or   Motto: Tenax propositi

For William Roundell, of Gledstone, eldest son of Danson Richardson
Roundell, who m. 1864, Harriet Jane, youngest dau. of Francis Beynon
Hacket, of Moor Hall, Warws, and d. 21 Oct. 1881.   (Sources, as 1.)

5. All black background
On a cartouche within ornamental gold framework
Arms: As 4.
For Harriet Jane, widow of William Roundell, who d. 30 Sept. 1895.
(Sources, as 1.)

MASHAM

1. Sinister background black
Gules on a fess argent between three cushions argent fringed or three
fleurs-de-lys gules (Hutton), impaling, Azure a fess ermine cotised
argent, in chief three stags' heads cabossed argent (Aggas)
Motto: Spiritus gladius   Three cherubs' heads above shield
For Harriet Aggas, of Bungay, Suffolk, who m. 1821, James Henry
Darcy Hutton, of Aldborough, and d.   He d. 31 Dec. 1844.
(B.L.G. 1937 ed.; Foster; Fisher's History of Masham)

2. Dexter two-thirds background black
Gules a griffin segreant or (for Batley), impaling, Azure a lion rampant
argent within a bordure or semy-de-lys sable (   )
Crest: A griffin's head erased or   Mantling: Gules and argent
Motto: Sapere aude
For John Lodge Batley, who d. 19 May 1820, aged 56.   (M.I.)

3. Sinister background black
Argent three chevrons braced sable, on a chief sable three molets of six
points argent (Danby), impaling, Qly, 1st and 4th, Or on a pile gules
between six fleurs-de-lys azure three lions passant guardant or, 2nd and
3rd, Gules two wings conjoined in lure or (Seymour)
Knot of blue ribbon above cartouche
For Caroline, dau. of Henry Seymour, who m. as his 1st wife, William
Danby, of Swinton Park, and d. 3 Mar. 1821.   (Burke's Commoners:
M.I.)

4. Dexter background black
Danby, impaling, Azure a fess or between two lozenges and an escallop
argent within a bordure engrailed ermine (Gater)
Crest: From a ducal coronet a crab or   Mantling: Gules and argent
Motto: Resurgam
Cherub's head at each upper corner of shield and winged skull below
For William Danby, of Swinton Park, who m. 2nd, 1822, Anne Howell,
2nd dau. of William Gater, and d. 4 Dec. 1833.   (Sources, as 3.)

5. Dexter background black
Gules two bars or (Harcourt), impaling, Gater
Crest: From a ducal coronet or a peacock proper
Mantling: Gules and argent   Motto: Resurgam
For Vice-Admiral Octavius Henry Cyril Venables Vernon-Harcourt, 8th
son of Edward, Archbishop of York, who m. 1838, Ann Howell (d. 26
June 1879), widow of William Danby of Swinton Park, and dau. of
William Gater, and d. 14 Aug. 1863.   (B.P. 1949 ed.)

METHLEY

1. All black background
Argent on a bend sable three owls argent (Savile)   In pretence: Gules
on a bend or three leopards' faces vert (Stephenson)
Earl's coronet   Crest: An owl argent   Motto: Be fast
Supporter: Two lions proper   Skull below
For John, 2nd Earl of Mexborough, who m. 1782, Elizabeth (d. 7 June
1821), dau. and heiress of Henry Stephenson, of East Burnham, Bucks,
and Cox Lodge, Newcastle-on-Tyne, and d. 3 Feb. 1830, aged 68.
(B.P. 1949 ed.; Foster; M.I.s)

MIDDLETON TYAS

1. All brown background
Or a chevron between three annulets gules, over all a fess argent
(Hartley)
No helm   Crest: On a mount vert a stag couchant proper attired
argent   Mantling: Gules and argent   Motto: Resurgam
Unidentified

2. All black background
Qly, 1st and 4th, Hartley, 2nd and 3rd, Sable a pale between four fleurs-
de-lys or (Gyll), in fess point a crescent argent for difference
Crest: A stag couchant proper   Mantling: Grey-brown
Possibly for George Hartley, of Middleton Lodge, d. 15 July 1841.
(M.I.)

3. Dexter background black
Argent on a chevron sable three quatrefoils argent (Eyre), impaling,
Argent a cross engrailed gules between four molets azure, on a chief or
three roses gules barbed and seeded proper (Allgood)
Crest: A mailed leg proper, ornamented and spurred or
Motto: Si je puis

138
                                                                    Yorkshire

For General Henry Eyre, of Garboldisham Hall, Norfolk, and West Hall,
Middleton Tyas, who m. 1840, Elizabeth Martha, dau. of Robert
Lancelot Allgood, of Nunwick, Northumberland, and d. 1889. She d.
1892.   (B.L.G. 1937 ed.; window in church)

GREAT MITTON

1. Dexter background black
Qly, 1st, Azure a fess nebuly between three crescents ermine (Weld),
2nd, qly 1. & iv. Argent a lion rampant gules (Shireburn), ii. & iii. Azure
an eagle displayed argent (Bayley), 3rd, Qly gules and gules a bordure
engrailed sable ermined argent (   ), 4th, Per fess or and gules a
pale counterchanged three trefoils slipped argent (Simeons), impaling,
Argent on a bend azure three stags' heads cabossed or (Stanley)
Crest: From a ducal coronet or a dragon's head azure, wings, collar and
chain or   Mantling: Gules and argent   Motto: Nil sine numine
Skull and crossbones below
For Thomas Weld, of Lulworth Castle, who m. 1772, Mary, dau. of Sir
John Stanley Massey Stanley, Bt., of Hooton, and d. 1 Aug. 1810.
(B.L.G. 1937 ed.; Foster)

2. Dexter background black
Or a chevron between three griffins' heads erased sable (Aspinall)
Crest: A demi-griffin segreant erased sable, legs beak and collar or
Mantling: Sable, gules, or and argent   Motto: Aegis fortissima virtus
Probably for John Thomas Walshman Aspinall, d. 1865.   (M.I.)

MOOR MONKTON, Red House

1. All black background
Qly, 1st and 4th, Gules a chevron between in chief two leopards' faces
and in base a hunting horn argent (Scriven), 2nd and 3rd, Argent a
griffin segreant sable, over all a bar gules (Slingsby), over all the Badge
of a baronet of Nova Scotia
Crest: A lion passant vert   Mantling: Gules and argent
Motto: Mors janua vitae
For a baronet of the Slingsby family who d. unm.   (B.P. 1859 ed.)
There are two similar hatchments at Knaresborough, but with supporters.

See p 333, Vol I, of Wotton's English Baronets 1727.   * given as rampant
                                                         ‡ given as' suppressed b
MYTON-UPON-SWALE   fess gules.

1. All black background
Qly, 1st, Argent a lion rampant sable (Stapylton), 2nd, Sable fretty or
(Bellew), 3rd, Argent a saltire and a chief gules (Bruce), 4th, Or a fess

dancetty between three cross crosslets fitchy gules (Sandys), over all
the Badge of Ulster
Crest: From a ducal coronet or a Saracen's head and shoulders proper,
wreathed about the head argent and sable
Mantling: Gules and argent   Motto: Fide sed cui vide
Supporters: Two talbots argent, ears and shoulders gutty gules
Probably for Sir Martin Stapylton, 8th and last Bt., of Myton, who d.
unm. 2 Jan. 1817.   (B.E.B.)

2. Sinister background black
Qly, as 1., impaling, Argent three bars and in chief three lions' heads
erased gules (Love)
Motto: Resurgam   Supporters: As 1.
For Leckie, dau. of John Love, of Bristol, who m. 1742, the Rev. Sir
Martin Stapylton, 7th Bt., and d. 11 Apr. 1797, aged 74.   (B.E.B., M.I.)

3. All black background
Arms: As 2.
For the Rev. Sir Martin Stapylton, 7th Bt., who d. 21 Jan. 1801.
(Sources, as 2.) Rector of Brightwell Baldwin, Oxon.

4. Dexter background black
Qly of thirteen, 1st, Stapylton, 2nd, Bellew, 3rd, Bruce, 4th, Argent
two bars gules, on a canton azure a lion passant or (Lancaster), 5th,
Chequy or and azure impaling Argent two bars azure (Richmond), 6th,
Barry of six or and gules (Fitzalan), 7th, Argent two bars gules (   ),
8th, Argent on a fess azure three fleurs-de-lys or (Usfleet), 9th, Argent
a bend gules between six martlets sable (Furnival), 10th, Gules two
crosses formy in pale between two flaunches chequy or and azure
(Sherington), 11th, Azure a bend argent (   ), 12th, Argent a fess
dancetty and in chief three lozenges gules (   ), 13th, Per pale
indented or and azure six martlets counterchanged (Fransham)
In pretence: Azure a fess dancetty argent between three ducal coronets
or (Curtis)
No helm   Crest, motto and supporters: As 1.   Cherub's head below
For Martin Stapylton, son of the Rev. John Bree and Ann Stapylton,
who took the name of Stapylton on succeeding to the Myton estates in
1817. He m. 2nd, Anne, dau. of William Curtis, of Chiswick, and d. 7
Mar. 1842.   (Sources, as 2.)

5. Dexter background black
Qly of twenty, 1st and 20th, Stapylton, 2nd, Bellew, 3rd, Argent a lion
rampant azure (Bruce of Skelton), 4th, Argent two bars and on a canton
gules a lion passant or (Lancaster), 5th, Chequy or and azure a bordure
gules semy of lions passant or, over all a canton ermine (Richmond), 6th,
Ermine (Brittany), 7th, Barry of eight or and gules (Fitzalan), 8th,
Bendy of six argent and azure (St Philibert), 9th, Argent on a fess azure

three fleurs-de-lys or (Usfleet), 10th, Argent on a bend between six
martlets gules a crescent or (Furnival), 11th, Or fretty gules (Verdon),
12th, Argent a lion rampant per fess gules and sable (Lovetot), 13th,
Gules a fess dancetty between six cross crosslets or (Engayne), 14th,
Azure semy-de-lys and fretty or (Morville), 15th, Gules two crosses
formy in pale or between two flaunches chequy or and azure
(Sherington), 16th, Azure a bend argent (   ), 17th, Argent a fess
dancetty and in chief three lozenges gules (   ), 18th, Per pale
indented or and azure six martlets counterchanged (Fransham), Or a
fess dancetty between three cross crosslets fitchy gules (Sandys),
impaling, Per pale azure and argent three greyhounds courant in pale
counterchanged, on a chief or a garb azure and a spear gules in saltire
(Tomlinson)
No helm   Crest, mantling, motto and supporters: As 1.
For Stapylton Stapylton, son of Martin Stapylton by his first wife, who
m. 1830, Margaret, dau. of Thomas Tomlinson, of York, and d. 8 July
1864.   (B.E.B.; Foster)

NEWBURGH Priory

1.   Dexter background black
Qly, 1st and 4th, Gules a bend between six unicorns' heads couped
argent (Wombwell), 2nd and 3rd, qly i. & iv. Argent a pale engrailed
between two pallets sable (Bellasis), ii. & iii. Argent a chevron gules
between three fleurs-de-lys azure (Bellasis), in centre chief the Badge of
Ulster   In pretence: Qly, 1st and 4th, Vert three greyhounds courant
argent, on a chief argent three hunting horns stringed sable (Hunter),
2nd and 3rd, Argent on a bend engrailed azure three bezants, a bordure
azure (   )
Crest: A unicorn's head erased argent, armed and crined or
Mantling: Gules and argent   Motto: In well beware
For Sir George Wombwell, 3rd Bt., who m. 1824, Georgiana, 2nd dau.
of Thomas Orby Hunter, of Croyland Abbey, Lincs, and d. 14 Jan. 1855.
(B.P. 1949 ed.)

SOUTH OTTERINGTON

1.   Sinister background black
Gules a sexfoil ermine (Boss), impaling, Qly, 1st and 4th, Gules a
chevron ermine between three spears erect proper (Pennyman), 2nd and
3rd, Gules a lion rampant within a bordure engrailed argent (Grey)
Motto: Requiescat in coelo   Cherub's head above shield
For Charlotte, dau. of Sir James Pennyman, 6th Bt., of Ormesby Hall,
who m. as his 1st wife, Capt. John George Boss, R.N., and d. 11 Sept.
1833, aged 55.   (M.I.; B.L.G. 1937 ed.)

OWSTON

1. Sinister background black
Or a chevron gules between two lions passant guardant sable (Cooke)
In pretence: Qly, 1st and 4th, Argent on a bend azure three molets
argent (Puleston), 2nd and 3rd, Gules on a bend argent a lion passant
guardant sable (Davies)
Mantling: Gules and argent   Motto: In coelo quies
Cherub's head above shield
For Frances, dau. and heir of Philip Puleston, of Hafod-y-wern,
Denbigh, by Mary, sister and co-heir of John Davies, of Llanerch, who
m. 1786, Bryan Cooke, of Owston, and d. 1 Jan. 1818.   (B.L.G.
1937 ed.; Foster)

2. Dexter background black
Qly, 1st and 4th, Cooke, 2nd and 3rd, qly i. & iv. Puleston, ii. & iii.
Davies, impaling, Gules two lions rampant combatant supporting a
dexter hand couped and erect argent (King)
No helm   Crest: From a mural coronet or, masoned sable, a demi-
lion rampant sable ducally gorged or   Mantling: Gules and argent
Motto: Spes tutissima coelis
For Philip Davies-Cooke, of Owston, son of Bryan Cooke, who m. 1829,
Helena Caroline, eldest dau. of George, 3rd Earl of Kingston, and d. 20
Nov. 1853.   (B.L.G. 1937 ed.)

PENISTONE

1. All green background
Argent on a bend sable three owls argent (Savile), impaling, Per bend
azure and or on a bend sable three escallops argent (   ), in centre
chief of shield, over line of impalement, the Badge of Ulster (field now
sable)
Crest: An owl argent   On a wood panel in polished oak frame
The arms on this hatchment are marshalled most incorrectly, the Savile
coat also occupying the lower third of the impalement, the bend
extending right across the shield
Unidentified

RAVENFIELD

1. Dexter background black
Qly, 1st and 4th, Argent a lion passant guardant sable (Oborne), 2nd
and 3rd, Gules a chevron between three escallops argent (Parkin),
impaling, Qly per fess indented or and argent (Laughton)

Crest: A demi-lion rampant sable   Mantling: Gules and argent
Motto: Mors janua vitae   Cherub's head below
For Walter Oborne, of Ravenfield Hall, who m. Mary Laughton, and d.
22 May 1778.   (Hunter, S. Yorkshire, I, 398; M.I.)

2. All black background
On a lozenge surmounted by a cherub's head
Arms: As 1.
For Mary, widow of Walter Oborne, who d. 5 Aug. 1785.   (Sources, as
1.)

3. Dexter background black
Argent five fusils conjoined in fess gules, in chief three bears' heads
erased sable (Bosvile)   In pretence: Qly, 1st and 4th, Azure three
swans' heads and necks erased argent (Hedges), 2nd and 3rd, Bosvile
Crest: A bull argent issuant from a holt of trees proper
Mantling: Gules and argent   Motto: Intento in Deum animo
Skull below
For William Parkin Bosvile, who m. Frances, dau. of Thomas Hedges,
of Tudeley, Kent, and d. 4 Aug. 1811.   (Foster)

4. All black background
On a lozenge   Arms: As 3.
Knot of ribbon above lozenge and cherub's head below, with sprays of
oak leaves and leaf-like ornament at sides
For Frances, widow of William Parkin Bosvile, who d. 19 July 1829.
(Foster; M.I.)

5. All black background
Qly, 1st and 4th, Bosvile, 2nd and 3rd, qly i. & iv. Bosvile, ii. & iii.
Azure three cups or, in each a boar's head couped and erect argent
(Bolle)
Crest, mantling and motto: As 3.
Probably for Thomas Bosvile, whose mother Bridget, was dau. and
co-heir of Thomas Bosvile, who m. Elizabeth, dau. and co-heir of John
Bolle.   He d. unm. 22 Jan. 1824.   (Foster)

RICHMOND Museum

1. Dexter background black
Argent a lion rampant within a dimidiated double tressure flory counter-
flory gules, in chief the Badge of Ulster (Dundas), impaling, Lozengy
argent and gules (Fitzwilliam)
Baron's coronet   Crest: A lion's head affronté crowned with an
antique crown or, within an oak wreath proper   Motto: Essayez

Supporters: Dexter, A lion argent crowned with an antique crown or, gorged with an oak wreath proper, and pendent therefrom an escutcheon, Or a saltire and a chief gules, on a canton argent a lion rampant gules, for Bruce   Sinister, A savage wreathed about the loins with a wreath of oak leaves and holding a club in his sinister hand proper
For Thomas, 1st Baron Dundas, who m. 1764, Charlotte, dau. of William, 3rd Earl Fitzwilliam, and d. 14 June 1820. (B.P. 1949 ed.)

2. Sinister background black
Dundas, with tressure undimidiated, impaling, Azure a chevron embattled counter-embattled or (Hale)
Baroness's coronet   Supporters: Two lions proper, crowned with antique crowns or, gorged with oak wreaths proper, pendent therefrom escutcheons charged, on the dexter, Bruce, and on the sinister, Lozengy argent and gules, for Fitzwilliam
For Harriott, dau. of General John Hale, who m. 1794, Lawrence, eldest son of Thomas, 1st Baron Dundas, later 1st Earl of Zetland, and d. 18 Apr. 1834.   (B.P. 1949 ed.)

3. All black background
Arms: As 2., but tressure dimidiated, and Hale field vert
Earl's coronet   Crest and motto: As 1.
Supporters: As 2., but Fitzwilliam shield, Lozengy or and gules
Hatchment inscribed on back, J. Westgarth, painter 1839.
For Lawrence, 1st Earl of Zetland, who d. 19 Feb. 1839. (B.P. 1949 ed.)

4. Sinister background black
Dundas, without Badge of Ulster, and with tressure dimidiated, impaling, Or a chevron gules between three trefoils slipped sable (Williamson)
Countess's coronet   Supporters: As 3., but crowned with ducal coronets or, and gorged with oak wreaths vert fructed or
For Sophia Jane, dau. of Sir Hedworth Williamson, Bt., who m. 1823, Thomas, 2nd Earl of Zetland, and d. 21 May 1865. (B.P. 1949 ed.)

5. All black background
Two oval shields   Dexter, Dundas, as 1., surrounded by the Garter, and pendent therefrom 'the George'   Sinister, Dundas, impaling, Williamson
Earl's coronet   Crest: A lion's head affronté proper crowned with a ducal coronet or, within an oak wreath vert fructed or
Motto: Essayez   Supporters: Two zoo lions proper, crowned with ducal coronets or, gorged with oak wreaths vert fructed or, pendent therefrom escutcheons, as 2.

Between the shields on green ribbon, the Badge of the Order of the
Thistle
Frame covered with velvet
For Thomas, 2nd Earl of Zetland, K.G., who d.s.p. 6 May 1873.
(B.P. 1949 ed.)
(There are duplicates of these hatchments at Marske, 2., 4. & 5., and
until recently, but now missing, 3.; and at Upleatham, 1., 4. and 5.)

RIPLEY

1. All black background

Qly, 1st, Sable an estoile of six points argent (Ingilby), 2nd, Gules a lion
rampant argent a bordure engrailed or (Mowbray), 3rd, Argent a saltire
gules, on a chief gules three escallops argent (Talbois), 4th, Argent a
chevron between three lions' heads erased gules (Roucliffe), over all the
Badge of Ulster
Crest: A boar's head couped erect argent tusked or langued gules
Mantling: Gules and argent   Motto: Mon droit
For Sir John Ingilby, 4th and last baronet of the first creation, who d.
unm. 14 July 1772.   (B.E.B.)

2. Sinister background black

Sable an estoile of six points argent, in dexter chief the Badge of Ulster
(Ingilby)   In pretence: Argent a tower between three cups azure
(Amcotts)
Esquire's helm   Crest: A boar's head erased erect tusked argent,
langued gules   Mantling: Gules and argent   Motto: Resurgam
Two cherubs' heads above and winged skull below
For Elizabeth, dau. and sole heir of Sir Wharton Amcotts, Bt., of
Kettlethorpe, Lincs., who m. 1780, Sir John Ingilby, 1st Bt. of the
second creation, and d. 21 Sept. 1812.   (B.E.B.; B.P. 1859 ed.;
Foster; Bloom: Compete Baronetage)

3. All black background

Ingilby, as 2., impaling, Amcotts
Crest, mantling and motto: As 1.
Two cherubs' heads above
For Sir John Ingilby, 1st Bt. of the second creation, who d. 14 May
1815.   (Sources, as 2.)

4. Sinister background black

Qly, 1st and 4th, Ingilby, as 1., 2nd and 3rd, Amcotts; with two Badges
of Ulster, one in dexter chief and one in sinister chief, impaling, Gules
a doubleheaded eagle displayed argent, on a chief or a rose between two
martlets sable (Atkinson)
Mantling: Gules and argent   Motto: Resurgam

Four cherubs' heads, two at top and two on lining of mantling
Winged skull below
For Louisa, dau. of John Atkinson, of Marple Hayes, Staffs, who m.
1822, as his 1st wife, Sir William Amcotts-Ingilby, 2nd Bt., of the
second creation, and d. 22 July 1836.   (Sources, as 2.)

5. All black background
Qly, 1st and 4th, Sable an estoile of six points argent within a bordure
engrailed compony or and gules (Ingilby), 2nd and 3rd, Amcotts, in
centre chief the Badge of Ulster
To dexter of main shield, arms as main shield, impaling, Atkinson A.Bl.
To sinister of main shield, arms as main shield, with in pretence, Vair
on a chief azure an annulet between two leopards' faces or, a canton
gules (Clementson) D.Bl.
Crests: Dexter, A boar's head couped erect argent tusked or, langued
gules, in his mouth an estoile of six points or   Sinister, A squirrel
sejant proper, collared or, eating a nut held in its forepaws
Mantling: Gules and argent   Motto: In coelo quies
For Sir William Amcotts-Ingilby, 2nd Bt. of the second creation, who
m. 1st, Louisa Atkinson (d. 1836), and 2nd, 1843, Mary Anne (d. 22
Dec. 1902), only child of John Clementson, and d. 14 May 1854.
(Sources, as 2; M.I.)

6. All black background
Ingilby, as 2., impaling, Azure a lion rampant argent crowned or
(MacDowall)
Crest: As 2.   Mantling: Or and argent   Motto: Mon droit
For the Rev. Sir Henry John Ingilby, 1st Bt. of the third creation, who
m. 1824, Elizabeth, dau. of Day Hort MacDowall, of Walkingshaw, co.
Renfrew, and d. 4 July 1870.   (Sources, as 2.)

RIPON Cathedral

1. All black background
On a lozenge, with escallop above and cherubs' heads at sides
Argent on a chevron between three molets sable three escallops argent
(Blackett), impaling, Sable three chevrons ermine between three snakes
argent (Wise)
For Patience, dau. of Henry Wise, who m. John Blackett, of Newby
Hall, son of Sir Edward Blackett, 2nd Bt., and d. 16 Jan. 1788, aged 92.
(B.P. 1949 ed.; Dean of Ripon)

2. Dexter background black
Qly, 1st and 4th, Sable three wild men ambulant in fess each bearing in
his sinister hand a shield argent charged with a cross gules and in the
dexter a club proper (Wood), 2nd and 3rd, Vert a chevron between

three ostrich feathers and a bordure argent (Perkins), impaling, Argent
on a bend between six martlets gules three lozenges argent each charged
with a saltire gules (Eckersall)
Crest: On a mount an oak tree proper   Mantling: Gules and argent
Motto: Resurgam   Two cherubs' heads above and one below
For Henry Richard Wood, of Hollin Hall, who m. 1810, Anne Elizabeth,
5th dau. of John Eckersall, of Claverton House, Bath, and d. 16 Apr.
1844.   (B.L.G. 7th ed.)

SANDAL MAGNA

1.   All black background

Argent a cross patonce voided gules, on a canton the badge of a baronet
of Nova Scotia (Pilkington)
Crest: A man reaping proper   Mantling: Gules and argent
Motto: Pax mentis honesta gloria
Probably for Sir Lionel Pilkington, 5th Bt., who purchased Chevet Park,
and d. unm. 11 Aug. 1778.   (Complete Baronetage)

2.   Dexter background black

Pilkington, as 1.   In pretence: Qly, 1st Argent a cross patonce sable,
over all a bend engrailed gules (Swinnerton), 2nd, Sable a chevron
between three leopards' faces or (Wentworth), 3rd, Per pale azure and
gules . . . (Rawsthorne), 4th, Argent a cross patonce sable (Copley)
Crest, mantling and motto: As 1.
For Sir William Pilkington, 8th Bt., who m. 1825, Mary, 2nd dau. and
co-heir of Thomas Swinnerton, of Butterton Hall, Staffs, and d. 30
Sept. 1850.   (B.P. 1949 ed.)

SANDBECK Hall Chapel

1.   Dexter background black

Qly, 1st and 4th, Argent a fess gules between three popinjays vert
collared gules (Lumley), 2nd, Gules six martlets, three, two and one
argent (Lumley), 3rd, Argent on a bend sable three owls proper (Savile),
impaling, Qly, 1st and 4th, Or three bars wavy gules (Drummond), 2nd
and 3rd, Or a lion's head erased within a double tressure flory counter-
flory gules (Drummond)
Earl's coronet   Crest: A pelican in piety on nest with young proper
Motto: Murus aeneus conscientia sana
Supporters: Two popinjays wings endorsed and inverted vert, legs and
beaks gules
For Richard George, 9th Earl of Scarbrough, who m. 1846, Frederica
Mary Adeliza (d. 2 Apr. 1907), dau. of Andrew Robert Drummond, and
d. 5 Dec. 1884.   (B.P. 1949 ed.)

SELBY

1. All black background
On a lozenge   Gules a bend or between two escallops argent (Petre),
impaling, Qly, 1st, Gules on a bend between six cross crosslets fitchy
argent the Augmentation of Flodden (Howard), 2nd, Gules three lions
passant guardant in pale or a label argent (Brotherton), 3rd, Chequy or
and azure (Warren), 4th, Gules a lion rampant argent (Fitzalan)
Baroness's coronet   Supporters: Dexter, A lion reguardant or,
collared azure   Sinister, A lion reguardant azure, collared or
For Juliana Barbara, dau. of Henry Howard of Glossop, who m. as his
2nd wife, Robert Edward, 9th Baron Petre, and d. 16 Apr. 1833.
(B.P. 1949 ed.)

SHERIFF HUTTON

1. Dexter background black
Per fess argent and sable a fess per fess embattled counter-embattled
between three falcons belled or all counterchanged (Thompson),
impaling, Argent three bulls' heads cabossed sable armed or (Waldron)
Crest: A dexter mailed arm qly or and azure, the hand proper grasping
a broken lance or   Mantling: Gules and argent
Motto: Je veux de bonne guerre
For George Lowther Thompson, of Sheriff Hutton Park, who m. 1805,
Mary Anne, dau. of the Rev. Edward Waldron, Rector of Hampton
Lovett, Worcs, and d. 25 Dec. 1841.   (B.L.G. 5th ed.)

SOWERBY

1. All black background
On a lozenge surmounted by a cherub's head
Gules on a chevron argent, between three towers argent issuant from
each a demi-lion or, three grappling irons sable (Priestley), impaling,
Argent a chevron between three crescents sable (Walker)
For Elizabeth, dau. of William Walker, of Crow Nest, Lightcliffe, who
m. John Priestley, of Thorpe, near Triangle, son of John Priestley, of
White Windows, Sowerby, and d. 27 July 1829.   He d. 21 Jan. 1801.
(R. Bretton, Local Funeral Hatchments; Trans. Halifax Antiq. Soc.
1952, p. 45)

SPROTBROUGH

1. All black background
Qly of five, 1st, Argent a cross moline sable (Copley), 2nd, Lozengy
gules and argent (Fitzwilliam), 3rd, Argent five fusils conjoined in fess

gules in chief three curlews' heads sable (Bosville), 4th, Gules a mule
passant argent (Moyle), 5th, Argent a saltire engrailed azure, on a chief
azure three cinquefoils argent (Hardwick), in fess point the Badge of
Ulster
Crest: From a ducal coronet or a panache of ostrich feathers argent
Mantling: Gules and argent
For Sir Lionel Copley, 2nd Bt., who d. unm. 4 Mar. 1806.   (B.P.
1949 ed.; M.I.)

2. Sinister background black
Qly, 1st and 4th, Copley, 2nd and 3rd, Gules a horse trotting argent
(Moyle), over all the Badge of Ulster, impaling, Qly, 1st and 4th, Gules
three cinquefoils argent (Hamilton), 2nd and 3rd, Argent a ship with
three masts and rigging sable (Lorne)
Motto: In cruce vinco
For Cecil, dau. of the Hon. & Rev. George Hamilton, Rector of Taplow,
Bucks, who m. 1790, Sir Joseph Copley, 3rd Bt., and d. 19 June 1819.
(B.P. 1949 ed.)

3. All black background
Arms: As 2.
Crests: Dexter, As 1.   Sinister, Two demi-dragons gules and argent,
addorsed, reguardant, necks crossed in saltire
Mantling: Gules and argent   Motto: In cruce vinco
For Sir Joseph Copley, 3rd Bt., who d. 21 May 1838.   (B.P. 1949 ed.)

STANWICK

1. All black background
Azure on a bend cotised argent three escallops gules, on a chief or
three martlets azure (Pulleine), impaling to the dexter, Argent ten
roundels gules four, three, two and one (Babington), and to the sinister,
Argent on a bend between three birds sable three lions' heads erased at
the neck or (Carr)
Crest: A pelican feeding its young proper   Mantling: Gules and argent
Motto: Nulla pallescere culpa   Skull and crossbones in base
For Wingate Pulleine, of Carleton Hall, who m. 1st, 1721, Catherine
Frances, dau. and co-heir of Philip Babington of Babington, and 2nd,
1727, Frances (d. 1735), dau. of Ralph Carr, of Cocken Hall, co.
Durham, and d. Aug. 1763, aged 62.   (B.L.G. 1937 ed.; Foster; M.I.)

2. Dexter background black
Pulleine, impaling, Argent a chevron between three stags' heads erased
sable (Collingwood)
Crest and motto: As 1.   Skull and crossbones below

For Thomas Babington Pulleine, of Carleton Hall, eldest son of Wingate Pulleine and his second wife, who m. Winifred, dau. of Edward Collingwood, of Dissington, Northumberland, and d. (B.L.G. 5th ed.; Foster)

3. Dexter background black

Pulleine, with martlets gules, impaling, Gules on a fess argent between three cushions argent tasselled or three fleurs-de-lys gules (Hutton) Crest, mantling and motto: As 1.   Additional motto: Resurgam Cherub's head below
For Henry Pulleine, of Carleton Hall, second son of Wingate Pulleine and his second wife, who m. 1764, Elizabeth (d. 1816), dau. of John Hutton, of Marske, Yorks, and d.   (Sources, as 1.)

4. Dexter background black

Two oval shields   Dexter, within the Garter, Qly, 1st, qly i. & iv. Or a lion rampant azure (Percy), ii. & iii. Gules three lucies hauriant argent (Lucy), 2nd, Azure a fess of five fusils or (Percy), 3rd, Gules on a saltire argent an annulet sable (Nevil), 4th, Qly gules and or, in the first and fourth quarters a molet argent (Vere)   Sinister, within an ornamental border, Vert on each of three escutcheons argent a bordure engrailed or (Burrell)
Duke's coronet   Crest: A fetterlock or within a crescent argent
Mantle: Gules and ermine   Supporters: Dexter, A lion rampant azure   Sinister, A unicorn argent, horned, crined, tufted, ducally gorged with chain flexed over back or   Motto: Esperance en Dieu
For Hugh, 2nd Duke of Northumberland, K.G., who m. 2nd, 1779, Frances Julia, dau. of Peter Burrell, of Beckenham, Kent, and d. 10 July 1817.   (B.P. 1949 ed.)

5. Dexter background black

Two oval shields   Dexter, within the Garter, Qly of six, 1st, qly i. & iv. Percy, ii. & iii. Lucy, 2nd, Percy, 3rd, Barry of six or and vert a bend gules (Poynings), 4th, Gules three lions passant in pale or over all a bend azure (Plantagenet), 5th, Or three piles in point azure (Brian), 6th, Nevil   Sinister, within an ornamental border, presumably as dexter, but covered by dexter shield, impaling, Azure a garb or (Grosvenor)
Duke's coronet   Crest: On a chapeau gules and ermine a lion statant azure   Supporters: Dexter, A lion rampant azure   Sinister, A lion rampant guardant or, collared compony argent and azure
Motto: As 4.   The George pendent below shields
For Algernon, 4th Duke of Northumberland, K.G., who m. 1842, Eleanor (d. 4 May 1911), dau. of Richard, 2nd Marquess of Westminster, and d. 12 Feb. 1865.   (B.P. 1949 ed.)

STILLINGTON

1. Dexter background black
Qly indented or ermined sable and gules, in the first quarter a lion
rampant guardant sable (Croft), impaling, Or a sinister quarter, qly, i. &
iv. Gules a pile or masoned gules (Zouch), ii. & iii. Azure a lion passant
argent (Fitz-Aer), over all a lion rampant gules (Charlton)
Crest: A lion passant guardant sable, dexter forepaw resting on a shield,
Sable ermined or, a lion passant guardant or
Mantling: Gules and argent
For Colonel Harry Croft, of Stillington Hall, who m. 1822, Elizabeth,
dau. of William Charlton, of Apley Castle, Salop, and d. 1853.
(B.L.G. 1937 ed.)

TADCASTER

1. All black background
On a curvilinear lozenge surmounted by a skull and crossbones and with
a cherub's head at each side
Argent a cross engrailed gules between four water bougets sable
(Bourchier)   In pretence: Qly, 1st and 4th, Or a fess gules between
three branches vert (Roundell), 2nd, Argent on a chevron sable three
fleurs-de-lys argent (Elwick), 3rd, Argent a chevron between three
fleurs-de-lys sable three rams' heads argent (Ramsden)
For Mildred, dau. of Richard Roundell, of Hutton Wansley, who m.
John Bourchier, of Beningborough, Yorkshire, and d. 12 Dec. 1796.
(Foster)

2. All black background (should be dexter black)
Qly, 1st and 4th, Azure five fusils conjoined in fess or (Percy), 2nd and
3rd, Gules three lucies hauriant argent (Lucy), impaling, Azure a cross
or between four birds argent (Wriothesley)
Earl's coronet   Two crests, one each side of shield: Dexter, A
crescent argent   Sinister, A crescent argent surmounted by an earl's
coronet
A small hatchment, c. 2ft. x 2ft, on wood panel
For Josceline, 11th Earl of Northumberland, who m. 1662, Elizabeth,
dau. of Thomas, 4th Earl of Southampton, and d. 21 May 1670.   She
m. 2nd, Ralph, 1st Duke of Montagu.   (B.E.P.; B.P. 1949 ed.)

TEMPLE NEWSAM House

1. All white background
Ermine on a fess gules three escallops or (Ingram), impaling, Sable three
greyhounds courant in pale argent collared gules within a bordure argent
(Machel)

Viscount's coronet   Crest: A cock or   Mantling: Gules and
ermine   Supporters: Dexter, a griffin qly argent and gules
Sinister, A greyhound argent collared gules
For Arthur, 3rd Viscount Irvine, who m. 1685, Isabella (d. 1764),
eldest dau. and co-heir of John Machell, of Hills, Sussex, and d. 21 June
1702.   (Foster; Complete Peerage)

2. Dexter background black
Ingram   In pretence: Gules on a chevron between three fleurs-de-
lys argent three molets of six points sable (Shepheard)
Viscount's coronet   Crest: A cock proper
Mantling: Gules and argent   Motto: In caelo quies
Supporters: Dexter, as 1.   Sinister, An antelope argent, horned,
hoofed and crined or, ducally gorged gules   Cherub's head below
For Charles, 9th Viscount Irvine, who m. 1758, Frances Shepheard, and
d. 19 June 1778.   (Sources, as 1.)

3. All black background
On a lozenge   Arms: As 2., but molets gules
Viscountess's coronet   Mantling and motto: As 2.
Supporters: Dexter, as 1.   Sinister, An ibex argent, horned and
hoofed or, ducally gorged gules
For Frances, widow of Charles, 9th Viscount Irvine, who d. 20 Nov.
1807.   (Sources, as 1.)

4. All black background
On a lozenge   Qly, 1st and 4th, Sable on a bend cotised argent a
rose gules between two annulets sable (Conway), 2nd, qly i. & iv. Or on
a pile gules between six fleurs-de-lys azure three lions passant guardant
in pale or, ii. & iii. Gules two wings conjoined in lure or (Seymour), 3rd,
Ermine on a fess gules three escallops or a canton gules (Ingram)
In pretence: Qly, 1st and 4th, Ingram, without canton, 2nd, Azure a
chevron between three lions passant or (Ingram), 3rd, Sable three
greyhounds courant in pale within a bordure argent (Machel)
Marchioness's coronet   Mantle: Gules and argent
Supporters: Two blackamoors, wreathed about the temples argent and
sable, habited in golden breastplates and buskins, adorned about their
waists and shoulders with green and brown feathers, their exterior hands
resting on oval shields, the dexter, Vert a sun in splendour or, and the
sinister, Vert a crescent or
For Isabella Anne, eldest dau. & co-heir of Charles, 9th Viscount
Irvine, who m. 1776, as his 2nd wife, Francis, 2nd Marquess of
Hertford, and d. 12 Apr. 1836.   (B.P. 1949 ed.)

5. All black background
On a lozenge surmounted by a cherub's head
Qly, 1st, Azure three boars' heads couped or (Gordon), 2nd, Gules
three lions' heads erased or langued azure (Badenoch), 3rd, Or three

crescents within a double tressure flory counter-flory gules (Seton), 4th,
Azure three cinquefoils argent (Fraser)   In pretence: Ermine on a
fess gules three escallops or (Ingram)
Supporters: Dexter, A greyhound argent collared gules   Sinister, A
griffin gules bezanty, clawed and beaked or, langued azure, with collar
and chain or
For Frances Shepheard, 2nd dau. and co-heir of Charles, 9th Viscount
Irvine, who m. 1781, William, 2nd son of Cosmo George, 3rd Duke of
Gordon, and d. 29 Sept. 1841.   (B.P. 1949 ed.; Foster)

THIRSK

1. All black background
Azure a chevron between three bells argent (Bell)
Crest: A falcon proper ringed and belled or   Mantling: Gules and argent
argent   Motto: Non omnis moriar
Unidentified

2. All black background
Per chevron azure and sable a chevron engrailed plain cotised between
three bells argent (Bell)
Crest: On a bell argent a falcon proper
Mantling: Sable and or   Motto: Spes mea copia fecit
Unidentified

3. All black background
Azure a chevron engrailed plain cotised between three bells argent (Bell)
Crest: As 2.   Mantling: Sable and argent   Motto: As 1.
Unidentified

4. All black background
Qly, 1st and 4th, Sable a chevron between three bells argent (Bell), 2nd
and 3rd, Argent a maunch sable, over all a bend compony ermine and
sable (Conyers), impaling, Argent a saltire and in chief a lion's head
erased sable (Barnett)
Crest, mantling and motto: As 1.
For John Bell, of Thirsk, who m. 1800, Frances Brady, dau. of the Hon.
William Barnett, of Arcadia, and d.   (B.L.G. 1937 ed.)

5. All black background
Argent two bars gules (Martin)
Crest: From a ducal coronet or an ass's head proper
Mantling: Gules and argent
Unidentified

6. All black background
On a curvilinear lozenge   Azure a chevron ermine (   )
Motto: Mors janua vitae   Cherubs' heads at sides of lozenge
This hatchment (still present) was formerly over a monument to
Amelia Sparre, only child of Charles Baron Sparre. She d. 5 Oct. 1778.

7. This hatchment was recorded in 1961, but is now missing. It was in
poor condition and impossible to blazon accurately. The arms were on
a lozenge, a quarterly coat impaling Bell.

THORNTON-LE-STREET

1. Dexter background black
Vert on a bend argent double cotised ermine between two covered cups
or a lion passant gules, on a chief azure three pheons or, in dexter chief
the Badge of Ulster (Crompton), impaling, Qly, 1st, Azure three cross
crosslets fitchy each issuant from a crescent argent (Cathcart), 2nd,
Gules a lion rampant argent (Wallace), 3rd, Or on a saltire azure nine
lozenges or (Dalrymple), 4th, Azure three covered cups or (Schaw)
Crest: A demi-horse salient azure vulned in the breast by an arrow or
Mantling: Gules and argent   Mottoes: above crest, Resurgam
below arms, Love and loyalty
For Sir Samuel Crompton, 1st and last Bt., of Wood End, who m.
Isabella Sophia (d. 9 Dec. 1896), dau. of the Hon. and Rev. Archibald
Hamilton Cathcart, vicar of Kippax, and d. 27 Dec. 1848.   (B.P.
1949 ed.; M.I.)

THORNTON WATLASS

1. All black background
On a curvilinear lozenge   Argent a bend engrailed sable between
three annulets gules (Dodsworth), impaling, Gules on a fess between
three lozenge cushions argent three fleurs-de-lys gules (Hutton)
For Henrietta, dau. of John Hutton of Marske, and sister of Matthew,
Archbishop of Canterbury, who m. 1719, John Dodsworth, of
Thornton Watlass, and d. 1797.   (Foster)

2. Sinister background black
Dodsworth, in dexter chief a martlet argent for difference   In pretence:
Ermine on a chief azure three talbots' heads erased argent (Barrell)
Motto: Give and Forgive   Cherub's head above shield
For Catherine, dau. and co-heir of Francis Barrel, of Rochester, who m.
as his first wife, the Rev. Frederick Dodsworth, Canon of Windsor, 4th
surviving son of John and Henrietta (see 1.), and d.   (Foster)

3. Dexter background black
Dodsworth   In pretence: Qly, 1st and 4th, Sable a chevron between
three millpicks argent (Mosley), 2nd, Gules on a bend cotised argent
three escallops gules, on a chief argent three martlets gules (Pullein),
3rd, Argent five bars gules a lion rampant sable (Estotville)
No helm   Crest: A dexter cubit mailed arm or, the hand proper
grasping a broken tilting spear or, embrued gules
Mantling: Gules and argent   Skull below
For the Rev. Frederick Dodsworth, Canon of Windsor, who m. 2nd,
Frances, dau. & co-heir of Thomas Pullein-Mosley, of Burley in
Wharfdale, and d. 31 Mar. 1821.   (Foster)

4. Dexter background black
Qly, 1st, Per saltire argent and sable two trefoils slipped in pale gules
(Smith), 2nd, Per chevron embattled or and vert three martlets counter-
changed (Hodgson), 3rd, Vert a bend between two stags' heads couped
or (   ), 4th, Argent a molet pierced sable (Ashton), over all the
Badge of Ulster, impaling, Dodsworth
Crest: From a ducal coronet or a boar's head couped at the neck azure
crined or   Mantling: Gules and argent
Motto: Pro lege senatu que rege
For Sir John Silvester Smith, 1st Bt. of Newland Hall, who m. 1761,
Henrietta Maria, dau. of John and Henrietta Dodsworth (No. 1.), and
d. 15 June 1789.   (B.P. 1949 ed.; Foster)

5. All black background
On a lozenge surmounted by a skull and crossbones
Smith, in fess point the Badge of Ulster, impaling, Dodsworth
For Henrietta Maria, widow of Sir John Silvester Smith, Bt., who d.
                                        (Sources, as 4.)

6. Sinister background black
Qly, 1st, qly i. & iv. Dodsworth, ii. & iii. Smith, 2nd, Hodgson, 3rd, as
4., but stags' heads erased, 4th, Ashton, over all the Badge of Ulster,
impaling, Gules a lion passant guardant or between two roses in pale
argent, on each of two flaunches or a lion rampant sable (Dawkins)
Motto: As 4.   Cherub's head above shield
For Susannah, youngest dau. of Col. Henry Dawkins, of Standlynch,
Wilts, who m. 1804, Sir Edward Dodsworth, 2nd Bt., and d. 13 Mar.
1830.   (Sources, as 4.)

7. All black background
Arms: Qly, as 6., but martlets argent, impaling, Gules a lion passant
guardant between a rose and another lion passant guardant in pale
argent, on each of two flaunches or a lion rampant sable (Dawkins),
in fess point of shield the Badge of Ulster

Crests: Dexter, as 3. Sinister, as 4. Mantling and motto: As 4.
For Sir Edward Dodsworth, 2nd Bt., who d.s.p. 31 Dec. 1845. Sir
Edward was the eldest son of Sir John Silvester Smith, 1st Bt., and
changed his name from Smith to Dodsworth in compliance with the
will of his uncle, the Rev. Frederick Dodsworth (No. 3.). (Sources, as
4.)

8. All black background
Qly, 1st and 4th, Dodsworth, 2nd and 3rd, Smith, over all the Badge of
Ulster, impaling, Gules three mailed armed embowed erect hands
clenched, two and one, proper (Armstrong)
No helm or crest   Mantling: Gules and argent
Motto: To die is gain   Three cherubs' heads above shield
For Sir Charles Dodsworth, 3rd Bt., who m. 1808, Elizabeth (d. 12
June 1853), dau. and heir of John Armstrong, of Lisgoole, co.
Fermanagh, and d. 28 July 1857.   (Sources, as 4.)
(The absence of helmet and crest suggests that the hatchment may have
been used originally for the wife and subsequently for the husband)

9. Sinister background black
Qly indented or ermined sable and gules, in the first quarter a lion
passant guardant gules a label of three points argent, in fess point the
Badge of Ulster (Croft), impaling, Gules a lion rampant between eight
cross crosslets fitchy argent (Warre)
Motto: In the midst of life we are in death
Two cherubs' heads above shield
For Amelia Elizabeth, dau. of James Warre, who m. 1816, as his first
wife, Sir John Croft, 1st Bt., of Cowling Hall, and d. 20 Oct. 1819,
aged 35.   (B.P. 1949 ed.; B.L.G. 10th ed.)

10. All black background
Gules on a fess between three lozenge cushions argent fringed and
tasselled or three fleurs-de-lys gules (Hutton), impaling, Per bend
indented argent and azure three cinquefoils counterchanged (Chaytor)
Crest: On a cushion gules, fringed and tasselled or, an open book
proper with the words, Odor Vitae   Mantling: Or and argent
Motto: Resurgam
For Timothy Hutton, of Clifton Castle and Marske Hall, who m. 1804,
Elizabeth, dau. of William Chaytor, of Croft and Spennithorne, and
d. 1864.   (Foster)
(There is another hatchment for Timothy Hutton at Downholme)

11. Dexter background black
Azure on a bend cotised argent three escallops gules, on a chief or three
martlets azure (Pulleine), impaling, Argent on a chief gules a cushion
between two molets of six points pierced argent (Marjoribanks)

Crest: A pelican in her piety with nest and three young argent
Mantling: Gules and argent   Motto: Nullâ pallescere culpa
For James Pulleine, of Crake Hall and Clifton Castle, who m. 1841,
Annie Caroline (d. Mar. 1889), eldest dau. of Edward Marjoribanks, of
London, and d. 23 Mar. 1879.   (M.I.; Foster; B.L.G. 1937 ed.)

12. All black background
Qly of sixteen, 1st, Argent a chevron between three hunting horns sable
stringed gules (Dodsworth), 2nd, Argent a chevron between three lions
rampant sable (Thoresby), 3rd, Azure a maunch or (?Conyers), 4th,
Argent crusilly gules a lion rampant azure (Mountford), 5th, Argent a
fess between six fleurs-de-lys sable (   ), 6th, Gules . . . a chief or
(   ), 7th, Azure a cross flory or (   ), 8th, Argent a chevron
between three birds sable (Lawson), 9th, Hutton, 10th, Argent a cross
flory between four birds sable, a canton sable ermined argent (   )
11th, Argent a lion rampant sable (Stapleton), 12th, Hutton, 13th, Per
saltire argent and azure three ?trefoils gules (?Smith), 14th, Dodsworth,
15th, Gules three arms in armour embowed two and one argent
(Armstrong), 16th, Per bend vairy or and azure, and gules a castle
proper (   ), the Badge of Ulster
No helm, crest, mantling or motto
Unidentified
(This hatchment, recorded since the Survey began in 1952, is now
missing)

TONG

1. Dexter background black
Ermine a bend vair contised sable (Plumbe)   In pretence: Qly of eight,
1st, Argent a bend between six martlets sable (Tempest), 2nd, Gules a
bend ermine (Rye), 3rd, Ermine five fusils conjoined in fess gules
(Hebden), 4th, Sable an escutcheon ermine within eight martlets in
orle argent (Bowling), 5th, Argent a wolf's head between three horns
sable (Bradford), 6th, Azure a bend argent between two cotises and six
martlets or (Tong), 7th, Vert two lions passant argent (Mirfield), 8th,
Argent on a bend sable three owls argent (Savile)
Crest: A greyhound sejant argent collared gules
Mantling: Gules and argent   Cherub's head below
For Thomas Plumbe, who m. Elizabeth, dau. of John Tempest, of Tong
Hall, and d. 7 June 1806.   (B.L.G. 1937 ed.; Foster)

2. Sinister background black
Qly of twelve, 1st, Tempest, 2nd, Plumbe, 3rd, Argent a chevron
between three martlets gules (Waddington), 4th, Rye, 5th, Bowling,
6th, Bradford, 7th, Tong, 8th, Argent two lions passant vert (Mirfield),
9th, Savile, 10th, Gules a cross formy or (Golcar), 11th, Gules two
esquires' helmets proper and a garb or (Cholmley), 12th, Gules a lion

rampant or a bordure vair (Scrimshire), impaling, Qly, 1st and 4th, Plumbe, 2nd and 3rd, Per fess gules and or a lozenge counterchanged (Kirk)

Crests: Dexter, A griffin's head sable (Tempest)   Sinister, A greyhound sejant argent collared gules (Plumbe)

Motto: Loywf as thow fynds

For Sarah, dau. of the Rev. William Plumbe of Aughton, Lancs, and Catherine, dau. of Samuel Kirk, who m. her cousin, John Plumbe-Tempest, of Tong Hall, and d. 31 Dec. 1856.   (Sources, as 1.)

3. All black background

Arms: As 2.

Crests and motto: As 2.

For John Plumbe-Tempest, of Tong Hall, who d. 6 Apr. 1859. (Sources, as 1.)

4. All black background

Qly, 1st and 4th, qly of six, i. Tempest, ii. Plumbe, iii. Waddington, iv. Rye, v. Bowling, vi. Bradford, 2nd and 3rd, qly of six, i. Tong, ii. Mirfield, iii. Savile, iv. Golcar, v. Chomley, vi. Scrimshire

Crests and motto: As 2.

Probably for Thomas Richard Plumbe-Tempest, son of John and Sarah Plumbe-Tempest, who d. 27 July 1881.   (B.L.G. 1937 ed.; Vis. of England and Wales, Vol. I, 35)

5. All black background

On a lozenge surmounted by a lover's knot

Arms: As 4.

Motto: Resurgam

Probably for Catherine Elizabeth Tempest, who succeeded her brother, Thomas Richard Plumbe Tempest, and d. unm. 17 Mar. 1884. (Sources, as 4.)

6. All black background

Qly of twenty-five, 1st, Tempest with the Badge of Ulster in chief, 2nd, Argent on a chevron azure between three roses gules two swords argent hilts and pommels or, their points passing through a wreath or, on a chief azure a naval crown between two anchors or (Ricketts), 3rd, Or on a fess wavy gules three molets argent, on a canton azure a fleur-de-lys or (Gumbleton), 4th, qly i. & iv. Tempest, ii. & iii. Plumbe, 5th, Tempest, 6th, Waddington, 7th, Rye, 8th, Hebden, 9th, Bowling, 10th, Mirfield as 2., 11th, Tong, 12th, Savile, 13th, Golcar, 14th, Argent on a bend gules three escallops or (Tankersley), 15th, Bowling, 16th, Or on a chief indented azure three roundels argent (Lathom), 17th, Argent a bend between a bird rising wings elevated and a cross patonce sable (Rishworth), 18th, Gules two bars and eight martlets in orle argent (Eland), 19th, Tankersley, 20th, Ermine three chevrons gules

(Pictavensis), 21st, Gules two bars gemel and a chief argent (Thornhill),
22nd Gules two esquires' helmets proper and a garb or, at the fess
point a fleur-de-lys or issuant from a crescent ermine (Cholmley), 23rd,
Gules three molets or (Belward), 24th Argent a cross patonce azure
(Malpas), 25th, Argent on a fess gules three roundels argent (Etton)
Crest: A griffin's head per pale argent and sable
Mantling: Sable and argent   Motto: Loywf as thow fynds
For Sir Robert Tempest Tempest, 3rd Bt., who assumed in 1884, the
surname and arms of Tempest in lieu of Ricketts, son of Sir Cornwallis
Ricketts, 2nd Bt. and Henrietta, youngest dau. of John Tempest,
formerly Plumbe. He m. 1861, Amelia Helen (d. 1869), dau. of John
Stewart, of Dalguise, co. Perth, and d. 4 Feb. 1901.   (B.P. 1949 ed.)

7. All black background
Qly of twenty-six, 1st to 25th, as 6., 26th, Or a lion rampant between
three molets vert, over all a fess chequy argent and azure (Stewart)
Crest, mantling and motto: As 6.
For Sir Tristram Tempest Tempest, 4th Bt., who m. 1902, Mabel Ethel
(d. 1906), dau. of Major General Sir George Hall MacGregor, K.C.B.,
and d.s.p. 23 June 1909.   (B.P. 1949 ed.)

ULSHAW BRIDGE (R.C. church)

1. Sinister background black
Azure a bend or (Scrope), impaling, Barry of six or and azure
(Constable)
Crest: Out of a ducal coronet or a plume of five feathers argent
Mantling: Gules and argent   Motto: Non haec sed me
Frame decorated with crossbands
For Mary, dau. of Robert, 3rd Viscount Dunbar, who m. as his 1st wife,
Simon Scrope of Danby, and d. 21 Feb. 1694/5.   (Foster)
(This hatchment, in poor condition when recorded in 1955, was
destroyed in 1972)

UPLEATHAM

1. Dexter background black
Or six annulets, three, two and one sable (Lowther), impaling, Argent a
chevron between three spear heads gules (   )
Crest: A dragon passant or   Mantling: Gules and argent
Frame decorated with skulls and crossbones
Unidentified

2. Duplicate of Richmond, 1.

3. Duplicate of Richmond, 4.

4. Duplicate of Richmond, 5.

WADDINGTON

1. Dexter background black
Qly, 1st and 4th, Vert a chevron between three stags' heads cabossed or (Parker), 2nd, Sable a stag's head cabossed or between two flaunches argent (Parker), 3rd, Argent a cross patonce gules between four martlets sable a canton azure (Goulbourne), impaling, Azure a cross moline or (Molyneux)
Crests: Dexter, A stag trippant or   Sinister, A dexter cubit arm erect, the sleeve gules three bars argent, cuffed argent, grasping in the hand proper a stag's antler or   Mantling: Vert and or
Mottoes: Nec fluctu nec flatu movetur & Resurgam
Sprays of leaves at the sides of shield, at top sun's rays shining down, in each corner at sides a cherub's head, and in base an hourglass
For Thomas Parker, of Browsholme, who m. Mary, dau. of William Molyneux, of Liverpool, and d. 22 April 1832.   (Foster's Lancashire Pedigrees; B.L.G. 1937 ed.)

2. Dexter background black
Qly of nine, 1st and 3rd, Vert a chevron between three stags' heads cabossed or (Parker), 2nd, Gules three cushions ermine (Redmayne), 4th, Argent a bend between six martlets sable (Tempest), 5th, Or on a cross sable five escallops argent (   ), 6th, Argent a lion rampant gules within an orle of ten fleurs-de-lys azure (Thorpe), 7th, Gules a chevron vair between three cross crosslets fitchy argent (Blakey), 8th, Sable a stag's head cabossed proper between two flaunches argent (Parker), 9th, Argent a cross patonce sable between four martlets gules a canton azure (Goulbourne), impaling, Per pale gules and azure on a chevron embattled argent three estoiles sable (Carr)
Crest: A stag trippant proper   Mantling: Vert and or
Motto: Resurgam
For Thomas Goulbourne Parker, of Browsholme, nephew of Thomas Parker, who m. 1845, Mary Anne, eldest dau. and co-heir of John Francis Carr, of Carr Lodge, Horbury, and d. 17 Apr. 1879. (Sources, as 1.)

WAKEFIELD

1. All black background
Argent a cross patonce voided gules, on a canton azure a saltire argent for the badge of a baronet of Nova Scotia (Pilkington)

Crest: A man reaping (hardly discernible)
Probably for Sir Lionel Pilkington, 5th Bt., who purchased Chevet Park,
near Wakefield, and d. there, unm. 11 Aug. 1778.   (Complete
Baronetage)

WALKINGTON

1. All black background
Qly, 1st and 4th, Or a lion rampant sable between two bugles gules, in
chief a cross crosslet sable, over all a bend compony argent and azure
(Fawsitt), 2nd and 3rd, Azure three buckles between three boars' heads
couped argent (Ferguson)
Crests: Dexter, A demi-lion rampant sable, forepaws against a column
gules surmounted by a bugle or   Sinister, An arm and hand proper
holding a dagger erect argent, in front of the arm a buckle argent
Motto (above dagger): Arte et marte   Mantling: Gules and argent
Motto: Dominus providebit
Across the top of the frame is nailed a metal band inscribed: Resurgam
For Major John Daniel Ferguson-Fawsitt, J.P., of Walkington Hall, who
m. 1866, Anne Eliza, dau. and co-heir of John Fawsitt, of Hunsley,
Yorks. Major Ferguson took the additional name and arms of Fawsitt,
and d. 1908.   (Armorial Families, 1902 ed.; J. Tindale)

WATH, nr Ripon

1. All black background
Sable on a fess between three crosses flory or three martlets sable
(Samwayes)
Crest: A lion's gamb erased and erect or holding a hammer proper
Mantling: Gules and argent, with gold tassels
A small hatchment, c. 15ins. x 15ins., on a wood panel
For the Rev. Peter Samwaies, D.D., Rector of Bedale and Canon of
Ripon, who d. 6 Apr. 1693.   (McCall, Richmondshire Churches,
1910)

WATTON Abbey

1. All black background
On a lozenge surmounted by a cherub's head
Argent a chevron between three boars' heads couped sable a crescent
on the chevron for difference (Bethell), impaling, Qly, 1st and 4th,
Gules a chevron ermine between three broken spears or headed argent
(Pennyman), 2nd and 3rd, Vert on a chevron argent a martlet between
two pheons gules (Warton)

Skull below
For Charlotte, dau. of Ralph Pennyman, who m. William Bethell, of
Rise Park and Watton Abbey, and was bur. 2 Nov. 1814. He d.s.p.
25 July 1799.   (B.L.G. 5th ed.; Foster)

2. All black background
Argent a chevron engrailed gules between three molets sable, on a chief
azure three stags' heads cabossed or (Parker), impaling, Sable a fess
ermine between three church bells argent (Bell)
Crest: A falcon, wings elevated and inverted, belled or
Mantling: Gules and argent   Motto: Pax piis solum
Unidentified

WENTWORTH (Old Church)

1. Dexter background black
Qly, 1st and 4th, Argent on a chevron engrailed azure between three
martlets sable three crescents or (Watson), 2nd and 3rd, Sable a chevron
between three lions' faces or (Wentworth), impaling, Argent a chevron
between three griffins passant sable (Finch)
Marquess's coronet   Crests: Dexter, A griffin's head argent ducally
gorged or (Watson)   Sinister, A griffin passant argent (Wentworth)
Mantling: Gules and argent   Motto: Mea gloria fides
Supporters: Dexter, A griffin argent ducally gorged or   Sinister, A
pegasus argent, winged and ducally gorged or
For Thomas, 1st Marquess of Rockingham, who m. Mary, dau. of
Daniel, 6th Earl of Winchelsea, and d. 14 Dec. 1750.   (Foster; B.P.
1949 ed.)

2. Dexter background black
Qly, 1st and 4th, Watson, 2nd and 3rd, Wentworth   In pretence: Qly,
1st and 4th, Per pale azure and gules a bend between two molets or
(Bright), 2nd and 3rd, Argent a fret gules, on a chief gules three lions'
faces or (Liddell)   Shield within the Garter
Marquess's coronet   Crest: A griffin passant argent ducally gorged or
Motto: Mea gloria fides   Supporters: Dexter, A griffin argent
ducally gorged or   Sinister, A lion or
For Charles, 2nd Marquess of Rockingham, K.G., who m. Mary, dau.
and heir of Robert Bright, of Badsworth, and d. 1 July 1782.
(Sources, as 1.)

(Both these hatchments were in a terrible condition when last seen in
1973)

WESTON

1. All black background
Qly, 1st and 4th, Or a fess dancetty sable (Vavasour), 2nd, Sable three
lozenges argent each charged with a bend gules (Benville), 3rd, Argent a
bend sable (Stopham), impaling, Ermine a mascle sable (Fawkes)
Crest: A cock gules, legs, beak, wattles and comb or
Mantling: Gules and argent   Motto: Firmus infirmum
Frame decorated with skulls and crossbones
For William Vavasour, of Weston, who m. 1696, Mary, eldest dau. of
Thomas Fawkes, of Farnley Hall, Otley, and d. Nov. 1753.   (Foster)

2. All black background
Or a fess dancetty in chief a crescent sable (Vavasour), impaling, Qly
gules and argent (Cooke)
Crest and mantling: As 1.
For William Vavasour, great-grandson of 1., who m. Sarah, dau. of John
Cooke, of Swinton, and d. 15 Jan. 1833.   (Foster)

3. Dexter background black
Sable a hound passant guardant or, on a chief argent three square
buckles sable (Carter), impaling, Ermine on a fess sable three molets or
(Lister)
Crest: Issuant from a mural coronet argent a demi-lion rampant proper
Mantling: Gules and argent   Motto: Resurgam
Sprays of leaves at lower sides of shield, and winged skull below
For William Vavasour Carter, who m. Elizabeth Emily, dau. of Ellis
Cunliffe-Lister-Kay, of Manningham Hall and Farfield Hall, and d. 17
Nov. 1852, aged 28.   (Foster; arm. ped. at Weston Hall)

4. Dexter background black
Ermine three pallets engrailed gules, on a canton sable a stag lodged
argent (Dawson)   In pretence: Per pale argent and sable a hound
statant counterchanged, on a chief gules three buckles or (Carter)
No helm   Crest: A hound statant sable charged with two buckles
or, in front of a quiver of arrows or   Mantling: Grey
Motto: Resurgam
For Christopher Holdsworth Dawson, who m. Emma, sister and heir of
William Vavasour Carter, and d. 22 Sept. 1864, aged 63.   (Fox-Davies,
Armorial Families; arm. ped. at Weston Hall)

5. All black background
On a lozenge surmounted by a cherub's head on a cloud
Arms: As 4., but hound is passant
Motto: Resurgam
For Emma, widow of Christopher Holdsworth Dawson, who d. 29 Oct.
1880, aged 65.   (M.I.; Fox-Davies, Armorial Families)

WESTOW

1. All brown background
On a lozenge surmounted by a skull
Sable a fess or, in chief two helmets proper (   )
Unidentified

2. All black background
Qly of eight, 1st, Barry wavy of six argent and azure a lion rampant or,
in chief two escallops sable (Field), 2nd, Gules a chevron vair between
three eagles displayed or (Wilmer), 3rd, Argent a chevron gules between
three popinjays vert, beaks, legs and collared gules (Thweng), 4th,
Argent a lion rampant azure, armed and langued gules (Bruce of
Skelton), 5th, Argent two bars and on a canton gules a lion passant
guardant or (Lancaster), 6th, Bendy paly argent and azure (   ),
7th, Argent a cross moline azure (   ), 8th, Sable a fess or in chief
two helmets proper (   ), impaling, Qly, 1st and 4th, Per pale
gules and azure a cross patonce or (Wainman), 2nd and 3rd, Argent a
chevron sable (Bradley)
Crests: Centre, A dexter hand and wrist proper holding by a gold handle
a globe argent ruled sable encircled in bend with a gold band inscribed
with signs of the zodiac, the whole surrounded by clouds   Dexter, A
demi-eagle displayed or wings vair   Sinister, A pelican vulning herself
and feeding her young in a nest all proper
Mantling: Azure and argent   Motto: Murus aeneus mens conscia recti
For Joshua Field, of Westow House, who m. 1801, Elizabeth, dau. of
William Wainman, of Carrhead, Craven, and d.   (B.L.G. 2nd ed.)

3. All black background
Azure five mascles conjoined in cross or a chief ermine (Norcliffe),
impaling, Argent three laurel leaves erect vert (Foulis)
Crest: A greyhound sejant or collared azure, the dexter forepaw resting
on a mascle argent
Mantling: Azure and argent   Motto: Sine macula
Pendent below shield, Star of the Hanoverian Order of Guelph, and a
medal with four bars
For Major-General Norcliffe Norcliffe, K.H. of Langton and Westow,
who m. 1824, Decima Hester Beatrix (d. 3 Feb. 1828), dau. and co-
heir of John Robinson Foulis, of Buckton, and d. 8 Feb. 1862.
(Foster; B.L.G. 5th ed.)

WHIXLEY

1. All black background
Argent a chevron between three escallops gules (Tancred)
Crest: On a mound a tree vert fructed or   Mantling: Gules and argent

A small hatchment, about 2½ft. x 2½ft.
Possibly for Christopher Tancred, of Whixley Hall, b. 1689, d. 1754.
(His tomb is below hatchment, with same arms, but a crescent for
difference)

WIGHILL

1. Dexter background black

Sable a wolf salient and in chief three estoiles or (Wilson), impaling,
Argent a fess couped gules between three birds wings raised sable
(Peirce)
Crest: A demi-wolf rampant or   Mantling: Gules and argent
Motto: Resurgam
For Christopher Wilson, of Oxton House, Tadcaster, who m. Sophia,
dau. of John Pearse, of London, and d. 25 May 1842.   (M.I.;
Foster)

2. All black background

On a lozenge surmounted by a cherub's head
Wilson, impaling, Ermine on a fess couped gules between three birds
wings raised sable three annulets or (Peirce)
Motto: Resurgam
For Sophia, widow of Christopher Wilson, who d.   (Sources, as 1.)

WINESTEAD

1. All black background (faded to grey)

Qly, 1st and 4th, Azure a chevron between three molets or (Hildyard),
2nd and 3rd, Azure six cinquefoils, three and three, between nine
crosses flory, three, three and three argent (Darcy), over all the Badge
of Ulster, impaling, Qly, 1st and 4th, Argent a fess azure in chief three
roundels gules (Dering augmentation), 2nd and 3rd, Or a saltire sable
(Dering)
Peer's helm   Crest: A cock sable wattles and comb or
Mantling: Gules and argent   Motto: ΠΑΕΟΝ ΗΜΤΣΤ ΗΑΝΤΟΣ
Skull below
For Sir Robert Darcy Hildyard, 4th Bt., who m. Mary (d. 1816), dau.
of Sir Edward Dering, Bt. of Surrenden Dering, Kent, and d. 6 Nov.
1814.   (Foster; B.L.G. 1937 ed.)

2. All black background

On a lozenge   Arms: As 1., but crosses are cross crosslets, and
Badge of Ulster in chief
For Mary, widow of Sir Robert Darcy Hildyard, 4th Bt., who d. 1816.
(Sources, as 1.)

3. All black background (should be dexter black)
Qly, 1st and 4th, Hildyard, 2nd and 3rd, qly i. & iv. Argent a fess
between three bugle horns sable (Thoroton), ii. & iii. Ermine three
bows palewise in fess proper (Bowes), impaling, Hildyard
Crest and mantling: As 1. Motto: Resurgam
For Thomas Blackborne Hildyard (formerly Thoroton), who m. 1815,
Anne Catherine, dau. of James Whyte, and eventual sole heiress of her
uncle, Sir Robert Darcy Hildyard, 4th Bt., and d. July 1830. She d.
1853. (Sources, as 1.)

WOOLLEY

1. All black background
Sable a chevron between three lions' faces or (Wentworth), impaling,
Ermine a mascle sable (Fawkes)
Crest: A griffin statant, wings elevated argent, beak and legs or
Mantling: Gules and argent Motto: En Dieu est tout
No frame
For either Godfrey Wentworth Wentworth, who m. 1794, Amelia, dau.
of Walter Ramsden Fawkes, of Farnley, and d. 1833, or for his son
Godfrey Wentworth, who m. 1822, Anne (d. 1842), dau. of Walter
Fawkes, of Farnley, and d. 22 Sept. 1865. (Foster)

WORTLEY

1. Dexter background black
Qly, 1st, Azure a stag's head cabossed within two branches of laurel or
(Mackenzie), 2nd, Argent on a bend between six martlets gules three
bezants, a canton of Stuart (Wortley), 3rd, Or a fess chequy argent and
azure within a double tressure flory counter-flory gules (Stuart), 4th,
qly i. & iv. Argent three lozenges conjoined in fess gules a bordure sable
(Montagu), ii. & iii. Or an eagle displayed vert (Monthermer), impaling,
Qly, 1st and 4th, Argent a lion rampant sable (Crichton), 2nd and 3rd,
Argent on a chevron sable between three sprays of three leaves vert
three boars' heads couped argent langued gules (   )
Baron's coronet Three crests: Dexter, An eagle rising from a rock
argent (Mackenzie) Centre, An eagle's leg erased or, issuant there-
from three ostrich feathers argent, the leg charged on the thigh with a
fess chequy argent and azure (Wortley) Sinister, A demi-lion rampant
proper, above his head a scroll with the motto, Nobilis ira (Stuart)
Motto: Avito viret honore Supporters: Dexter, A white horse,
ducally gorged gules Sinister, A stag proper, ducally gorged gules
For James Archibald, 1st Baron Wharncliffe, who m. 1799, Elizabeth
Caroline Mary, dau. of John, 1st Earl of Erne, and d. 19 Dec. 1845.
(B.P. 1949 ed.)

2. Dexter background black

Qly, 1st, Mackenzie, 2nd, Wortley, 3rd, Stuart, 4th, Montagu, impaling,
Sable a cross patonce and a bordure or (Lascelles)
Earl's coronet   Four crests: 1. An eagle rising from a rock argent,
and above a scroll inscribed, Firma et ardua (Mackenzie)   2. Wortley
3. A lion rampant gules, and above a scroll inscribed, Nobilis ira
(Stuart)   4. A griffin's head couped or (Montagu)
Motto and supporters: As 1.
For Edward Montagu Stuart Granville, 1st Earl of Wharncliffe, who m.
1855, Susan Charlotte, dau. of Henry, 3rd Earl of Harewood, and d. 13
May 1899.   (B.P. 1949 ed.)

3. All black background

Qly, as 1., impaling, Argent a shakefork sable (Cuninghame)
Crests: As 1., but with Mackenzie crest over helmet
Mantling: Gules and argent   Motto: As 1.
For the Hon. James Archibald Stuart-Wortley-Mackenzie, who m. 1767,
Margaret, dau. of Sir David Cuninghame, Bt., of Levingstone, and d.
1 Mar. 1818.   (B.P. 1949 ed.; Foster)

WRAGBY, Nostell Priory

1. Sinister background black

Qly, 1st and 4th, Ermine on a fess vert three eagles displayed or (Winn),
2nd and 3rd, Per pale azure and gules three lions rampant argent
(Herbert), in centre chief the Badge of Ulster   In pretence: Qly, 1st
and 4th, Argent on a chevron between three heronshaws sable five
bezants (Henshaw), 2nd and 3rd, Per fess azure and or a pale counterchanged three bucks' heads erased or (Roper)
Crest: Within an annulet a demi-eagle displayed or
Mantling: Gules and argent
For Susannah, dau. and co-heiress of Charles Henshaw of Eltham, Kent,
by his wife, Elizabeth, only dau. and heir of Edward Rooper, who m.
1729, Sir Rowland Winn, 4th Bt., and d. 24 Mar. 1741.   (B.P. 1949
ed.; Foster)

2. All black background

Arms: As 1.
Crest: A demi-eagle displayed or collared ermine
Mantling: Gules and argent
For Sir Rowland Winn, 4th, Bt., who d. 23 Aug. 1765. (Sources, as 1.)

3. Dexter background black

Qly, 1st and 4th, Winn, 2nd, Qly gules and azure an imperial crown or
between four lions rampant argent (Harbord), 3rd, Henshaw, but no
bezants   In pretence: Argent an owl standing on a cushion gules
(Du Hervert)   In centre chief of main shield the Badge of Ulster

Crest and mantling: As 2. Motto: Tout pour Dieu et ma patrie
For Sir Rowland Winn, 5th Bt., who m. 1768, Sabine Louise, only dau.
and heir of Jacques Phillippe, Baron d'Hervert, and d. 20 Feb. 1785.
(Sources, as 1.)

4. All black background
On a lozenge   Arms: As 3.
Motto: As 3.
For Sabine Louise, widow of Sir Rowland Winn, 5th Bt., who d. Sept.
1798.   (Sources, as 1.)

5. All black background
Arms: As 3. (but arms should be quartered and not in pretence)
Crest, mantling and motto: As 3.
Probably for Sir Rowland Winn, 6th Bt., who d. unm. 14 Oct. 1805.
(Sources, as 1.)

6. All black background
Winn arms only
Crest: A demi-eagle displayed or   Mantling: Gules and argent
Motto: Virtute et labore
Probably for John Winn, who d. unm. 17 Nov. 1817.   (Sources, as 1.)

7. Dexter background black
Winn, impaling, Gules a chevron between three crosses formy or, on a
canton ermine a buck's head erased sable (Strickland)
Crest, mantling and motto: As 6.
For Charles Winn, who m. Priscilla, dau. of Sir William Strickland, 6th
Bt., of Boynton, and d. 17 Dec. 1874, aged 79.   (Sources, as 1.)

8. Dexter background black
Winn, impaling, Gules three escallops or, an annulet argent for
difference (Dumaresq)
Baron's coronet   Crest: As 2.   Motto: As 3.
Supporters: Two dragons reguardant vert, gorged with a ribbon or,
pendent therefrom an escutcheon gules charged with a rose argent
seeded gules
For Rowland, 1st Baron St Oswald, who m. 1854, Harriet Maria Amelia,
dau. of Col. Henry Dumaresq, and d. 20 Jan. 1893.   (Sources, as 1.)

9. All black background
Winn, impaling, Qly, 1st and 4th, Azure three bears' heads couped
argent (Forbes), 2nd and 3rd, Azure three cinquefoils argent (Fraser)
Baron's coronet   Crest, motto and supporters: As 8.
Mantling: Azure and argent
A small hatchment, c. 2½ft. x 2½ft.
For Rowland, 2nd Baron St Oswald, who m. 1892, Mabel Susan, dau.
of Sir Charles Forbes, 4th Bt., and d. 13 Apr. 1919.   (Sources, as 1.)

WYCLIFFE

1. Dexter background black
Barry of six or and azure (Constable), impaling, Azure a fess dancetty
the two upper points flory or (Plowden)
Crest: A dragon's head argent, charged on the neck with three bars
gules, on each bar three lozenges or
Mantling: Gules and argent   Motto: Sans mal desir
Cherub's head at each upper corner and winged skull in base
For Francis Constable (formerly Sheldon, who assumed the name of
Constable on succeeding to the estates), who m. Frances Xaveria, dau.
of Edmund Plowden, of Plowden and Aston, Salop, and d. 12 Feb.
1821.   (B.L.G. 1937 ed.)

YORK, St Crux Hall

1. All black background
Vert a chevron between three stags at gaze or, in chief the Badge of
Ulster (Robinson)   In pretence: Azure a maunch ermine over all a
bend gules (Norton)
Crest: From a marquess's coronet or a mound vert, thereon a stag at gaze
or   Mantling: Gules and argent   Motto: Amore animose
For Sir Tancred Robinson, Bt., Rear-Admiral of the White, Lord Mayor
of York in 1718 and 1738, who m. Mary, only dau. and heiress of
Rowland Norton, of Dishforth, and was bur. at St Crux, 7 Sept. 1754.
(Foster; B.P. 1875 ed.)

YORK, St Cuthbert

1. Dexter background black
Or three cinquefoils between nine cross crosslets gules (Saltmarshe),
impaling, Gules three lions rampant or (Fitzherbert)
Crest: The rudder of a ship proper   Mantling: Gules and argent
Motto: Virtus et astrea
Two cherubs' heads at upper corners of shield and winged skull in base
For Philip Saltmarshe, who m. Constantia, dau. of Thomas Fitzherbert,
of Staffs, and d. 22 Mar. 1797.   (Foster)

2. All black background
Gules three lozenge cushions ermine tasselled or (Redman), impaling,
Argent a lion rampant sable collared or (   )
Crest: A dexter hand gules   Mantling: Gules and argent
Unidentified

3. All black background

On a lozenge surrounded with gilt decoration and surmounted by a skull
Per chevron embattled or and azure three martlets counterchanged (Hodgson)
Below the lozenge, very small and largely illegible letters, is an inscription which has been added later as part of the decoration has been painted out to make room for it. The following is all that can be deciphered: '. . . Elizabeth Daughter of Christopher Hodgson of Beeston New Hall in the parish of Leeds Esq. & Daughter by Law by marriage of her Mother to Henry Watkinson, Dr of Laws & Chancellor of Diocese of York. She died . . .'

YORK, Holy Trinity, Micklegate

1. All black background

Vert on a bend argent cotised argent between two covered cups or a lion passant gules, on a chief or three pheons azure (Crompton)
In pretence: Qly, 1st and 4th, Argent a fess between three rooks sable (Rookes), 2nd and 3rd, Sable three goats passant argent (Stansfield)
Crest: A demi-horse sable vulned in the chest with an arrow proper
Mantling: Gules and argent   Cherub's head in base
For Joshua Crompton, of York, who m. 1786, Anna Maria, dau. and co-heir of William Rookes, of Roydes Hall, and d. 13 Feb. 1832.
(Foster; B.L.G. 5th ed.)
(There is another hatchment for Joshua Crompton at Guiseley)

The following four hatchments were all recorded since the Survey began in 1952, but their present whereabouts is unknown.

1. All black background

On a lozenge surmounted by a cherub's head
Ermine on a fess sable three molets or (Lister)
Skull and crossbones below
Unidentified
(Formerly in the possession of Mr. E. G. Bayford, 16 Rockingham Street, Barnsley; originally in Bawtry church)

2. Dexter background black

Two coats per fess, 1st, Gules on a chevron argent three roundels sable a chief sable, a crescent for difference, in dexter chief the Badge of Ulster (Coghill), 2nd, Argent on a chief indented azure three fleurs-de-lys or a canton ermine (Cramer), impaling, Azure a cross or in dexter chief a rose argent (Hort)

Crests: Dexter, a cock with wings expanded or   Sinister, A fleur-de-
lys or   Mantling: Gules and argent
For Sir John Coghill, 1st Bt., son of Balthazar John Cramer, assumed
the name of Coghill, m. 1754, Mary, dau. of the Most Rev. Josiah Hort,
D.D., Archbishop of Tuam, and d. 8 Mar. 1790.   (B.P. 1939 ed.)
(Formerly in the possession of Mrs Prince, Knox Manor, Low Laithe)

3.   Dexter background black

Qly, 1st and 4th, Coghill, 2nd and 3rd, Cramer without canton
In pretence: Azure a lion rampant guardant between eight fleurs-de-lys
argent (Holland)
Crests: Dexter, as 2.   Sinister, A fleur-de-lys azure between two
wings argent
Mantling: Gules and argent   Motto: In coelo quies
For Oliver Coghill, of Coghill Hall, who m. 3rd, Jane Holland, of
Shrewsbury, and d.   (B.P. 1939 ed.)
(Formerly in the possession of Mrs Prince, Knox Manor, Low Laithe)

4.   Sinister background black

Qly, 1st and 4th, Argent a chevron sable ermined argent between three
griffins' heads erased sable (Pemberton), 2nd and 3rd, Argent a lion
rampant sable crowned or (Hindmarsh), impaling, Qly, 1st and 4th, Per
pale sable and gules three talbots courant argent, on a chief argent a
celestial crown between two buglehorns stringed sable (Hunter), 2nd
and 3rd, Argent a chevron sable ermined argent (   )
Shield surmounted by a bow of ribbon
For Jane, dau. of Thomas Hunter, of Beoley Hall, Worcs, who m.
George Pemberton, of Bainbridge Holme, co. Durham, and d. 22 Feb.
1826.   (B.L.G. 2nd ed.)
(Formerly in King Richard House, Scarborough)

ADDENDA

YORK, St William's College

1.   Dexter background black

Two oval shields   Dexter, within the Garter, Qly, 1st and 4th, England,
2nd, Scotland, 3rd Ireland   Sinister, Or semy of hearts gules three lions
passant guardant azure (Denmark)
Royal helmet, crest and crown above   Mantle: Ermine
Motto: Dieu et mon droit   Supporters: Lion and unicorn (but unicorn
sable)
Normal hatchment shape, c. 4½ft. x 4½ft.
On the frame the words: Blessed are the Peacemakers for they shall be
called the children of God + The Peacemaker of the World +
For H.M. King Edward VII, d. 6 May 1910.

2.   All black background

Within the Garter, Qly, 1st and 4th, England, 2nd, Scotland, 3rd, Ireland
Royal helmet, crest and crown above   Mantle: Ermine
Supporters: Lion and unicorn (but unicorn brown)   In dexter angle,
a red rose, in sinister, a white rose, in base, Tudor rose, thistle, leek and
shamrock.
Shape and size: As 1. On the frame the words: Blessed are the dead
which die in the Lord + Her children rise up and call her blessed +
Presumably also For H.M. Queen Victoria, d. 22 Jan. 1901.

SELECT BIBLIOGRAPHY

P. G. Summers, *How to read a Coat of Arms* (National Council of Social Service, 1967), 17-20.

P. G. Summers, *The Genealogists' Magazine*, vol. 12, No. 13 (1958), 443-446.

T. D. S. Bayley and F. W. Steer, 'Painted Heraldic Panels', in *Antiquaries Journal*, vol. 35 (1955), 68-87.

L. B. Ellis, 'Royal Hatchments in City Churches', in *London and Middlesex Arch. Soc. Transactions* (New Series, vol. 10, 1948), 24-30 (contains extracts from a herald-painter's work-book relating to hatchments and 18th-century funerals).

C. A. Markham, 'Hatchments', in *Northampton & Oakham Architectural Soc. Proceedings*, vol. 20, Pt. 2 (1912), 673-687.

T. H. Brown, *Coats of Arms in Cleveland*, 1973.

C. Roy Hudleston and R. S. Boumphrey, *Cumberland Families and Heraldry*, with *A Supplement to An Armorial for Westmorland and Lonsdale*, 1978.

C. H. Hunter Blair, lists and illustrates most of the Durham and Northumberland hatchments and armorial panels in *Archaeologia Aeliana*, 4th series, xix, xxxii & xxxv.

R. Bretton, 'Local Funeral Hatchments', *Transactions of the Halifax Antiquarian Society*, 1952, 43.

R. S. Boumphrey, C. Roy Hudleston and J. Hughes, *An Armorial for Westmorland and Lonsdale*, 1975.

Bloom, Rev. J. Harvey, M.A. *The Heraldry in the Churches of the West Riding of Yorkshire*, published in six parts, 1891-1895.;

INDEX